'His humanity, his humour, his perceptiveness changed sports-writing from mindless posturing into something for an intelligent person to enjoy. This book is a delight. No one tells it like Keating.' *The Times*

'a gleeful triumph ... relish the sheer joy of the writing' *Mail on Sunday*

'utterly compelling' *New Statesman and Society*

'The tension between Keating's old-hand tabloid instincts and his erudition has always been part of his success ... chief among his many virtues is his recognition that sentimentality and nostalgia are crucial to sportswriting.' Nick Hornby, *Sunday Times*

Classic Moments from a Century of Sport

Frank Keating

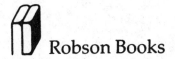

Robson Books

Published in paperback in 1998 by Robson Books Ltd.,
Bolsover House, 5–6 Clipstone Street, London W1P 8LE

First published in hardback as *Frank Keating's Sporting
Century* in 1997 by Robson Books Ltd.

British Library Cataloguing in Publication Data
A catalogue record for this title is available from the
British Library

ISBN 1 86105 229 4

Printed in Finland by W.S.O.Y.

Contents

Introduction

Herewith not only the best of the twentieth century but the best of the best; and in some cases, the worst. Comparisons are invidious, I know, even more so provocative comparisons. Nevertheless, while it has been fun making them, don't all write in at once to berate this dolt for neglecting so-and-so or forgetting a true-great such-and-such . . .

I might well have forgotten, but much more likely is the fact that we must simply agree to disagree. A print of my Cartoon of the Century, for instance, is framed on the wall of my loo; it shows the (great) Bill Tidy's archetypal brawny best-of-Brit in his Sunday breakfast braces in front of his QPR-striped teapot and, spread rumpled all over the kitchen table, some dozen and more newspapers from all over the world, each turned to the sports pages – *La Stampa, L'Equipe, Il Messagero, Der Zeitung, Herald-Trib, South China Post, Cape Argus, Giornale d'Italia, The Hindu,* the *Sydney Sun,* and the *Cork Examiner* . . . He had obviously read every one before tossing it away and, as he dismissed from his presence the last sports page, he was saying to his hair-curlered put-upon wife, 'Blimey, you wouldn't think the bloke had been at the same bleedin' match . . .'

Precisely. So, as I say, don't all write in at once. What follows here has to be subjective and, because it is subjective then sentiment also, and always, must clamour for inclusion.

Of course, in a few cases there is no need for debate about 'the greatest'. Some moments and men and women demand indisputable nomination and immediate acclamation for the Oscar and the only discussion is, as Walter Hagen used to taunt as he waggled his driver at the first tee, 'Okay, who's gonna come second?'

For instance, Don Bradman's batting figures at cricket simply defy any injection of sentiment. Even if he was a mass murderer, *Wisden's* small-print brooks no argument about Bradman being far and away the batsman of the century. With others – the likes, say, of Garfield Sobers, Lew Hoad, and Mark Ella – sentiment and 'presence' come into it, as Chesterton understood when he defined, 'There is a great man who makes every man feel small. But the really great man is the man who makes every man feel great.'

This true greatness relies as much on period and personality, opportunity and context, as on the record books. It is also a precious generational thing – in the Gloucestershire of my childhood there lived men who could swear at first-hand that Jessop was better than Hammond and that Graveney was better than both of these. Context is all: was Seb Coe's 1,500m gold medal in 1980 only the more glistening for his defeat a couple of days before as favourite in the 800m? Was Matthews better than Finney for posterity because venerable Sir Stan invariably excelled on the national stage at Wembley, whereas 'the Preston plumber' did not? Was Pelé only better than Best because the Brazilian played in four World Cup finals and Ulster's George not one?

In all these comparisons from different ends of the century, too, there has been a presumption of peak form, matching equipment and, to be sure, a level playing field.

Nor have we had to bother with the last century – no Renshaw or Dod who founded tennis's rolls of honour, no Smith at soccer, nor prizefighting's Sullivan and Fitzsimmons. Although at the age of 66, WG Grace scored his last half-century as late as July 1914 – 69 not out for Eltham v Grove Park – the Doctor remains an eminent singular Victorian and thus qualifies for no mention here. Two who do, however, are the successive and generous long-serving sports editors and friends on my beloved *Guardian*, John Samuel and Mike Averis, who dispatched me actually to witness many of the events I chronicled, judged and one-man juried here – and those of the century which obviously I couldn't maxboyce ('I know 'cos I was there') myself, well, happy library poring and no end of video patrols allowed me, like the man said,

To weigh the stars in the balance, and grasp the skies in a span
So take, if you must have an answer, the word of the common man.

Gratitude as ever to my wife Jane for typing and tidying the manuscript (and pouring the half-time drinks); to her father John for some valuable suggestions and, at Robson Books, Jeremy himself, Kate Mills and copy editor, Charlie Richards, for being particularly helpful and helpfully particular.

Real life selectors in sports must be sensible and coldly objective, dry-eyed, unfeeling and heartless. This one hasn't had to be. He even subscribes to the certainty that 'great' is, well, a really great word.

Football

Goal of the Century

With a pub to prove it

Where do you begin? More crucially for the matter in hand, where do you end? So many goal-nets the world over have been billowingly spinnakered (and Linekered) down the century with so many billions of goals that the choice of the best can only be personal – and the judge's decision ruthlessly final. The yardstick here: no free-kicks or penalties, and only international matches, international cup ties, and Cup finals . . . but that's still an awesome chorus of stadium-erupting clamours of Y-E-SS!

It might seem a shame to some to preclude free-kicks, those dramatic one-crack net busters which have turned and won many a match down the years. But analysis of all of them would keep us up all night. The Brazilian Garrincha is said to have 'invented' and perfected the curling 'banana' shot in the 1950s, but that is probably because it was the first time the world was able to gasp collectively when they saw the 'Little Bird' on television. Certainly, Garrincha's free-kicks inspired no end of stars to become superstars as 'bending' specialists in the Uri Geller class, notably his successors in the Brazilian shirt, Gerson, or the estimable Zico and later, as the century ran its course, Roberto Carlos, whose spectacular long range late swerver against France in the 1997 pre-World Cup le Tournoi de France was a breathtaking, pluperfect strike. It was timed at a blistering 85 mph and as it left the boot you could see the photographers behind and wide of goalkeeper Fabian Barthez's left-hand post beginning to cower and duck. Carlos had hit it with the outside of his left boot to conjure the vicious late swing. Apart from that, 'practice, practice, and more practice is how I do it' said probably the game's finest left-back of the 1990s.

In the Italian SERIE A, I daresay well into the 21st century that top-corner blind-spot of about 12-inches square and high to the goalkeeper's left hand will still be known as 'Zona del Piero', for that is where the grand dead-ball artist Del Piero thrillingly and killingly scored with so many of his long-range free-kicks.

The eruptive art-form has never been a particular speciality of the British game – perhaps others practise it far more diligently while the Brits 'hit and hope'. Even the idea of hitting left-footers with the outside of their foot with such finesse and at such speed would give most British players an immediate hernia. Stuart Pearce was an England captain who cracked it straight and furious, like Paul Gascoigne who once scored with a memorable drive from around 30 yards for Tottenham Hotspur against Arsenal in the 1991 FA Cup semi-final – but any English preening at that whizzbang was put in its place in a matter of months when the Brazilian Branco, playing for Genoa in the UEFA Cup, dismantled Liverpool with a coldly aimed for and sensational straight 45-yarder, after which the Liverpool goalkeeper Mike Hooper admitted, 'I have never been passed by a ball travelling so hard and fast, even when hit from the penalty-spot; to have that flash past me, inch perfect, from 45 yards was simply unbelievable. It must be the hardest free-kick ever struck.' Not many of us in Genoa that night doubted him. Nevertheless, for invention, the Brits might take the free-kick palm. Twenty seasons before Branco's astonishing clap of thunder, playing for Coventry against Everton and about 20 yards from goal, Willie Carr stood directly over the ball at a free-kick, in one movement flicked it backwards and upwards with his heels and dived sideways out of the way – and, behind him, Ernie Hunt volleyed the ball into the net. The goal stood, but the ploy was at once outlawed by the FA. So, for cunning invention, Free-Kick of the Century to Ernie Hunt – and so on with the genuine motley . . .

Goals by the bagful had to be collected, considered, and then discarded or not. And not your delicate little Lancaster Gate velvet bag containing sixteen numbered billiard balls – these goals, which came in all shapes and sizes, are crammed and jampacked into umpteen Santa-type sacks. Just as an example, take this sackful of nominations at random, empty them out and scrutinize them as either discards or worthy of going through to the next round ...

Look, here's a real gem for starters: Bobby Charlton v Portugal in 1966 ('... as I carried the ball forward at speed, I remembered Jimmy Murphy telling me years before, when I was a kid, "Don't bother taking aim from long range – when it seems the right time, just give it a heck of a hump."'). Or what about this one, same type of tumultuous clap of thunder for all sorts of reasons, namely Hidegkuti's first in the 6–3 in '53? Or Mario Kempes, unforgettably, through the firecrackers and blue-and-white confetti of extra-time at Buenos Aires in 1978? Does Dennis Bergkamp's dazzling circus trickery for Holland against Argentina 20 years later win the palm? Or even Michael Owen's speed, daring, and deadly strike for England in those same 1998 finals?

Ditto, for sure, Jimmy Greaves's against Burnley in 1962: 'They tell me there were five blokes in claret-and-blue defending the goal-line; they thought I'd whack it, but I noticed a chink and carpeted it softly past them along the floor.' Or some similar stealth by another all-time maestro, Billy Meredith for Man City against Bolton at Crystal Palace in 1904? Were either of those two better or worse than Norman Whiteside's thumping inswinger in extra-time in '85, or Paul Gascoigne's two-card trick against Scotland in Euro 96? And who could ignore nerveless Bill Perry in the last minute in 1953 when the score was 3–3 and – WHACK! – he just hit it. Or Derek Temple likewise when the score was 2–2 and he just ran it in from forty yards, thirteen years later? Or, same sort of scenario in 1979, with United still celebrating at the other end, Arsenal steal away, and Brady to Rix to Sunderland, game, set and match?

See what I mean? Sackfuls of them. Open another sack at random ... and out tumbles Raich Carter's silky beaut for Sunderland in 1937, Tommy McLean's for Blackburn in 1928, founder-of-the-feast David Jack's (white horse and all) in 1923 ... and on and on. But each one of the above ultimately, some sadly, rejected.

Hey, here's a genuine candidate for the prize. Nayim in Paris, 1995 – remember that unbelievable lob from the touchline and almost on halfway which seemed to ricochet off the raging moon and down again to fall, inch perfect, behind an incredulous, ambushed Seaman, Arsenal's goalkeeper of England? And in a Cup final, too. Was that the goal of the century? Or was it a fluke? Many said it was, for the scorer didn't even look up, just mishit a half-volley hoof and got lucky. Pele himself almost scored one like that in the 1970 World Cup, and sent it the wrong side of the post by a whisker, but the great man had noticed the goalie off his line so the 1000–1 shot was 'on'.

It might be a calumny, but even suspected flukes are out. Again, when England beat Italy 4–0 in the sun-drenched heat and dust of the passionate Stadio Municipali in Turin in May 1948, Stan Mortensen scored in the fourth minute a goal since fêted in the lore as just about the best ever by an Englishman. But no TV pundits and slo-mo replays from every angle in those days. Italy kicked-off intent to over-run England, and goalkeeper-captain Frank Swift had to make two frantic and telling saves before, it seemed, any other Englishman had even touched the ball. Then Billy Wright stabbed a clearance to Stanley Matthews, on the halfway touchline. The right-winger inim-itably slipped his marker Eliani, and noticed his Blackpool confrère Mortensen haring from midfield. Stanley pushed it into Stan's path. Mortensen, spindly-legged but barrelly-tough with it, could run like a gale. He did so, being forced diagonally in the direction of the right corner-flag by the covering central defender, the great Barola. Meanwhile, at a lick, England's other attackers, Wilf Mannion and the Toms, Lawton and Finney, crammed on full-sail, shouting for the pass, as they bore down on goalkeeper Bacigalupo's territory. For a moment, it seemed that Mortensen's fulminating, careering sprint would either overrun the ball itself or the fast approaching bye-line. Still at full tilt he began a tumbling fall, but as he did so, now almost on the line, he whacked the ball fiercely with his right foot – and its late swerve curled it dramatically over the startled goalkeeper's head and into the near roof of the net.

The 85,000 Italians were stunned. So was Morty from his somer-saulting tumble into the bank of photographers. So, with astonish-ment and delight, were the three England forwards who'd been lining up for the pass. Many years later, Matthews would not be drawn: 'Typical Morty. We got lots like that. I'd just give him the ball, and it was in the net in a flash.' Finney also remembered, and with the fond flicker of a smile, 'It was a really sensational run alright, but I'm convinced to this day that he was shaping to cross to one of us. But he caught it with the outside of his right boot as he fell and, as the goalie came out to take it off our heads, the ball sailed like a boomerang into the top corner. However hard I chaffed him down the years, till the day he died Morty would never agree with me, but I was always certain it was the best fluke the dear chap ever scored.'

Alas, poor Morty, no goal of the century can realistically have the slightest whiff of fluke. One unquestioned laurel-wreathed goal for posterity was not, by any means, a fluke, but the famed scorer of it admits that he was not in the least bothered at the time whether the ball finished in the net behind the goalkeeper or on the northbound platform of Wembley Park station. It was, of course, Geoff Hurst on that (for the English) golden afternoon in the midsummer of 1966. Hurst had scored twice, England were 3–2 up, and already injury-time was up and they were playing out the final seconds – and high in the BBC commentary box, Kenneth Wolstenholme's mind was about to compose for him immortally, off the cuff, the three short sentences which would make him as enduringly famous as the scorer.

Hurst's quite tremendous left-footer, on the run and seventeen yards out when he thumped it, made for an unforgettable *coup de grâce* as well as for a seminal moment in English and world football for any amount of reasons. But as a boomingly unfussy and no-nonsense, very English curtain-call, its true glory was in the pass which led to it. The throng was whistling, impassioned, for the end and for victory celebrations to begin. Deep in his own penalty area, the England captain Bobby Moore emerged with the ball as one more last-ditch German attack was repelled, yet another furious wave dying against a sea wall. Alongside, the heroic, hard-nut crag of a centre-half Jack Charlton bellowed for Moore to 'Get rid of it, Bob! Hump it into the stand!' Even at that frenzied time, such a thing was simply contrary to the meticulous nature of England's patrician leader. He nothing common did or mean, upon that memorable scene. The unflappable Moore caressed the ball, nudged it unhurriedly ahead of him, looked up and saw Hurst standing alone, arms akimbo, on the halfway line. With scarcely a backlift, the captain exquisitely slippered the ball some fifty yards for it to run, millimetre perfect, into the now clear and galloping path of his West Ham comrade . . .

Hurst admits, 'It was the most perfect of passes but, 3–2 up and the whistle about to blow, you're not necessarily looking for another goal. I heard a defender puffing after me, and the irrepressible Alan Ball coming up too, screeching for the pass. But all I could think of was letting fly in the general direction of goal, almost saying to myself in that split-second, "Just kick it as hard and as high as you can, and if it flies clean out of the ground they'll take ages to get it back – and we've won!" '

So he did hit it as hard and as high as he could – a thunderclap of a rising screamer – and it probably would have gone on rising far out of the stadium had it not been dramatically ensnared, indeed netted, in a singularly violent havoc immediately behind the gymnast's trembling flutter and dying fall of the black-clad goalkeeper Tilkowski . . . *Some people are on the pitch. They think it's all over. It is now.*

Great stuff. But can the greatest of all remotely be the one in which the scorer would just as happily have seen the ball soaring into the crowd? I think not. And still the sacks are emptied – individual ones as well, bulging with glittering goals from the century's true greats of this greedy art and science, from Bloomer and Camsell and Dean, McGrory and Gallacher, Lawton and Law, Rowley and Rush, Atyeo and Aldridge, Osgood, Dalglish, Lineker, and good ol' Cloughie too; not to mention Steve Bull, the Wolf, and Terry Bly of Peterborough; and that's only individual sackfuls from the British Isles.

Is the one-man judge and jury allowed to be totally personal about this? Again, I think not. Personal time-and-place might impassion one's choice and make it too glisteningly gilt-edged in the memory bank. So, for what it is worth, 'my' best four Cup goals, I reckon, were Ron Radford's hooraying hump for Hereford to help put out Newcastle; Charlie George's socks-down rasper for Arsenal's 1971 double; Argentinian Ricky Villa's hopscotch replay run and metaphorical V-sign to the Spurs management after they had substituted him in the first match; and Keith Houchen's classic horizontal header for the photographers on that sky-blue day in 1987. But each far too personal and hometown-domestic to take the palm.

Can it be won by defenders? Rare things of beauty in their way, but not quite what we are looking for. David Webb's delirious Old Trafford winner off his ear-lobe in 1970 was crucial all right, and brazen, but not as crucially brazen as Tommy Smith's whizzbang classic of a header from Heighway's corner in Rome in 1977. It could have been his namesake Lawton. At the carousing Koppite party afterwards in Rome's Hilton, Tommy came in with his hair unkempt. 'I'm never going to wash my hair again,' he said.

But special prize for the best Defender's Goal of the Century must go to Bill Foulkes in Man United's second European semi in Madrid in 1968. Two–three on the night, 3–3 on aggregate, twelve minutes left on a seethingly operatic and wondrous European winner-take-all passion play. Smith's goal in Rome was from a set-play, it had been planned and the timing of his run, the presentation of the corner and the convulsive header were its glories. There was nothing predetermined about Foulkes's score. It was in open play and it was sheer instinct and inspiration from an ageing warrior, fully sixteen years in the colours. And red was the colour. And it came out of the blue. Foulkes was the very epitome of the old-fashioned defensive centre-half who knew his place, and his place was inside his own penalty area defending the ramparts. Then Paddy Crerand took a throw-in on halfway, down the right touchline. He threw to George Best and, of a sudden and inexplicably, something stirred in old Bill Foulkes's breast. From the sandbags' fastness of defence alongside his goalkeeper, Foulkes was inspired to ease forward. What urged him was no last-fling desperation; there were more than ten minutes left, for heaven's sakes. 'I still cannot say for the life of me what made me do it, I'd never done it before and would never do it again,' said Foulkes a quarter of a century later. The genius Best wriggled past the Spanish defender Sanchis. From the deep, far behind, Foulkes's hesitant edge forward now became a trot, and he was up to the halfway line now. Young Best, in his glory, unbalanced and then left for dead the full-back Zoco, and corkscrewed on inimitably towards the bye-line, tugging a wary central defender towards him. The fire in Foulkes's breast was now stoked red hot. He was galloping now, with the skip of a released colt, and he passed the eighteen-yard line just as Best, from almost the bye-line, intricately threaded the ball diagonally between goalkeeper Betancourt and Pirri – and precisely into Foulkes's path.

Foulkes did not have to break stride as he exultantly clipped the pass first-time into the net. United were on their way to the final which, of course, they won. 'To this day, I don't know what I was doing there,' said Foulkes. 'It can only have been divine inspiration.'

The incomparable (eponymous?) Best had been Foulkes's ravishing provider that memorable night. The truth was that Best's goal, the only one of the first leg of the semi at Old Trafford, had itself enabled Foulkes to beat down the door to the final itself. For the rest of the century, Best himself would keep that one particularly warm in his memory: 'It satisfied me almost more than any other. A snap shot with my weaker, right foot, it fair screamed in.' This time from the left, the two providers were the eighteen-year-old Brian Kidd and underrated winger John Aston. In *The Times*, doyen reporter Geoffrey Green described how 'from Aston's diagonal, in came Best to thunder it first-time into the roof of Real's surprised net – it might have been Walter Hammond driving a half-volley gloriously past extra-cover off the full face of the bat.'

In his own crammed sackful, two of Best's against another auld enemy from Europe must also take the big-time biscuit. In 1966 and 1968, Benfica and Eusébio stood in United's way. Best's feathered touch did for them both times. The first, in Lisbon's Stadium of Light, was sheer incandescence by the teenager as he shimmered past one, two, three defenders as if they were shadows and then put the ball low into the net as if with a single shot from a high-calibre pistol. Eusébio and his men came to London for the final two years later: extra-time and the slight, wee Irishman begins the settling of it, to all intents, by insouciantly nutmegging the Portuguese centre-half and then drawing in and teasing the goalkeeper as would a contemptuous matador a bull. Best explains: 'I was still a cocky kid then – the nutmeg was more enjoyable than the goal itself. Then the goalie made a lunge far too soon, so I knew I had to just show him the ball and just dummy around him as he sprawled. I just slid the ball in and as I did so I remember regretting I hadn't dribbled on up to the goal-line, stopped the ball, knelt down and just, say, "nosed" it into the net. Or something daft like that. Then I thought of Sir Matt and thought better of it.'

I think I saw George's last ever League goal in England. He was now cavorting – second childhood with Rodney Marsh, two Huckleberries down by the riverside – through his last days at Fulham, when, 1977? Twenty yards out, on a skid-pan pitch, he looks around, flips the ball from his instep, bounces it once, twice on his knee then, as it falls, he drop-kicks it in an exquisite and gentle little parabola – and it kisses the crossbar and falls PLOP! over the line with the poor admiring Oldham goalkeeper flat on his backside in the mud.

I wonder if anyone in the next century will see any player remotely resembling the all-round glories of George Best. They will be mighty lucky if they do. Or the man himself, Pelé of Brazil and all the universe. I saw Pelé score one of his copper-bottomed classics, with his head in the 1970 World Cup final in the wondrous Aztec Stadium. He really did hang up there like a sparrowhawk considering his prey. Then WHOOSH! – by golly, the rigging didn't half hiss behind the Italian goalkeeper Albertosi. I wonder how many of the great Brazilian's 1,281 goals (in 1,263 games) would get on an infallibly computerized shortlist of the greatest of the century. Lots, I should think. 'One goal is never like another,' said Pelé, 'but each and every one is very, very good.'

The mesmerizing South American samba-beat carnival on that final Sunday in the Azteca was ceremoniously rounded-off by Pelé in tandem with his captain Carlos Alberto. But that was a defender's goal – although, I agree, with Brazilians that rule is banished forthwith. They are all attackers. Anyway, I happily concede that the vivid image of Carlos Alberto's eruptively emphatic score, which sealed Brazil's victory by 4–1, has ever since been lodged in the souls and spirits of those of a certain generation as the very best of the bunch, and the certainty of its place atop the pantheon was confirmed in a poll on Sky Television which also pronounced it the World Cup's best of the century. I saw him when he came to London to receive the prize.

The once straight-backed defender with the puma's stride remembers the goal, of course he does. Clodoaldo's compelling dribble out of defence, Jairzinho's take and turn and caressing pass to Pelé, mid-pitch inside-left and twenty-five yards from goal . . . but as the Italian defence bristled en masse behind its confidently, timelessly impregnable fortifications, Pelé does not run at them but senses the express thundering through the station on his right and, like a meticulous carpet-bowler, he serenely rolls the ball into its path.

Carlos Alberto, at full steam, has no need minutely to alter stride or direction as his instep convulsively meets the ball and in a blink the missile is nesting in the far corner of the netting behind the duped and deluded Italian goalkeeper.

Was it, for Carlos Alberto as well, the best ever? 'The best ever? There were so many. Well, I played eleven years with Pelé at Santos. You cannot pick just one as the best among so many.' He remembers the finest actual match, as opposed to moment, of those epic finals being Brazil's narrow win over England, 'although a few days later, for the first half-hour against Romania, we were playing so beautifully we looked at each other with wide-opened eyes, saying, "Wow! Isn't this great?" After that, although we won 3–2, we played like shite, like manure.'

'Shite'? What's he talking about? I saw that match. Brazil were simply Brazil, and quite stupendous all through. But was that final-clinching flourish in the Azteca the very best of the best? Well, those ten million TV viewers apparently voted it so. But at the end of the 1990s, the couch-spuds of soccer would only deign to consider for selection anything in glorious technicolor plus multi-split screen replays. If they wanted a genuinely illuminating goal of poster-paints brightness to be tops of the tops, the winner might have to be the richly-gifted Argentinian Maradona for his sublime goal of atone-ment in the 1986 World Cup, in which he butter-knifed through a third of the England team to score ravenously – only four minutes after his wretched cheater's 'Hand of the Devil' goal had suckered both goalkeeper Peter Shilton and the Tunisian referee. But, however breathtaking it was, for TV viewers in England to be asked to vote for that second confessional *mea culpa* goal as best of all would have been stretching too far collective forgiveness. Equally, its potency must be diluted somewhat, being scored against a team still diverted, once Shilton and defender Fenwick had furiously passed on the news, by the understandable lather of fury they were feeling at the allowance of the handball goal only minutes before.

So no Maradona. Nor would the pink-shirted TV competition-setters even consider entering any footage from history which depicted fuzzy little faraway monochrome blobs flickering about on a sad grainy-grey backcloth. But just after the half-century was posted, two singular and almost blindingly iridescent blooms – goals, that is – vividly lit up the grey 1950s. Another true great also came to London as the century reached its end. On his seventieth birthday, Ferenc Puskas revisited Wembley. He had first set foot on that green field of dreams with his Hungarian comrades on 25 November 1953. Now, well over forty years later, an adversary that day, Sir Stanley Matthews, was there to greet him. The two old men embraced. England had been beaten by 6–3. Four months later they went to Budapest for revenge. They lost by 7–1. The now even more podgy Puskas never stopped chuckling all through his birthday: 'How we scored six I don't know. To us, your heavy footballs were like blocks of wood.' Said the octogenarian Sir Stanley, fiddle-fit and still bright-eyed: 'We never thought England could lose at Wembley. It was simply an impossibility. But Hungary were tremendous, every move was an eye-opener with their interchanging attack. Puskas's left foot must have been the greatest in all football. I can still see his third goal in my mind's eye. I still say I have never seen better. It was truly remarkable.'

Puskas had bamboozled the England captain and right-half Billy Wright as he confidently came in for the tackle. Puskas allowed Wright to commit himself – Geoffrey Green wrote next morning that 'Wright's tackle resembled a fire engine rushing to the wrong fire' – then the Hungarian dragged the ball back with the sole of his left foot before, in a blur of instinct and speed, pirouetting and, with the same left foot and with no discernible backswing, magically thunderclapping the ball past goalkeeper Merrick.

Said Puskas all those years later, and still chuckling as he tells his interpreter: 'The "drag-back" is still my favourite score of all. My friend Czibor gives it to me from the right wing. I am on the corner of the six-yard box, my back to goal. I sense Wright charge in for the tackle with a great leap. I fear for my safety. Will he take us both into the grandstands? I drag-back the ball like I practised for fun as a little kid sometimes, but now it was only to escape from Wright. So he tackles thin air, and vanishes past me . . . and, still on my right foot, I turn ninety degrees and whack it into the net. So you see, I had to do the "drag-back" simply for my own safety and to escape your Mr Wright.'

England had been too insular to be forewarned about the

Hungarians' collective genius. After all, only fifteen months before, that same Hungary side had been crowned the 1952 Olympic champions. At those Games, in the six rounds including the final they had scored an astonishing twenty-seven goals and forfeited only five. Before that Hungarian side, themselves mostly army officers, had with such a multi-coloured starburst carried all before them at the Olympics, *the* crack team of Europe, generally acknowledged (except by the ivory-towered English) for the previous couple of years, had been Austria. With nice symmetry, three months before those Olympics, England had played Austria in Vienna. The match was considered by many (some years, of course, before such things officially happened) as a sort of play-off to determine the national championship of Europe. The year before, for instance, Austria had come to Wembley and played sparklingly enough to come very close to destroying England's proud unbeaten home record against foreign teams, drawing 2–2. Since when, if further warnings were necessary, the two visiting sides to Vienna before the English came had been Scotland and the Republic of Ireland, and they had both been thrashed respectively by 4–0 and 6–0. To be sure, in their previous fifteen international matches, fielding such supreme talents as Ocwirk, Huber and Dienst, Austria had scored fifty-seven goals, almost an Hungarian Olympics 'average'. So Austria v England was going to be a competitive match alright.

In hindsight, knowing what was to shatter England's soccer pride in the following year at Wembley, a romantic could readily settle for this match in Vienna, on 25 May 1952, harshly and in bold outline representing the End of an Era – the end of the evocative, cosy and comfortable, almost aspic-bottled football of olde England which had scarcely been stirred throughout the first half of the century. Thus does the plot throw up in the leading part, and with pluperfect casting, a man who could not be more fit for the job and ready for the historic role. Roll the drums, open the envelope, and, applause, applause . . .

Step forward . . . Nat Lofthouse, of Burnden Park, of Bolton Wanderers, of England. One-club man in the white shirt. He not only scored the Goal of the Century but, in doing so, provided a proud old lion's last roar.

Nat was a coal-bagger's son who signed for the Wanderers on his fourteenth birthday, 4 September 1939 – you just don't need scriptwriters for this movie – the very morning after War was declared and things-would-never-be-the-same. So, instead, he went down the pit at the Mossley colliery. When he came up, with the Peace he paraded his full pomp. The celebrated football correspondent of the *Manchester Guardian*, Donny Davies, was the critic who watched him most. 'Lofthouse is,' he wrote, 'a superbly built, athletic fellow with a frank, open countenance, a ready smile, a cheerful disposition, and the men on the terraces acclaim "Nat's a toff" and they can't say fairer than that.' And they couldn't say fairer than that in Vienna on 25 May 1952. Nor can you, a full half-century after those words were written. The old man came to the turn of the century still 'the toff' of his town and, with it, a gentle, parfait knight.

Lofthouse *was* Burnden Park all through those post-war years when the white-shirted Wanderers were such a force in the land and any smart film-director knew that Bolton's ground was the place to go to depict the rich flavours of a century of working men's Saturdays: that steeply-raked ocean of flat caps, great waves rolling down to the goal at the Railway End; the throng's communal chorus of fevered oohs and aahs; and that winter-warm fug of Woodbine smoke. Burnden Park, of course, is where LS Lowry painted his masterpiece, 'Going to the Match'. And Burnden Park, almost naturally, was home to the bullocking hero in the number nine shirt, whom the multitude serenaded in song:

> *Like a Centurion tank is our Nathan*
> *Wi' a turn of speed like a bomb*
> *Many a goalie's said sadly*
> *'I wonder where that came from?'*

How many soccer men have had a pub named after them in their home town? For sure, Nat Lofthouse has. On the edge of Bolton still stands the stately 'The Lion of Vienna'.

It was the war-ravaged Vienna of Carol Reed's *The Third Man*. Harry Lime was Vienna's most celebrated name. Before our Nat hit town, that is. Over forty years later, he remembers: 'We had played Italy a few days before in Florence. I'd mucked it up a bit and we only drew. When we got to the British zone in Vienna, I managed a phone-call home to the wife.

"Oh, love," she said, "Desmond Hackett in the *Express* is screaming for you to be sent home and for Jackie Milburn to be flown over for the Austria match."

"Oh, crikey," I thought, but Walter Winterbottom (the manager) stuck by me, although I knew it was a last chance.'

The match was played in the Russian zone, at the Prater Stadium. The Vienna Boys Choir sang the anthems. 'Suddenly when we got out there it was a fantastic feeling. Hundreds of thousands of Tommies from our zone had been allowed across to cheer us on. It was like a home match.'

At once Lofthouse scored with his 'nice old twenty-yard daisy-cutter'. Then Jack Sewell hit 'a peach'. Austria made it 2–2 by half-time and then set about Merrick in England's goal. It was desperate stuff.

Far across Europe, back home, Mrs Lofthouse cupped her ear along with millions towards the BBC wireless Light Programme as the fruity cackle of Raymond Glendenning, sea-shelled with static and crackle, described the live drama in his familiar and passionate crescendos:

'Ten minutes left, another corner to Austria . . . inswinger from the left, right across the goal, a good one indeed . . . oh, well pulled down by Merrick there on the far post . . . Merrick comes out and throws it up towards the centre circle . . . Finney collects it. It's put through to Lofthouse, and Lofthouse is racing through all on his own . . . he's veering right as the goalkeeper comes out . . . he shoots . . . Lofthouse has scored . . . It's 3–2. Goalkeeper Musil ran straight into him and Lofthouse looks badly injured.'

Lofthouse listens in silence to the recording, then chuckles: 'I were. I were right down and out. I'd run like the wind. Musil came out. I let fly from about thirty yards. I knew I'd hit it true, but didn't know where it went till [the trainer] Jimmy Trotter's magic sponge had done the trick and he said to me: "Nathan, lad, you've never scored a better – and you never will." And then I sat up and heard the roars of all those regiments of ours, and I was that proud.

'At the whistle we were all chaired off the pitch. It was like a sea of khaki. They took us all off to the British barracks. We started in the officers' mess, then supped more in the sergeants' mess, then to the privates' mess. They treated us like royalty. It was the finest night of my life and I was as drunk as a monkey.'

And next day, above Desmond Hackett's unapologetic eulogy in the *Express* was the bold banner headline, LOFTY THE LION OF VIENNA. And so he is – and there's a pub to prove it.

Goal of the Century
NAT LOFTHOUSE

Only think of two things – the gun and the tape. When you hear the one, just run like hell until you break the other. *Sam Massabini, coach, Paris, 1924*

Never play cards with a man called 'Doc'! *Nelson Algren (1909–81), US novelist*

I would not advise any pro to marry until after the age of thirty. Marriage demands a division of interests and golf, particularly tournament golf, demands every minute of a man's time. *Henry Cotton, 1936*

Save of the Century

Did you see that!

For humour's sake, one is tempted to give the palm to the wizard Colombian goalkeeper, that moustachioed and dreadlocked tubby ball of fun Rene Higuita, for his delicious handstand and 'heel-kick' circus save against England at Wembley in September 1995. The beguiling nutter enchanted the old stadium with the wheeze – he said afterwards it was a regular part of his repertoire back home and he had even baptized the save with a name, 'the Scorpion'. But that match was a dull and uncompetitive friendly with no needle. As context goes, this game was as flat as a board.

We need needle. In the European Cup final of 1968, Manchester United's three forwards, Best, Kidd and Charlton, scored the goals in extra-time which ensured their ultimate victory by 4–1 – but just before the end of the ninety minutes, two point-blank saves from the Portuguese star Eusébio in, memory demands, almost the same breathtaking moment by United's goalkeeper Alex Stepney would have handed the Cup to Benfica there and then had he not made them. Said Stepney, 'They were just saves on total instinct. I didn't break out in a cold sweat till I saw them replayed on television months later. Eusébio loved to hit "netbreakers". If he had just tried gently to slide either of them in, he'd certainly have scored.' In a European Cup tie almost thirty years later, against Rapid Vienna in 1996, another Man United goalkeeper, Peter Schmeichel, made a dramatically difficult and elastic save, right-handed and falling to scoop the ball up and over the bar – yet another to make you appreciate Eamon Dunphy's definition of the polo-necked breed (he was talking about the grand Irish keeper Pat Jennings): 'The grace of a ballet dancer joins with the strength of an SAS squaddie, the dignity of an ancient king and the nerve of a bomb-disposal officer.'

A pile of similes never better earned than by Jim Montgomery of Sunderland when he ensured that FA Cup win of 1973 for his Second Division club at Wembley against then narrow-eyed and mighty Leeds United. Sunderland had scored the only goal of the game after half an hour and Leeds spent the next hour bearing down on Montgomery's goal. His save from Peter Lorimer, considered at the time to be the hardest shooter in British football, has been gold-framed in the legend of the lore as simply 'Montgomery's Save' – but in fact, here was another 'double' save. In the sixty-sixth minute, Leeds full-back Reaney's cross was met with a strong diving header by Trevor Cherry. Montgomery hurled himself to his left to parry it, which he did brilliantly but, from the goalkeeper's arm, the ball now invitingly sat up and begged to be lashed in by Lorimer. With Montgomery still floored, Lorimer licked his lips with relish and, with cold aim, swung his famed right foot to send the ball mercilessly for the net to Montgomery's right – but in a blur of agility the goal-keeper had half-risen, turned and flung himself across his line . . . and clawed with his 'wrong' left hand the unerring thunderbolt onto the underside of the bar, and away to safety. Nineteen years later, when Sunderland again reached Wembley and he was a 'backroom boy' with the club, I asked Montgomery if I could, for memory's sakes, shake his left hand. 'When I die, it's going to be embalmed and put in a glass case,' he joked. I told him that up in the press box that memo-rable afternoon in May 1973, following 'The Save' a colleague remarked that, somehow, Sunderland's name had been pre-ordained to be on the Cup that year and that it was, in fact, Fate which had conspired to save Lorimer's cannonball. 'No,' I'd replied, 'Fate could never have reached it . . .'

Something of the same sort of mighty testament to the flexibility of the human body had happened three years before, at Guadalajara on 7 June 1970, in the heat and altitude and dazzling light of the Mexican mountain range. England, the world champions, versus Brazil, soon to be so. It was also, in this context, a heavyweight contest – Pelé, the finest forward in the world, versus Gordon Banks, at the time considered the finest goalkeeper in the world. It was 0–0, the tension of the match dagger-sharp. The night before, I had envied my friend John Moynihan of the *Sunday Telegraph* covering the game – I had been despatched to another match in Puebla.

On television all the following is over and done with in one distant, long-lensed blink of agitation. Not having to file a running story, Moynihan and our friend Harry were actually standing right behind Banks's very net as . . .

'Pelé hurtled in his header, leaping over Mullery, and all for one were shouting "GOAL!" and rising to acclaim "the King". Then an outrageous flash of movement, a combination of sprawling arms and legs. Banks was suddenly over to his right of the goal, lying sideways with his left leg thrust out straight, his other bent at right angles, and his groping right hand scooping the ball up and over the crossbar. In this attitude of a preying mantis after spinning to a new twig, Banks had played the ball up and away with an extended palm into oblivion. It tumbled over the bar and rolled slowly onto the other side of the net with the sudden abatement of an ocean wave after breaking on a rock. And one wondered amid all the shouting and screaming and commotion whether England's goalkeeper had broken his arm and suffered grievous damage; he lay on his back with his shoulders on the grass, his colleagues around too nonplussed to yell their praise (till the cockney Mullery broke the spell, looked down at him in wonder and said to his goalkeeper, "Why didn't you catch it?") – and already the moment had become a legend, a piece of unique folklore, a gymnastic impossibility. "Did you see that?" roared Harry, turning round to me. His nicotined fingers were trembling with tension. "Christ! Johnny, did you see that?" '

Save of the Century
GORDON BANKS

Footballer of the Century

Bestest first, Best second

During West Africa's bloody Biafran War, a three-day ceasefire was strictly adhered to when both sides needed time to travel to watch a long-arranged exhibition soccer match in which the Brazilian Pelé was booked to appear. He did so. Next day, once he had flown home, the war resumed. That is the measure of this grandest of sportsmen: he could stop a war; enough said. Pelé played in four World Cups, three times on the winning side. Like Muhammad Ali in the ring or Don Bradman at the crease, at his sport Pelé bestrode the century as the greatest of such greats as Best, Puskas and Di Stefano, or Matthews or Finney, Eusébio or Cruyff, Platini or Maradona or Ronaldo. All those attackers, except Northern Irishman George Best, were allowed to grace the World Cup stage and illustrate their genius to the world. Had Best been able to, well, who knows, he might have been inspired to raise his own brazenly brilliant game. As it is, for his voluptuous all-round talents, he is still probably runner-up here. The critic who saw Best play more than any other, David Meek, who was for thirty-seven years the football correspondent of the *Manchester Evening News* says: 'The man was incredible, and not only for his dribbles and goals, he was the best tackler ever. He'd chase back, slide in, get his foot round the ball and then stand up and be balanced and ready to go all in one movement, like an ice skater rising up from a crouch but still going at full lick. People say he wasted his career. Nonsense, he was hunted down by defenders for eleven full seasons, starting at seventeen. He paid his dues to the game all right.'

Footballer of the Century
PELE

Never catch a loose horse. You could end up holding the ruddy thing all day. *Lester Piggott*

If you're up against a girl with big boobs, bring her to the net and make her hit backhand volleys. *Billie Jean King*

When I was ten, all I ever dreamed of was playing at Wimbledon with the greats, and having my ears pierced. *Tracey Austin*

Defender of the Century

And the greatest was . . .

Pelé said, 'Two men who marked me were head and shoulders above any other defender, Beckenbauer of Germany and Moore of England – and the greatest of them was Moore.'

Defender of the Century
BOBBY MOORE

Personally, I look upon cricket as organized loafing. *William Temple (1881–1944), Archbishop of Canterbury*

Jog and die healthier. *Anon*

At another year, I would not boggle, Except that when I jog, I joggle. *Ogden Nash (1902–71)*

England Forward-line of the Century

Five for a fantasy

Which was English soccer's finest ever forward-line? How about the attack that the already legendary GO Smith led into the new century in 1900, Athersmith–Bloomer–Smith–Wilson–Plant? Or was it, perhaps, when the great Dixie was centre-forward in the late twenties, Hulme–Brown–Dean–Rigby–Page? For sure, the Matthews–Carter–Camsell–Westwood–Bastin quintet must have been pretty good when it saw off the Germans in 1935, and so for sure was the famous five of a quarter of a century later, Douglas–Greaves–Hitchens–Haynes–Charlton.

There is general agreement that 1966's luminaries, Ball–Hurst–Charlton–Hunt–Peters, were less of a vibrant force than Lee–Ball–Charlton–Hurst–Peters a World Cup later in 1970. Of fives that followed, take your pick of such mix 'n' matches as Coppell–Keegan–Francis–Brooking–Woodcock in the seventies, Waddle–Robson–Lineker–Beardsley–Barnes in the eighties, or the young bloods of 1998, Anderton–Beckham–Shearer–Owen–Scholes. Such musings, however, are so academic as to be pointless. For any pub quiz know-all can recite England's very best, the forward-line of supreme and everlasting grandeur, namely Matthews–Carter–Lawton–Mannion–Finney.

Even my cat knows that.

There is one tiny problem for posterity and truth, however. That immortal line of resplendence never once played an international match together. But they so nearly damn well did when, in May 1947, England embarked on their most 'congested' ever series of matches, which included their longest trip by air to play an international. On the previous, pre-war tour in 1939, for matches in Milan, Belgrade and Bucharest, the England team had travelled by ferry and the Orient Express.

In 1947, England warmed up against France at Highbury on 3 May winning 3–0 with goals from Tom Finney, Raich Carter and Wilf Mannion. Finney had stood in at right-wing for Stanley Matthews, but the great man was fit by the following Saturday when, with four others of that England XI, Great Britain beat the Rest of Europe 6–1 at Hampden Park to celebrate the four home countries making peace with FIFA.

An awesome 134,000 ungrudgingly acclaimed Mannion and Tommy Lawton, who each scored two, as the best players of the afternoon – although both afterwards had to travel south on the packed night train, perched throughout on their cases in the corridor. First and second-class carriages were empty, but their FA rail vouchers allowed only third-class travel.

Five days later, the England party flew from Croydon airport in a chartered four-engined Skymaster to Zurich. On 18 May, the Swiss beat them 1–0. In an autobiography published later that year (*Football Is My Business*), Lawton called it a 'rough-and-tumble sort of affair' with the pitch narrow and the ball 'old and scuffed'. In his memoir (*Feet First*, 1948) Matthews wrote that 'the Swiss tackling was always first-time stuff' and he seemed more wide-eyed at staying in the 'luxurious' Dolder Grand Hotel in Zurich, 'where I noticed with delight that the hotel actually had its own golf course'.

The England forward-line was Matthews, Carter, Lawton, Mannion and Bobby Langton, the knobbly-kneed Blackburn Rover. Before they left for Lisbon, Winterbottom told Finney he would be taking Langton's place against Portugal. So at last, the romantics' line-up for posterity would actually take the field together: the mesmerizing virtuoso Stanley, already a global totem; Raich, the all-rounder with the silvery sheen; Tommy at his utter peak as, simply, England's best ever number nine; golden boy Wilf, with his grace and charms; and the already richly gifted Finney. The football world drooled at each one of them.

Famous poets, such as Alan Ross, had already published hymns of praise to Matthews:

> *Expressionless enchanter, weaving as on strings*
> *Conceptual patterns to a private music, heard*
> *Only by him . . .*

Carter had been alongside Matthews in England's white shirt since they had, together, made their debutant's curtsey a full thirteen years before, in 1934, and the reporter from the *Daily Mail* had next morning made the prescient prophecy: 'The boys made a storming right-wing and appear to have come to stay.' It was said of Whistler that he mixed his paint with brains. That is what Carter did in his football. All the sciences and, to be sure, all the arts: of the younger, less grave, Mannion, the northern football critic Donny Davies enthused: 'Mannion is Mozartian in his exquisite workmanship. His style is so graceful and so courtly that he wouldn't be out of place if he played in the lace ruffle and peruque.' A later writer, David Miller of *The Times*, had idolized Mannion: 'As with most sublime players, there was no apparent effort. Ball-control was instantaneous. It was common to see Mannion make a sudden sprint, taking two or three opponents with him, only for them to discover that he had left the ball behind. He would then turn and amble back to it.' The other four fondly 'fathered' Wilf. 'He was our darling boy,' Matthews told me many years later, 'willing and generous to a fault on the field, a smiler, and a maker of goals as well as a taker.'

In between Carter and Mannion, the sleek, dark Prince Rupert and leader of the line, Lawton had it all. Goalkeepers the world over had nightmares about his ruthless heading abilities. Right up to his death, almost half a century later in 1996, when ageing sages told him there had never been a finer player in the air, not even his loved mentor Dixie Dean, Tom would smile wide, make a little grimace and say, 'I didn't think I were too bad on the deck as well.' Even in utter modesty, he never denied the wonder of his gifts. In the year Tom died, I happened to watch Newcastle United, with the new and mighty good number nine champion of England, Alan Shearer, wallop by 5–0 Manchester United with an old friend who had seen Lawton displaying his genius in his prime. The most memorable of quite a few thunderclaps that afternoon was when Shearer, with no backlift and all of twenty-five yards out on the angle, suddenly let rip and laced the thing against Schmeichel's right post before the giant goalkeeper could say 'Frank Swift'.

The dramatic, daring finesse and sheer oomph of that moment was not to be replayed nor reported because of the upcoming hatful of goals. But I was out of my seat hollering 'Wow!' as the fulminating shell left the upright twanging and rebounded away. 'Great,' said my friend, 'but a Lawton shot like that would have been just inside the post. That's the difference.'

Tom Finney was so versatile that when Lawton retired, he moved in from the wing to lead the line for England. His wing play was clean cut and shining bright, like a yacht on a millpond on a lovely summer's day. Finney's admiring comrade and wing-half at Preston North End, Bill Shankly, said that to give other teams a chance of making a game of it, 'Tom should play in his overcoat.' Even then he would, added Shankly, 'still make monkeys of them'.

On the subject of clothing, in his seventies Finney looked back to his international days and, with a smile, was amazed they had all played so well together. 'They had one size of shirt for everyone in the England squad,' he said, 'so if you were six foot two it strangled you and if you were my size it came down below your knees. Same with the socks. When you put them on, they reached to the top of your thighs. Then those boots. Remember? Stiff leather, up over the ankles, bulbous toe-caps. Felt like diver's boots. When it rained and the shirt collected the water and the socks were soaked, we must have weighed a ton apiece. Don't know how we moved.'

But move they did, and all for a pittance, for they were garlanded only with grandeur, not green ones: at this peak of their glory they earned a maximum of £15 a week in the season, £8 in the summer, with a bonus of £1 for a win, 10 shillings (50p) for a draw. The fee for an international match, be it in Wembley or Rio or here in Lisbon, was a flat £20. On England's tour of Italy the following year, after England won so famously in Turin, Finney was offered £10,000 on signature, £150 a month and huge bonuses to play in the Italian league for Palermo. He told his Preston chairman, a bluff northern builder called Nathaniel Buck, that he was very seriously considering the offer. Said Buck: 'What's that money t'thee, Tom? You're Preston. Tha'll play f'Preston or tha'll play f'nobody.'

All five of these differently glittering forwards, of course, had the full bloom of their careers dulled by the war in which, at one time or another, each had been posted abroad. Yet their almost boyish wide-eyed enthusiasm on these football travels together remains appealing. From the dull match in Switzerland, they determined to pull those thick long socks up for the journey to Lisbon, which was improved, Lawton noted, as 'by permission of General Franco, we were allowed to fly over the Pyrenees and cut an hour off the journey . . . Much gratitude to the Generalissimo.' Matthews was still enchanted with his Euro-digs: 'With its white buildings and exquisite display of geraniums, the gardens were the finest I have ever seen, and our Estoril hotel was a millionaires' playground.'

They were fêted at a bullfight and Matthews remarked, 'I don't approve, but confess the skill and horsemanship of the matadors is to be admired.' Some of the team, to their merriment, were warned by the police for illegal jay-walking, others for swimming without wearing singlets. The match was played at the 'breathtaking' National Stadium, 'where every spectator sits on white marble seats', said Matthews. 'The turf was the finest I have ever seen', wrote Lawton.

After breakfast consultation with the FA selectors, Winterbottom announced the team. Finney, as he said, was in. But Carter was dropped, never to play for England again. The quintet of dreams – and pub quizzes – would never be.

Matthews had recently left Stoke City for Blackpool. So they gave a first cap to his new club's breezy young inside-right Stanley Mortensen, a South Shields boy who had in the war been shot down in his RAF Lancaster bomber. His bravery on the field matched the legend: he was as teaky-tough as a rugby forward, as keen as Colman's, and as athletic as a greyhound. He and Matthews became a two-named byword just as, at the time, Hutton and Washbrook were at cricket. Somebody said that while old Merlin Matthews called up the thunder on the wings with his magic, Morty was the lightning that struck immediately afterwards.

Oh, yes, and England beat Portugal by 10–0 (Lawton 4, Mortensen 4, Finney and Matthews), and for the next umpteen matches the attacking line Matthews–Mortensen–Lawton–Mannion–Finney became itself immortal, and England's best ever in history – as well as reality.

England Forward-line of the Century
MATTHEWS–MORTENSEN–LAWTON–MANNION–FINNEY

> In football, it is widely acknowledged that if both sides agree to cheat, cheating is fair. *Charles B Fry (1872–1956), sportsman*

> Were cricket and football abolished, it would bring upon the masses nothing but misery, depression, sloth, indiscipline and disorder. *Lord Birkenhead (1872–1930), Attorney-General*

Cup Final of the Century

Signs of the cross

Brazil's winning finals in 1958 and 1970 were sumptuously satisfying for all soccer, and the home victories by Uruguay in 1930 and Argentina in 1978 were so resonant as to inspire national carnivals for weeks. In contrast, Hungary's 'impossible' defeat (after being 2–0 up) against the solid West Germans in 1954's final caused gloom among soccer purists worldwide, except in Germany, that is. But cup finals increasingly became wracked with too much tension and expectation. Certainly domestic ones – England's best at Wembley is still considered 1948's between Manchester United and Blackpool, with its only competitor since being 1977's between the same United and Liverpool. In the European Cup, the same tight, dull caution has usually prevailed year on year, although AC Milan did let the sunshine in with their 4–0 drubbing of Barcelona in 1994. But if you want iridescence, the 1960 European Cup final played at cold, grey Glasgow's Hampden Park on 18 May still glows with it. It was a golden night, gleaming with skill, competitiveness, sensational goals and good vibes. In all logic, the Cup Final of the Century should be that glory which ended Real Madrid 7 (Puskas 4, Di Stefano 3) Eintracht Frankfurt 3 (Stein 2, Kress).

But it is not. Still a Scottish connection, however. Seven springs later, on 25 May 1967, Celtic were the first British club in a European Cup final and, quite spectacularly, they revived in only an hour and a half a competition which had allowed itself to become debased by

Latin insecurities. Next morning, the *Daily Express* banner headline screamed 'CELTIC SUPERMEN!' and, below it, the master of hooraying hyperbole Desmond Hackett had, the day before from Lisbon, managed to out-Hackett Hackett . . .

'Glasgow Celtic, super superb Celtic, marched proudly into soccer history when they became the first British team to win the European Cup. "Won" is a tame word. They shattered Inter Milan and the 2–1 score was an affront to the magnificence of Celtic. They were *demanding* the cup from the first moments of this final in the golden mould of the National Stadium. Then their fans took over. They kissed the turf. They embraced the goalposts. They danced, they cried, they waved their banners with the defiance of the defenders of Bannockburn . . .'

Inter Milan were considered thoroughbreds of the lore under the legendary management of Helenio Herrera. A negative and over-cautious attitude prevailed in Italian club football. Inter Milan were pre-eminent in that regard: score once, then close the wall up with chained defence – *catenaccio*. On this occasion, such a tactic looked even more likely for Inter were missing through injury their prodigiously gifted Spanish 'playmaker' Luis Suarez.

That sun-baked afternoon in the evocative tree-ringed stadium, Inter did indeed score after only seven minutes, with a penalty after Craig tackled Cappellini from behind. It took almost an hour of relentless Scottish attack before Gemmell equalized with a dramatic twenty-five yarder. Five minutes from full-time, Chalmers diverted a cross-shot from Murdoch into the net for 2–1 and an announcement for the party to begin.

The Celtic captain, and later distinguished manager, Billy McNeill remembers that although it seemed they had left it mighty late for the winning score, each Celtic player 'played the match as if, somehow, victory was pre-ordained'. He reckoned Inter knew it too: 'From the very first our skill and spirit shocked the Italians. Even beforehand, when we were waiting in the tunnel to take the field, we spontaneously burst into a Celtic sing-song, all the supporters' songs and chants. That really amazed them, almost frightened them; well, certainly set them back. You could see it in their eyes. They were white with nerves when we walked out. They were more than a wee bit surprised as well, I think, to see that we could match them for Signs of the Cross.'

Celtic played with such bonny verve and unshakeable contempt for the very idea of defeat that it was not only a heartening victory for Scottish and British football (Manchester United were to win the trophy the following year), but it exposed and shamed the static and neurotic Italian game.

Celtic's grandest of managers, Jock Stein, had announced before the match that he and his players considered themselves on a mission: 'Inter will play it defensively. That's their way and it's their business. But we know we have a duty to play the game our way, and our way is to attack. Win or lose, we want to make the game worth remembering. We have an obligation. We can be as hard and professional as anybody, but I truly mean it when I say we just don't want to win this cup – we want to win it by playing great football, to make neutrals glad we've done it, glad to remember how we did it.'

And so they did. Next morning, Lisbon's *Mundo Desportivo* spoke for football: 'The meaning of this is that the Inter of Herrera, of negative and marginal victories, have paid for their refusal to entertain.'

Despite the extreme tension Stein must have felt as the match approached, he never lost the bantering humour that kept the morale of his expeditions unfailingly high. The impact of Celtic's supporters' invasion on Lisbon's Catholic churches was a rewarding theme for him. 'They're getting some gates already since we came in. The nine and ten o'clock Masses are all-ticket. They've had to get extra collection plates to take round. How do they divide the takings here? Is it fifty-fifty, or in favour of the home club?'

When Hugh McIlvanney filed to the *Observer* from the airport on the Saturday, two days later, he described 'the most hysterically exuberant occupation any city can ever have known . . . with pockets of Celtic supporters still holding out in unlikely corners, noisily defending their own carnival atmosphere, and even among the refugees at the British Embassy bereft of everything but the rumpled clothes they stand in, the talk is of that magical hour and a half under the hot sun on Thursday.' At the airport, McIlvanney wrote, 'the impression is of a Dunkirk with happiness'.

Thirty years on and, they will tell you in Glasgow, some still haven't made it to that airport. All round Iberia, some Celts are celebrating still.

Cup Final of the Century
CELTIC 2, INTER MILAN 1

> In cricket it separated Bradman and Sobers from the rest; Pelé had it in football, Borg had it in tennis, Ali had it in boxing, Barry John had it in rugby. Those who try to pin down everything in life like so many butterflies to a board would call it genius. I prefer it nameless. *George Allan, sportswriter, 1983*

> Unquestionably, TV is saving sports, although I am not sure if sports is worth saving. *Howard Cosell, US TV commentator*

Club Team of the Century

Record realities

Ignoring the – okay, domestically passionate – tedium of annual victories all down the century in Glasgow's two-horse race between
Rangers and Celtic, Liverpool have by far the best British claim,
winning the European Cup four times (in 1977, 1978, 1981 and 1984);
they were runners-up once. The European Cup is by far the most
competitive knockout tournament in world soccer. It was begun in
1956 – and won and held for five successive seasons by Real Madrid's
regal side which included at times such luminaries of the legend as Di
Stefano, Puskas, Del Sol and Gento. Real Madrid have also been
European Cup runners-up three times.

Club Team of the Century
REAL MADRID

> Bernard Darwin and Neville Cardus took the shine off
> the ball in the battle against penny-a-line journalese and
> then Henry Longhurst came along to win the match.
> *Peter Dobereiner, sportswriter, 1978*

Penalty Save of the Century

Unworried Reds in Rome

The last quarter of the century, when penalty shoot-outs were introduced, made two-a-penny of this category, so an extremely long and repetitive list has been whittled down to three contenders.

League Cup semi-final, 27 February 1972, West Ham United v Stoke City. It was a filthy night at Upton Park, and with only a couple of minutes to go West Ham were surely through when they were awarded a penalty. England's centre-forward Geoff Hurst, with a kick of a mule, was to take it against his England colleague in the polo-neck, Gordon Banks. Hurst ran up long and really let fly with a hell of a whack, head-high to Banks's right. The goalkeeper flung his body and right fist at the blur and punched it onto the crossbar and away into the crowd and up into the night. Stoke went on to win the final. 'In terms of what that save allowed us to go on and achieve, it was the most vital I ever made,' said Banks.

FA Cup final, 14 May 1988, Wimbledon v Liverpool. Incredibly, this was the first penalty ever to be saved (or missed) in an FA Cup final at Wembley, all of sixty-five years since they began playing there. In 1988, Liverpool's grandeur at its zenith, the upstarts from Wimbledon came to Wembley to challenge them for the prize. What did John Motson call it – 'the Crazy Gang versus the Culture Club'? But Wimbledon take the lead before half-time and then continue to hold out any old how. Liverpool get rattled, very ratty – till, all's well, they are awarded a penalty. The dead-eyed hoofer John Aldridge saunters up to the oche and places the ball. No problem: he has scored eleven out of eleven penalties in the season, hasn't he? And, Liverpool being Liverpool, nearly all of them were on television. Which was one reason why Wimbledon's big, lurching, busby-haired goalie, Dave Beasant, had bought himself one of those newfangled video recorders and the week before had sat up late studying Aldridge's twelve-yard art. 'If the goalie stands on his line straight and still, Aldridge always plays it to their left,' Beasant confided to Motson before the game. And so it came to pass. Liverpool 0, Wimbledon 1 – and within weeks Beasant was sold to Newcastle for almost a million pounds. The goalkeeper's love of the penalty.

European Cup final, 30 May 1984, AS Roma v Liverpool. Penalty shoot-out in the raucously seething din of the Stadio Olimpico. 'No worry, boys, I'll put them off,' reassured Bruce Grobbelaar, the Liverpool goalkeeper, in his Zimbabwean razor-slice twang. At once the penalty count stood 2–1 to Roma. Up steps the Italian international Bruno Conti to settle it. He places the ball, looks up at Grobbelaar – and the crazy Koppite in gloves is crouching on his line, knees swaying and hands crossing like he's Max Wall doing his 'Black Bottom' dance routine. Conti panics and clears the bar by yards. Next, Falcão, the Brazilian: as he prepares to run up, Bruce is gnawing at the netting near the goalpost like a caged tiger; Falcão hesitates, resettles, but is lost. Liverpool are ahead. Roma's last chance is with ace man Francesco Graziani. As the Roman makes an elaborate Sign of the Cross after placing the ball, Grobbelaar sways into his limp-kneed, drunken matelot act. Graziani misses by miles. Liverpool win 4–2 on penalties. That 'all goalkeepers have a slate loose' was an axiom right down the century. Never better illustrated than by Grobbelaar on that passionate Cup final night in Rome. But Penalty Save of the Century? He never touched the ball. Unquestionably the Zimbabwean Liverpool's Kop knew as 'the Joker from the Jungle' conspired by his madcap antics to unsettle the Italian side's penalty-takers – certainly they complained afterwards that he had. Not that there was anything new under the crossbars of the penalty area. There was a precedent to Grobbelaar's mime show. In the 1922 FA Cup final at Stamford

Bridge, with 0–0 on the scoreboard, the England and Huddersfield Town forward Billy Smith was brought down inside the area. As he ran up to take the penalty-kick himself, Smith hesitated – Preston North End's amateur goalkeeper James Mitchell, who habitually played in spectacles and with a knotted and spotted handkerchief on his head, was dancing about on his line and waving his arms like a crazed octopus in an attempt to distract Smith – who continued his run-up and scored. It was the first time in history a final was settled by a single penalty goal, and the outcome was a new FA law forbidding goalkeepers to move at a penalty till the ball was struck. Had Smith missed that kick in 1922, Mitchell might well have taken the prize in this category; as he did not, sixty-two years later in Rome, any one – take your pick – of three missed penalties against Grobbelaar qualifies to be the

Penalty Save of the Century
BRUCE GROBBELAAR

> For when the great scorer comes to write against your name, He marks: Not that you won or lost, but how you played the game. *Grantland Rice (1880–1954), US sports-writer*

> Sports do not build character. They reveal it. *Heywood Broun (1888–1939), US humorist and writer*

Giantkillers of the Century

'A blur, a trice, a flash . . .'

In the World Cup finals, the two giantkillers of the century are surely the United States, who beat England 1–0 in 1950, and North Korea, who did for Italy by the same score in 1966. But let us wallow in more homely pastures here and stay with the one enduring cup competition which was already in rude annual health when the nineteenth century became the twentieth. All down the years, the FA Cup has been speckled with Davids defeating mighty Goliaths. As the longtime BBC radio football correspondent Bryon Butler so evocatively put it once: 'The giantkillers shred the form book, bulldoze their way across rigidly defined social barriers, steal a lead role in the show from the back row of the chorus and earn the sort of headlines normally reserved for wars and pretty princesses. They are mice which roar and oblige the nation to listen. They prevail, like David, with a sling and a stone. They, above all, provide the fun.'

You can reel off in your sleep the roll of honour through the century. Walsall and Woking, York City and Yeovil Town, and those bonny Uniteds – Colchester and Peterborough, Hereford and Sutton – who each united all right to slay the giant at their door. And quite a few more where they came from, not to mention Blyth Spartans, seeing as you ask. Oddly, many of these teams have Cup-fighting traditions inbuilt in the psyche and, by fluke of the draw, seem to be given regular silk-ruffed dandies from the top division to rough up in the ambush. Just as readily, some hoity-toity patrician teams seem to be more susceptible than others to being slain. None more than the two North London swanks. Even at century's end, rheumy old men at Arsenal, for instance, will wince when simply you say 'Walsall 1933', and their sons and grandsons do the same at mention of Bradford Park Avenue (1948) or Northampton ten years later.

The haughty Hotspurs from Tottenham, too, are famously liable, and their traditional Cup vulnerability was never put better to me than by that stalwart Port Vale player and manager Roy Sproson in a confident prophecy the day before Terry Venables brought his swaggering stars to the Potteries. 'It will be such a culture shock for them, especially if the weather's raw,' he said. 'Out of their thick-pile carpets and centrally-heated stockbroker houses and then their snug luxury coach, and for all their international caps and snazzy blazers and Italian shoes they'll have to head straight into our barn-like, concrete-floored visitors' dressing-room with its cold-white tiles, no coat-hangers, only a couple of wonky benches to sit on, and just one communal bath-tub. Our draughts can chill the marrow. And they only get a lukewarm cup of tea at half-time.'

Inevitably Venables and his snazzy blazers teeth-chatteringly slunk away, well beaten.

Into our hat went every FA Cup giantkiller of a century of this truly, madly, deeply magical phenomenon of glorious comeuppance and triumph. Many, indeed most, of these perky aforementioned bandits were, of course, in the lower recesses of the Football League, so were at least officially considered as one of the leading ninety football teams in the country.

Nevertheless, into this book's little velvet bag they all go for a romantic shake-up, for old times' sake as it were – but only two of them are taken out to play this exquisite final to decide the Giantkiller of the Century. Neither were even members of the League at the time, they were fun 'part-timers'. In both cases, every player came to Saturday's football after a full-time working man's week. And the dragons they slayed were unquestionably fierce powers in the land. One of our giantkillers was from Wessex, the other from the quiet Welsh Marches. Both were minnows of the small-pond Southern League. But both had ambitions for fresher, wider and deeper waters.

In 1947 a British Army officer, an expert in tank warfare who had been invalided out with punctured eardrums after the battle of Caen, was now farming a small-holding back in his native Somerset, where his father had been a miner. One evening he was enthused to read an ad in the *Bath Chronicle* for a post which might help brighten up his life on the farm. Alec Stock had, before his 1940 commission, after all, played some sterling games of football for both Charlton Athletic and Queen's Park Rangers.

It was Yeovil Town, dozy Southern Leaguers snuggling down in the balmy Blackmoor Vale, who had advertised roughly thus: '£10 a week, part-time coach, trainer, player, captain, secretary, manager, preferably a goalscoring forward with a knowledge of first aid.' Major Stock just couldn't resist. The only other fellow on the staff was the groundsman at thirty bob a week. Stock recalled to me many moons later how the job, and his passion for it, concentrated his mind so much that he was mentally numb by the time Saturdays came round; he was invariably sick in the dressing-room during his half-time pep talks.

Then, in the following 1948–49 season, Yeovil painstakingly, amazingly, won through to the third round proper of the FA Cup. They were drawn against Bury, who were quite a force then and the Second Division leaders. On a dull Thursday ten days before the game, Jack Milligan of the *Daily Graphic* drifted back from Peels in Fleet Street after lunch to do the first edition throwaway Soccer Bits. Anything for an intro, and luckily Enquiries didn't take long to get him Yeovil Town's number. For something to say, Stock told him that Bury should really be bothered about Yeovil's incredible sloping pitch.

Though Milligan didn't know it, Yeovil's pitch was the flattest by far in the area (if not the whole Southern League) but it was a good enough angle for a quiet sports-desk day. Stock's quotes ran in all editions: 'We'll keep banging the ball up the slope to our winger on the top side. He'll just blow his crosses over. It's hard work for our men on the bottom side, but I can assure them that it'll be a lot harder for Bury if they don't grasp the idea.'

It was the perfect con. Bury by no means grasped it. Yeovil won into the fourth round and a stupendous home draw against the stars in stripes from Sunderland – Watson, Shackleton, Elliott, Ramsden, Daniel and all, the most expansive and expensive line-up of the day, a team of invention and talent and nine of them internationals. They were second in the First Division at the time. Stock's near-genius invention of his slope and all the trumpeting follow-ups to Milligan's story made Sunderland hesitate; daily, it seemed, Stock was photographed on his centre-circle with a spirit-level; he had the local brewery ring the ground with tiered terracing in the form of beer crates, not only to let 17,500 of Yeovil's 23,000 population see the game but to help cramp the Sunderland forwards; and he even persuaded the local Casterbridge-type grain merchants to be Yeovil football's first sponsors and to put up his team of part-timers in a hotel for the week before the match.

And sure enough on 29 January 1949, Sunderland went to bits. Player-manager Stock himself scored a beauty, a twenty-yard left-foot volley, on the half-hour. Sunderland equalized, on instinct as it were, then settled back into a right old flap. Yeovil went ahead again and then set about kicking everything out of sight – 'over the grandstand and into the allotments,' recalled Stock. When Stock hoofed one clearance into Devon with two minutes left, the immortal Len Shackleton complained to him, 'Come on, old matey, don't spoil a good game.' But they did and they were through. Glory be, for their next trick they drew Manchester United at Maine Road (Old Trafford was still a bomb site). It was 81,000, no slope and an 8–0 drubbing in the fifth round. And when Matt Busby came to the visitors' dressing-room afterwards to say sorry about the volume of goals, Stock told him in his 'officer-Zummerzet' burr, 'Don't worry, my dear, at least we've lived a little.'

Yeovil and Alec Stock's 'slope', by the way, remained famed throughout football till the very last decade of the century, when the club, still thriving in non-League backwaters, built itself a new, small and perfectly formed (pitch pancake-flat) mini-stadium on the outskirts of town. The Major himself remained Yeovil's most celebrated citizen till Ian Botham was bred and schooled there, by which time Stock ('I'd actually always wanted to be an estate agent, my dear') had left Wessex to become a highly successful manager of such vibrant teams of their times as Luton Town and Fulham (whom he led out at Wembley itself for the 1975 Cup final). In 1969, Stock had signed for Luton from Fulham for £17,500 a raw centre-forward whom he sold on to Newcastle United 18 months later for £180,000. His name was Malcolm Macdonald.

By the winter of 1971–72, the appealing Macdonald had become not only a national figure through a handful of goalscoring splurges but one of those idolized icons they so take to their hearts at Newcastle United's hotbed at St James's Park, cult figures down the century such as Gallacher, Milburn, Keegan and Shearer. When January's third-round draw was made, Newcastle were drawn at home to Hereford United, like Yeovil, of the Southern League. Hereford had already caught the public's imagination by battling through three second-round replays against Football Leaguers Northampton Town. Now on their own sacred patch at St James's, Tyneside was stunned when their Magpies and Macdonald were held to a 2–2 draw by the battling non-League side. They promised the upstarts painful retribution in the replay back at Hereford's folksy paddock on Edgar Street – indeed, when the coach carrying the Newcastle team arrived for the match and parked in the neighbouring cattle market, Macdonald announced with smiling confidence that Newcastle would break all Cup goalscoring records, 'and I'll get eight of them at least.' He said he felt sorry for Hereford's impudence in the first match and that this time the tiny non-Leaguers would be shown 'the difference between Sotheby's and Steptoe and Son', the latter being rag-and-bone merchants of a popular TV comedy.

The clouds brooded, pewtery grey, and the rains sloshed in from Wales. The pitch glistened, and squelched underfoot. Fifteen thousand sardined around the rickety low-slung arena and, it seemed, the same number stood outside following the action simply through the different cadence of the tense, full-throated oohs and aahs of those inside with tickets.

Newcastle strutted their stuff. Hereford chivvied, chased. Goalkeeper Fred Potter made some unlikely saves, and at half-time the player-manager Colin Addison told them, 'Keen battling for every blade of grass.' Macdonald had been heroically policed by Hereford's own Mac, Mick McLaughlin, but now the England player scored and celebrated with abandon. Newcastle would surely set about making good their boasts as the part-timers ran out of puff and, well, expectations. Not a bit of it. Hereford dug deep, rallied even, and now Newcastle's Irish international goalkeeper Ian McFaul was having to do some serious mudlarking. In the eightieth minute, the stout

Hereford defender Roger Griffiths, a canning factory engineer, finally collapsed. In the fourth minute of the game he had injured his leg. Now he realized, seventy-six minutes later, that he had broken it: 'I don't think we had a stretcher at Hereford then. They carried me off, but I refused to go to hospital, I just lay on the touchline watching to see if the lads had anything left.'

Had they? Just four minutes remaining. Newcastle had settled for 1–0 now. They just wanted a shower and a quick getaway north.

Ron Radford, the joiner, picked up the ball in the centre-circle's tangent for Hereford, passed to fellow midfielder Brian Owen, who prodded it back to him . . .

In a blur, a trice, a split-second, a flash – call it what you will, a blinding coruscation if you like . . . anyway, in a single blink, and from a distance of nearly forty yards, the ball was billowing the netting behind McFaul and then bobbling merrily down into the mud to mock him: 'It was by far the best goal that has ever been scored against me. It simply screamed past. I never had a chance.' It was BBC TV's Goal of the Season. It was in Sky's Top 20 Goals of the Century. It was scored by Ron Radford. He is still a joiner, a quarter of a century later.

'I pushed it through from midfield to Brian, and he gives it straight back,' he says. 'Tell you what, it was a memory to last a lifetime, wasn't it? Ask anyone. My philosophy was always to have a dig. Suddenly, no rhyme nor reason to it, your instinct tells you there's a chance. You don't look up; no question of placing it; just the basics, head down, eye on the ball, good contact. In other words, as the old saying goes, "If you can see them white sticks, then have a go at getting it between them." Mind you, though I got quite a few like that, a heck of a lot went over the bar or nearer the corner-flag.

'That day it just happened, and television captured it. Years later, sure, we sat down and taped it when it came up as a BBC Great Sporting Moment. So the family have got it logged for posterity. And after it, Hereford gave me a lovely rosebowl to remember it by. But you don't have to be given anything tangible, do you, that can better the warm recollections that are up here in your head?

'Anyway, why be talking to me? When it comes down to it, everything in football is a team effort. We were playing that day for ourselves, sure, but honestly far more for the supporters of that little place, and for the lovely old market town itself. The whole place was in a lovely fever. The rest of the world hadn't even heard of Hereford, had it? And if they had, they didn't exactly know where it was. If our team in those days had character – and by heck, it did – then the club, the support and the whole area itself had helped to create it.'

The utter grandeur of Radford's forty-yard, ravishing, aimed-for score knocked the stuffing out of Newcastle. In extra-time, Ricky George clipped in Hereford's winner to inspire outpourings of local jubilation. In the next round, although they were to lose in the replay, Hereford again forced a noble draw with First Division West Ham in the first match to ensure that every resident in the old black-and-white city with its rosy-red cathedral walked about on a high for months like so many Mrs Fezziwigs – 'one vast substantial smile'.

No non-League club in the century had forced three successive replays – and won two of them – against Football League opposition. Hereford was assured immortality. And, in his way, so too was Ron Radford: 'We all had a bit of skill, but most of all we had that indefinable thing called "character", the sort of quality that gave us, if you like, an intellectual resilience to overcome all the hype and flannel of a Cup run.

'We all had our daily jobs, so had no time to get worked up. Full-timers, in a way, have nothing else to think about but the Saturday. We had Fred Potter in goal, he worked a skilled job all week on the motor-ways; Ken Mallender and Dudley Tyler were both top reps; Mike McLaughlin was an exporter; Alan Jones was a prison warder . . .' and he goes through the whole legendary list of his old mates. 'Every one of us will be proud to have been part of it till our dying day.'

Giantkillers of the Century
HEREFORD UNITED

Careless Hands of the Century

Dan, Dan, the Teflon man

On 12 May 1971, keeping goal for England against Malta, Gordon Banks did not have to touch the ball once. The ball never crossed England's bye-line to necessitate a goal-kick, nor did he have to make one save. Ten years earlier, those 100,000 who were there say that in the England v Scotland match at Wembley on 15 April 1961, the Scottish goalkeeper, Celtic's Frank Haffey, had only to make nine saves during the match. The match finished England 9 Scotland 3. 'Slap' Haffey became a successful crooner on the Scottish nightclub circuit. Peter Bonetti in his turn bought a faraway Scottish hotel when he retired. Away from it all. There was a rotten joke about the England reserve goalkeeper in the 1970 World Cup finals being nearly run over and killed by a bus as soon as he arrived back at Heathrow – 'but don't worry, the bus passed straight under him'. Bonetti was Chelsea's agile goalkeeping 'cat' but, as Gordon Banks's deputy, he let a couple of perceived soft goals through against West Germany in the World Cup's crucial quarter-final in which England, 2–0 up, ended 2–3 losers.

Next in the England jersey was Ray Clemence, athletic and balanced, a real gymnast. But not at Hampden Park in 1976. Playing for the Scots was Kenny Dalglish, a terrific goalscorer. Clemence agrees he might have too tensely lined up and braced himself for one of the howitzer shells Dalglish was famed for. But this time the electric Scot scuffed the shot – and it dribbled between Clemence's legs and over the line as if he was a schoolboy. It was the winning goal.

Clemence, in turn, was to hand over England's last-line duties to Peter Shilton, big and brave and a perfectionist. But only perfect sometimes. One of the most calamitous nights for England in their World Cup history was against Poland at Wembley in 1973. The decisive score had Peter Shilton flopping like an undertrained dolphin only after the ball had passed. He blames himself to this day: 'I had it covered, but as I came out I let him hit it under my body. It was an idiotic goal – I will go to the grave knowing I should have easily had it.'

Leeds United's Welshman Gary Sprake let in a sitter against Chelsea in the 1970 Cup final – and overnight the nation's perception of a hitherto brilliant goalkeeper changed. Leeds always seemed to be on television, so any mistake by Sprake was magnified, rather in the manner of Liverpool's David James a quarter of a century later – England champion one week, Liverpool joke the next. Once, against Liverpool, in front of the Kop, centre-half Jack Charlton passed back to Sprake. The goalkeeper caught the ball and made to throw out to Paul Reaney on the touchline. As he noticed the forward John Toshack moving to cover the throw Sprake aborted it – or not quite. As he checked the throw and turned, his arm followed through with the plan and he hurled the greasy ball into his own net. Pop-song hit of the time was 'Careless Hands'. The Kop's chorus rendered it full-throatedly. Thirty years later, by now a successful social-worker in the west Midlands, Sprake admits there are still occasions when someone recognizes him in the street and he hears the hummed tune 'Careless Hands'. If that Liverpool v Leeds fixture had not been on national television, few would have been any the wiser. The same would go for famous gaffes by Fulham's Peter Mellor in the 1975 Cup final ('Teflon', they called Pete, meaning 'non-stick'), Watford's Gary Plumley in the 1987 semi-final, and an alleged host of Scottish keepers down the century . . .

On 23 April 1927, the FA Cup left England for the one and only time when Cardiff beat Arsenal 1–0 at Wembley. It was, by all accounts, a nondescript match which the London club's pressure should have long settled before Cardiff's flukey seventy-third-minute goal. But one particular peripheral item, seemingly unimportant at the time, held a resonance for history and the future – and for goalies.

Did the fact that the match is remembered for being decided by a goalkeeping gaffe have anything to do with it being the first Cup final broadcast live by the fledgling BBC wireless station? In other words, did Captain Teddy Wakelam at the microphone get as worked up as a latter-day Alan Green over the one incident of much interest, thus settling goalkeeper Dan Lewis's boob indelibly into the minds of thousands of listeners?

The match was going nowhere on a greasy Wembley pitch when Cardiff's centre-forward Hugh Ferguson mishit a gentle daisy-cutter straight at the Arsenal custodian Lewis. The turf was not the only greasy thing. The story goes that Lewis had, for this special occasion, worn a brand-new jersey. As he knelt to gather Ferguson's shot, the ball skidded off the 'shiny' unwashed wool and slid under his left arm. He turned to clamp his right arm on the ball, but it only trickled further – and calamitously over the line. Thanks to the wireless, poor Dan's reputation was never the same again – and Arsenal made a ruling, still strictly adhered to at the end of the century, that no goalkeeper must take the field with a new, *unwashed* jersey.

Careless Hands of the Century
DAN LEWIS

There's a simple recipe about this sports business. If you're a sporting star, you're a sporting star. If you don't quite make it, you become a coach. If you can't coach, you become a journalist. If you can't spell, you introduce *Grandstand* on a Saturday afternoon. *Desmond Lynam*

The sports page records people's accomplishments; the front page has nothing but man's failure. *Judge Earl Warren (1891–1974), Governor of California*

Cricket

Batsman of the Century

Thirty-seven not out

The only possible way is to divide cricket's twentieth century into two distinct blocks – the twenty-six years before 10 November 1926, and the seventy-four years after that immortal, luminous and neon-winking date. BD and AD, you might say.

Cricket had long come out of its languid 'golden age' and had become hard-edged and professionally skilful. On either side of the doleful 1914–18 War, England and Australia had played regular and seriously competitive (albeit socially convivial) series against each other. The 'Ashes' captured the public imagination and huge crowds collected to watch the matches in both countries. Ditto when each played less regular matches against the white English-speaking colonials of South Africa.

Only a matter of weeks before that seminal, never-the-same-again day in 1926, the Australian cricketers had disembarked at Melbourne at the end of a five-week voyage from England, having surrendered the Ashes for the first time in fourteen years after losing the final Test match at The Oval on 18 August amid scenes of Kennington jubilation. Most of the genuine greats of the cricketing century thus far had played in that evocative match under the gasometers – such legendary figures as Woodfull, Ponsford, Macartney, Bardsley, Ryder, Gregory and Mailey under the Australian captain Herbie Collins; and, in an English side led by the dashing young 'golden age' throwback Percy Chapman, such accepted giants as Hobbs and Sutcliffe, Woolley and Hendren, Geary and Strudwick, as well as the tyro tearaway Larwood and, at forty-eight, the venerable but still mighty Rhodes. Many of these twenty-two would never play Test cricket again.

Once the travellers landed on the quay, they were chastened to realize the extent of that truth they had supped with their mother's milk – that Australia was a country not best pleased at being beaten by Poms. Recriminations were nasty. Selectors resigned and scapegoat number one was the hitherto-admired captain Collins, whose popular nickname 'Lucky' had been cancelled forthwith by the nation.

Within a few days of returning home, Collins announced his retirement from cricket and he at once took out a licence and became a bookmaker at the Sydney racetrack – a 'fresh start' to what was to become a sad personal downward spiral. Anyway, had Herbie not been so enamoured of reading, for his new professional reasons, the race-card lists of runners and riders in the *Sydney Morning Herald* on the morning of 11 November, he might have noticed on the adjoining sports pages of the newspaper this small-print, one-paragraph, abridged cricket score from a one-day match the day before at the Sydney Cricket Ground: SCG. One-day boys' trial match. Probables 302 for nine (AF Kippax 58, AA Jackson 53 retd). Possibles 237 (D Mullarkey 64 retd, DG Bradman 37 not out; JN Campbell 5 for 79).

Don Bradman was just eighteen. He was from upcountry Bowral where he was an estate agent's clerk, having left school at fourteen. It was the first time he had trod the Sydney Cricket Ground. At home the pitches were of coir or canvas matting on concrete, and this was the first time he had played on a turf wicket. He batted at number seven. On the same sports page, a *Herald* report had ended: 'Although on the slow side, Bradman showed supreme confidence, and the further he went the better he shaped. He was one of the few batsmen to leave his crease to the slow deliveries of Campbell.' A month before, Bradman had been asked by the New South Wales Cricket Association to attend boys' net practice in Sydney: 'We are prepared to pay your fare from Bowral and return, and we sincerely trust you will give this matter the consideration its importance warrants.' His father, a carpenter, accompanied him by train – Bowral is eighty-two miles south-west of Sydney – just as he had on the only two previous occasions the country boy had visited the big city. The first time was as a twelve-year-old, still in schoolboy knickerbockers, when they had watched the fifth Ashes Test in February 1921, and the first batsman he saw score a half-century was England's lissom Frank Woolley.

In fact, in his early teens, tennis was the boy's first great passion. He won a couple of local junior tournaments, encouraged by his uncles George and Richard, and when at fourteen he began work at Percy Westbrook's estate agency, his boss urged him to continue concentrating on his tennis. So in the summer of 1924–25 he played only one game of cricket – making a duck and 66. But the Bowral town side knew a good prospect and they asked the small lad with the clerk's neat handwriting if he would like to be their match secretary. He would – and in the summer of 1925–26 he batted twenty-three times in Berrima District League matches. He averaged 94.14 and the word soon reached Sydney, and led to his invitation to the boys' trial match the following November.

The second trip to Sydney had been when he was seventeen. His mother had promised him a new bat 'of real English willow' if he scored a century for Bowral in the final of the Berrima District Cup final. He scored exactly 300. In Sydney's biggest department store, according to his father later, the young man deliberated for more than an hour before deciding on a close-grained bat manufactured by the Yorkshire firm of William Sykes and signed 'Roy Kilner'. It was to serve him well. But not for long. That boys' trial match of 10 November led to Bradman being selected for the NSW Southern Districts team for the annual Country Week cricket tournament a fortnight later, where one-day matches were played on five successive days. For each match he batted at number three. He had never before faced first-class bowling. At the SCG he scored 43, 24 and 27; at the Parramatta Oval he made 41; and at Manly, 25.

His captain that week, the Sheffield Shield player LW Sieler, remarked: 'A fine boy, a good sport, the game is treated by him as a business and he has great ambition to succeed.' So much so that the day after his 25 at Manly, the senior Sydney grade club St George picked him for their Saturday away match against Petersham, who fielded the Test bowler Tom Andrews and NSW stalwart Sam Everett.

Bradman batted at number five. His first fifty took an hour. He had reached 98 in ninety minutes when he danced out to on-drive to the boundary for his century. He middled it, but the ball dribbled, as if punctured, to mid-on. No run. His new bat had snapped in two at the splice.

A player trotted on with a substitute willow. Next ball, Bradman went to his century with a venomous pull through midwicket. Ten runs later he was run out. It was his first century in grade cricket. Just two seasons later he was playing for Australia.

With 'Lucky' Herbie, alas, winning fewer big-money coups at the racecourse than he had hoped, the England team's SS *Otranto* docked at Fremantle in October 1928 to begin their defence of the Ashes under the dashing gaiety of young Chapman (another whose life as an ex-captain after cricket would become sadly unsteady, in his case after he had become director of a brewery). Melbourne's Jack Ryder, the much-liked and leathery all-rounder – 'the good ol' King of good ol' Collingwood' – was now the Australian skipper, and he was none too sure, in his kindly way, when the Sydney lobby demanded that 'the boy' Bradman should be pitched straight in against the English attack in the first Test at Brisbane's Exhibition Road ground.

Ryder put Bradman in after himself, at number seven. The kid made 18, clean bowled by Maurice Tate, England's bonny and tireless pro from Sussex. With little thought of his future, Maurice cheerfully told the press that, no problem, 'this boy's my bunny'. By the end of the series, in which England confidently retained the Ashes, Tate's 'bunny' nevertheless had played himself in for life dramatically with, respectively, 40 and 58 in the Adelaide match, and 79 and 112 and 123 and 37 not out in the two Tests at Victoria's MCG.

The following English summer of 1930, Sussex's good apple-cheeked Maurice – who remains, at century's end, almost best-of-the-best – was still, well, rabbiting on about 'bunnies'. In the first Test at Trent Bridge, true to his word, he clean-bowled Bradman for 8. The Brighton grin was from ear to, well, there. Bradman saw it, and responded with a pinched, shy-boy's determined half-smile. In the next five Test innings of the series, the diminutive, almost hopscotch-dancing, and cruelly dissecting Bradman humiliated Tate and his toiling English confrères for 131, 244, 334 (309 in a single day), 14 (c Duleep b leg-spinner Peebles), and 232 in the final match at The Oval.

And after that, Bradman quite phenomenally just, well, took it from there . . . Till 1948 when, back for the last time at The Oval, he took his farewell curtain-call. Quite outrageously, and unbelievably, he walked in needing only to hit just one single boundary-four to average exactly 100 every time he had been to the wicket in a Test match. Eric Hollies bowled him, second ball with a googly, for 0.

So Bradman ended with a Test match batting average of 99.94.

Think about 99.94. Nobody in the annals has remotely challenged it. To Sir Donald's Neil Armstrong, first man on the moon, every other leading and fêted Test match batsman in history is but as high as Sir Edmund Hillary and Sherpa Tensing, the first men to climb Everest. Great and mortal earthly men compared with, well, a heavenly feat beyond compare.

Of men who played around as many Test matches as Bradman's fifty-two, only England's Herbert Sutcliffe (60.73) managed to average roughly within forty each innings; far away in the distance from Bradman. Throughout the century – BD, before Don, and AD, after Don – no player has remotely got to within one-third of his scoreboard accomplishments. Simply buy 1999's *Wisden*, look at the facts – and then pour yourself a drink.

You might only gulp, and then say to yourself that the two nearest, the sublime South African leftie Graeme Pollock (60.97 in twenty-three Tests) and the quite stupendous, at the time, 'one-man band' West Indian George Headley – the cricket world knew him as the 'Black Bradman' – (60.83 in twenty-two) were prodigiously promising enough to have batted themselves even nearer to the Don's 99 had they not, for totally different reasons (respectively, wicked whites-only apartheid and, in the 1930s, the white establishment's patronizing fixture-list), been denied top cricket through their prime. But even those two all-time greats could never in truth have out-Bradmanned Bradman.

In Test cricket Bradman hit twenty-nine centuries (including doubles or trebles) in only eighty innings; in all first-class cricket he hit 117 in 338 innings, and here averaged 95.14 every time he went to the wicket – again leaving every other batsman (nearest here was a reasonable challenger at least, that deliciously stylish, but concentrating, Indian VM Merchant, with 71.22 in 229 innings) more than a despairing, and unbelievable, twenty-three points behind. In fact, history has to tell, Bradman did comparatively fail with that first cricket club he joined as a callow, pale boy in Sydney, St George. After he had broken his beloved first bat 'of English willow', he played for St George for another seven seasons before he moved to business in Adelaide. For St George, in seven full seasons, his batting average was, alas and alack, a scrimpy, dodgy 91.57.

That small-print throwaway paragraph in the *Sydney Morning Herald* of a boys' trial match on 10 November 1926 – 'DG Bradman 37 not out ... Bradman showed supreme confidence' – logged the first time a child trod on a first-class cricket field and was a prophecy which, in its way, changed all sport. For in no time, no sportsman had been so globally recognized as undeniably the best. Except, perhaps – and with very different resonance – the American boxer Jack Johnson. Certainly, the already grand old game of cricket was never remotely the same after 10 November 1926.

Batsman of the Century
SIR DONALD BRADMAN

I hate this attitude the media have that just because someone is good at sport means that their opinion on any topic is of fantastic importance. *Steve Ovett*

Journalism and batting are not so different – a few good strokes are often better remembered than all the padding in between. *Ted Dexter*

And when you rub the ball on rump or belly, Remember what it looks like on the telly. *Sir AP Herbert, poet and humorist*

Delivery of the Century

Whistling through his beard

Test match cricket's very Delivery of the Century might actually have been only the second one delivered in the very first Test of the brand-new twentieth century – on the first day of the first Test of the Ashes series on 1 January at Melbourne in 1902:
Trumper b Barnes 2

Then again, it could have been at Adelaide twenty-three Januaries later when another first-morning, first-over delivery – this time a leg-cutter, fashioned far away in Sussex – snortingly pinged out the Aussie captain's middle peg:
Collins b Tate 3

Who is to say the best of them all wasn't delivered just a year later in south London, in August 1926 at The Oval, when England blooded the square-shouldered young miner Harold Larwood? The twenty-one-year-old Nottinghamshire prospect led the attack with the recalled and supreme old forty-niner, Wilfred Rhodes. This time, doughty Bill Ponsford was on strike, and almost three score and ten years later Larwood, aged and stooped and blind, was to sit me down and recall that delivery as vividly as if it had been only the week before:

'Rhodes was pure genius. I got Woodfull for a duck and after a bit Rhodes came on. That Ponsford was a vicious cutter of the ball, vicious. I was at point but Rhodes keeps signalling me closer to the bat. Still fetching me up till I'm almost standing on Ponsford's crease.

Sure I'm a bit scared. Rhodes comes up, just two paces from behind umpire. But he stops dead, and stares at me.

'I'd involuntarily taken a pace back from Ponsford's crease. He fetches me in again. First ball nips through and smacks into Struddy's gloves. Second ball breaks back – and Ponsford, surprised, pops it up and I jump across and catch it left-handed. Rhodes walks down the pitch to me and says softly, "You can go back a bit now, sonny, we got him." '

Ponsford c Larwood b Rhodes 12

Or again, three full-bloom summers after that, and with Surrey's same gasometers standing sentry, might the Ball of the Century have been the skidder with which dark-haired Alan Fairfax did for the greybeard and Master, Jack Hobbs, in his very own kingdom and in his very last Test innings:

Hobbs b Fairfax 9

Nine! What sort of score was that for a forever curtain-call? Hobbs's biographer, the always evocative Ronald Mason, described it poignantly:

'You could hear the cavernous gasp as the bails fell . . . as for just that second longer than usual Hobbs stood motionless, looking at the broken wicket. If it had been 0 now, as Bradman's last innings was, there had been some perverse distinction in the failure; but 9 was neither here nor there. The foundations were kicked away from the excitement, the evening dusk gathered above the players . . . and the crowd sloped home in sadness, feeling for their hero.'

To be sure, for such evocation's sake, that medium-fast delivery from Fairfax, which pitched middle-and-leg and took Hobbs's middle, will remain logged and indelible for more than this century, not for more than a passing moment for the bowler who bowled it, but for the giant of an old batsman it dismissed. Context is crucially important here, as everywhere in history. How about this scorecard line, for instance, at the very top of the innocent innings in Australia's first Test at Sydney against Jardine's Englishmen of what was, within weeks, to be known as the Bodyline tour? It was December 1932 and if this was not prophecy, what was?

Woodfull b Larwood 0

So was this, by Jove, in the second Test of that notorious series, moments after the mighty young Bradman, having missed the first Test, took guard at Melbourne:
Bradman b Bowes 0

That was, in fact, an aberration by both Bradman and Bowes. Bradman did not often miss long-hops. But did the ball from the resplendently hostile Larwood during the next Test at Adelaide in January signpost the way bowling would develop through the next two-thirds of the century?
Oldfield retired hurt 41

Certainly, those deliveries by Larwood and Bowes reverberated around cricket's British empire.

So, mercifully, and in solely sporting terms, did this nippy, left-arm back-of-the-hander which cut off Walter Hammond, again at ever lovely Adelaide, in February four years later. It had the onliest Neville Cardus cabling back to the *Manchester Guardian*, 'If one single ball ever won a Test match, this was it.'
Hammond b Fleetwood-Smith 39

... and continuing, 'In the morning's first over, Fleetwood-Smith practically settled the issue. A lovely ball lured Hammond forward, broke at the critical length, evaded the bat, and bowled England's pivot and main hope. The crowd roared out their joy, and sent three cheers into the sunshine for Fleetwood-Smith, while skipper Bradman ran to him and shook his hand.'

Same Australian captain, same month, same place, ten years later, and another famed English journalist, EW Swanton, was due to dine that balmy Adelaide evening of 1946 chez Bradman and was escaping the rush by leaving the ground an over or so before the close with Jessie Bradman and her son John: 'Suddenly a tremendous uproar. "That'll be Dad," said John.' It was:
Bradman b Bedser 0

... and the one delivery to which the most prolifically breathtaking batsman the game had known later gave, and always has, the ultimate palm of palms. Says Bradman:

'The ball with which Bedser bowled me in the Adelaide Test was, I think, the finest ever to take my wicket. It must have come three-quarters of the way straight on my off stump, only to turn off the pitch and hit the middle and off stumps.'

In their totally different ways, the Australians Lindwall and Miller, each utterly hostile, were, as the century thought of coming out for its second-half, followed by the West Indian wiles and often unreadable guiles of Ramadhin and Valentine. The four of them bowled many a ripe peach, jaffa and plum in their celebrated careers in tandem. This solitary *Wisden* small-print line, in the very first Ashes Test after the war at the Gabba in Brisbane in November 1946, was to serve salutary and immediate notice of what lay in store for world and English cricket for more than the next decade:

Hutton b Miller 7

So did this top-of-the-card double-legend announcement at Lord's on 26 June 1950 – the very beginning of the first Test match the West Indies were ever to win in England – when the captain Goddard made a double bowling-change after his ineffective new-ball seamers, King and Worrell, had bowled the opening twenty-odd trundling overs and everybody was yawning and looking to lunch and the Thermos flask. Within minutes, it was:

Hutton st Walcott b Valentine 35
Washbrook st Walcott b Ramadhin 36

... and international cricket was, quite deliciously, never the same again.

And after which the Test batsmen of the world were, more often than not, equally stumped – 'ramanvalled' was the collectively ambushed word – for answers for more than half-a-dozen years. And if they hadn't got you, some time that year, or next, then the demon-fast Lindwall would. Few weren't 'lindwalled' either and, to be sure, the Australian's spearing yorker was a thing of lethal beauty – ask Graveney after Lord's in 1953, or Hutton after Headingley in 1956. Two deliveries of the century? Quite possibly. Well, Hutton said it was the finest yorker that had ever bowled him, and Lindwall himself told me before he died in 1996 that, yes, the inswinging blockhole job which had done for Graveney 43 years earlier, was his best of all: 'Tom jammed a lot of bat on it, but it still got through.'

Only students of some of the outstanding Indian mystics of the century's second-half might oppose the motion that Jim Laker was the best off-spinner of the whole 100 years. Every delivery from his raw index-finger, twisted off that high-stepped pirouette, whizzed with menace. Long after his summer *mirabilis* in 1956, and till his death, Jim would hold your gaze, knowing all, and grin that Yorkie's clenched, but always amiably confiding, clothes-peg grin and tell you (seeing you pushed him) about Old Trafford in July 1956: 'After my first few overs, if May (Peter, the captain) hadn't switched me to the Stretford End and given Lockie the other, you know, I daresay I would not have taken one wicket; Lockie might have had the lot. First over after the switch, I had McDonald caught and then at once clean-bowled the great RN Harvey. I was on my way.'

Harvey b Laker 0

Might that one wicket have been the most potent delivery of all the century? It was, after all, the trumpeting Elgar-like overture to Laker's unassailably glorious and, surely, unbeatable nineteen-wicket Test match sackful which, for this book's purpose, must be the most voluptuous and glitteringly sustained one-match bowling feat of the century – well, what can match it really, but Massie's one-off? – and however much the Manchester groundsman might have helped, he wasn't at the time actually bowling or digging ditches at the other. Tony Lock was, seething with jealousy and fury the while, and he ended with just the solitary twentieth wicket. So possibly – well, mischievously –

Burke c Cowdrey b Lock

– might even, for those judges of a nicely perverse nature, be *the* delivery of the century.

Not long after Laker, the one-shot bingo, blast-'em-for-pace era was upon us. Like Larwood and Lindwall and Constantine before him, Frank Tyson had blown a thrilling gale and now, together, did Hall and Griffith, and later Lillee and Thomson. Then they began to hunt in fours. Not so good. The Batsman's Fear of the Battery. Armour and helmets came in, with only sheer courage inside them; subtlety went out the pav windows. Soon, the fast bowlers were not simply making inroads for the spin bowlers, with deft cunning, to continue the infiltration, but captains were happy with sometimes five unvaried bumper-bowlers of out-and-out nasty, ramparts-blasting pace. From behind the ropes, anyway, the eye could not follow the arrow, and the interminable, relentless legend was once more wearily inked-in – c Marsh b Lillee . . . c Murray b Holding . . . and on and on.

So as the century neared its end, there came upon us, unheralded and quite astonishingly out of the blue, the most dappily unlikely young man from Melbourne with peroxide hair, an insouciant charm and a carefree smile which could light up the day. All cricket had, by now, long mournfully presumed that the art of spin bowling had, with just one or two last-gasp exceptions, died with the retirement of, as the affectionately yearning Christmas carol spoof had it:

> *We three tweaks of Orient are*
> *Bedi, Venkat, Chandrasekhar*

This new fellow had hitherto, and ludicrously, only a paltry fourteen first-class wickets in his locker, and in his first Test match, against India in New Year's week, 1992, at Sydney, the selectors were dumbed and humiliated by his figures of 45-7-150–1. For romantics, however, that solitary wicket will remain something to savour far into this upcoming century:

Shastri c Jones b Warne 206

At that moment of Shastri's being caught, the seemingly dead art and craft and science and daring of the leg-spin and googly bowler could be said to have been vibrantly revived, single-handed, by the nous and skill and *joie de vivre* of Shane Warne. An apt century's anniversary too, for Australians have always called the googly (the disguised sleight-of-wrist which turns a seemingly delivered leg-break into a bamboozling 'offie') a 'bosie', after its inventor and first practitioner, the English public schoolboy Bernard Bosanquet. Dramatic unities are precisely served, for Bosanquet's first public experiment with the delivery took a wicket in the very first spring of the century, in May 1900 at Lord's, when a bemused Sammy Coe of Leicestershire was stumped by the proverbial mile. Bosie took his invention to Australia with Pelham Warner's England team of 1903. In the first afternoon of the first Test at Sydney on 11 December, Warner gave him a first bowl against the Australian champion who looked set for a big score:

Armstrong b Bosanquet 48

And Bosanquet's wristy-twisty joke went on to clinch the series and win the Ashes for England on the return to Sydney in February when he took 6 for 51 as the home side was skittled for 171. So in celebration, let the Ball of the Century be decided by the leggies – and before opening the envelope, the shortlist is announced as:

Trumper st Hayes b Mailey 8, Sydney 1906
The twenty-year-old Arthur Mailey bowled two leg-breaks to his hero, Victor Trumper. Both went for sumptuous fours through extra cover. Next, he tried the googly. *Howzee!* 'As he walked past me,' wrote Mailey, 'he patted the back of his bat and said, "It was too good for me." There was no triumph in me as I watched the receding figure. I felt like a boy who had killed a dove.'

Woolley b Grimmett 46, Sydney 1925
England had won the fourth Test by an innings, and Australia gave an unlikely début to a wizened and weather-beaten, thirty-four-year-old, coot-bald leggie who walked up to the wicket like Charlie Chaplin. Answering 295, England were past 100 and proceeding well enough through Woolley and Hearne when Australia introduced its fourth bowler. In his second over, Grimmett tried the googly. Photographs show the left-hander Woolley in a fearful pickle – as he misses the ball, he has pirouetted on his right leg in the crease by ninety degrees and is now facing leg slip and attempting to play the ball one-handed. Having introduced himself, Grimmett ended with 5 for 45.

Bradman c Duleepsinhji b Peebles 14, Old Trafford 1930
The merciless Don had scored 131, 254 and 334 in his first innings in the series' previous three Tests. At Manchester England called up

young Ian Peebles. Bradman at once hit him for a rasping boundary. 'Next ball, he came down the wicket for the same off-drive,' wrote Peebles. 'It turned, nicked to second slip and Duleep made no mistake. A roar went up which lasted for a full minute. I had fulfilled my purpose. I heard later that the well-known artist named Nevinson had returned to these shores that very day, in the midst of a bank crisis and various other Government disasters, to find, much to his disgust, that all the evening newspaper headlines said simply, "PEEBLES DOES IT!" '

Hardstaff b O'Reilly 11, Headingley 1938
Young Joe beguilingly drove 'the Tiger' for two successive fours, the second of which Frank Chester had called 'no ball', an added insult to O'Reilly's injury. 'Thus enraged,' wrote Jack Pollard in his *Australian Cricket History*, 'O'Reilly bounced up to the crease next ball, arms flailing, wrists cocked, face strained in anger ... and knocked back Hardstaff's stumps with a vicious leg-break! The Australians believed umpire Chester had won the game for them.'

Bradman considered O'Reilly the best bowler of his time: 'To hit him for four would arouse a belligerent ferocity, almost like disturbing a hive of bees.' Cardus thought he was better than Barnes as the bowler of the century because O'Reilly's repertoire included a hissing cobra-strike of a googly. (Sir Neville put this point to Barnes once. 'It's quite true. I never had the googly,' admitted Barnes – then, after a pause and a twinkle in the keen, steely eyes, he added: 'I never needed it.') I never saw O'Reilly bowl, of course, but have enough old sepia newsreel on video to get the message. He approached the wicket with no nonsense, no finery – all venom and malevolence. Just like his journalism and his views of modern cricketers. Robertson-Glasgow described his run-up as 'a sort of fierce galumph, the right forearm working like a piston, at delivery the head ducked low as if to butt the batsman at the bowler's end onto the stumps'.

Bradman b Hollies 0, The Oval 1948
Picked for the fifth Test, Hollies had bowled to Bradman in Warwickshire's county match against the Aussie tourists only a few days before. 'Don't show him your googly, Eric,' urged his county

captain Dollery to the tubby, Pershore-cheeked leg-spinner, 'and when you get to The Oval, only show it to him second ball.' Hollies obeyed orders to the letter – as John Arlott described to the nation in his BBC wireless commentary, which can still be recited, by heart and word perfect, by no end of schoolboys of that generation. Well, this one anyway. The recital demands an attempt at least of the beloved Arlott burr:

'. . . here's Hollies, then, from the Vauxhall End . . . and Bradman goes back across his wicket and pushes the ball in the direction of the Houses of Parliament, which are out beyond mid-off. It doesn't go that far, it merely goes to Watkins at silly mid-off. No run, still 117 for 1. Two slips, a silly mid-off, and a forward short-leg, close to him . . . as Hollies pitches the ball up . . . and he's bowled! . . . Bradman, bowled Hollies, nought . . . Well, what do you say in such circumstances? I wonder if you see a ball very clearly in your last Test in England . . . and the opposing team has just stood around and given you three cheers . . . I wonder if you really see the ball at all?'

John Arlott's lyrical immediacy sealed the legend that Bradman's last-Test duck was caused by sentimental tears in the great batsman's eyes – and many years later I mentioned this to the England fieldsman at first slip that day in 1948, doughty Jack Crapp of Gloucester. 'Tears? That bugger Bradman never had a tear in his eye in all his life,' scoffed Jack.

May b Benaud 0, Old Trafford 1961
England packed the batting (Close, Pullar, Subba Row) with left-handers to counter Richie Benaud's leg-breaks. Just before tea on the last day, England needed only 106 at a run a minute with nine wickets left. Then Benaud's extravagant turners into the rough gobbled up four for nine in four overs, including the captain Peter May, round his legs, for an ignominious duck. Australia kept the Ashes. 'When you try something and it comes off, it gives you a very good feeling,' admitted the ever laconic Benaud.

Randall c & b Qadir 7, Hyderabad 1978
The bounding, soon-to-be-great Abdul Qadir had nervously introduced himself to England in the first Test on a low, slow pitch at

Lahore three weeks before, but with just a solitary wicket (Willis, no less!), Brearley's Englishmen sniffed no dangers. In the second Test at Hyderabad, Boycott, Brearley and Rose had together posted a calm enough 130 for 3 when Qadir came on as fifth change. In his first over, Randall fidgeted back, forward, and back again to give a return dolly, and at once Roope did almost exactly the same. England all out for 191, Qadir on his way with 6 for 44. He ended with 236 Test wickets; a match-winner, he took five in an innings fifteen times, ten in a match five times – better than O'Reilly and Benaud, but not as 'striking' as Barnes or Grimmett. After every one of those 236, Qadir would offer gratitude, simply and with a shy smile, 'to the Maker'. It can be no sacrilege to surmise that the Muslim nature embraces the leg-spinner's mystique. Thus it is a pity that in terms of cricket, England's national religion inspires bowlers mostly to be, as another crafty 'legger' Ian Peebles used to complain, 'just good old straight up and down, no nonsense, military medium, Church of England trundling.'

After that first Test wicket for plenty against India, the young Australian Shane Warne was persevered with by the Australian selectors and had won plaudits enough in two following short series – not least from rival batsmen and captains Richie Richardson of the West Indies and Martin Crowe of New Zealand – to be assured of his inclusion for the 1993 Ashes tour to England. I had been commissioned to write a detailed profile of the Australian tour manager and former captain, Bobby Simpson, and caught up with him and his side, captained by Allan Border, at the first opportunity at the traditional pipe-opener at Worcester. Warne was picked to play and my initial reaction, voiced to Simpson and Border at a convivial party down by the Severn on the eve of the match, was to question the wisdom of throwing the tyro in at once against England's perceived star bat who had wintered well. Indeed, Graeme Hick of Worcestershire certainly was pawing the earth determined to consolidate his suddenly re-awarded five-star rating. Border replied, almost callously, 'Sure, it might upset his confidence if he doesn't put the ball on the right spot and Graeme gets a pile of runs off him; then it will be a taste of what will happen to our young leggie if he doesn't get it right.'

The feeling was that Border had gone quietly bonkers, when Warne dished up a diet of gently turning, lollipop leggies all pitching around or outside off-stump. Hick clocked him all over the apple-blossom orchards for a mega-century, hitting 96 off seventy-seven balls from Warne.

Over the next few weeks it became clear to me that a devious and delicious plot was being hatched. At Worcester, and at other grounds where England possibles were batting, those commiserating, worry-pot bits of advice and condolence which Border was giving his young spinner from mid-off, as they waited for the ball to be retrieved from the adjoining pastures, were nothing of the sort. What the captain was insisting was that Warne stuck resolutely to The Game Plan: toss down gentle coddlers and keep the repertoire under your top hat for the real show. Warne was kept under wraps through the international one-day games – where a carefree and still unsuspecting Robin Smith went brilliantly barmy.

The match before the first Test was at Leicester. Last afternoon, the county trying to bat out time. No hope. On came Warne for a lengthy pre-Test bowl. Wowzee! The full works. Three Leicestershire fellows were bowled round their legs, although they were probably none the wiser, such a tizz were they in from the mesmerizing mix of wrong 'uns, fizzing flippers and top-spinners.

Few at the Leicester ground that afternoon took much notice – its local football team, the City, were involved in a crucial First Division play-off match at Wembley and one's first feeling was that its county batsmen were, in fact, making fools of themselves out in the middle the quicker to get back to the dressing-room TV and the soccer. Till I heard one of them – Vince Wells, I think – come in muttering, 'I've never seen anything like that before.' Warne's figures were 25–12–58–6; it was just the private dress-rehearsal Simpson and Border needed from him for the Test match two days later, and this is what I filed to the *Guardian* from Leicester that evening:

'Two or three batsmen rolled back to the pavilion in a daze of eye-rolling double-takes after being scrambled and poached by an outrageous right-angled extravagance which dips in serenely to land on the uncut edges of the strip far outside the left peg before snapping back a full yard to nip away the off-bail.

'A rare bird, Warne stands out more luminously for his peroxide haircut and electric-blue wraparound sunglasses. Handed the ball, he gives the thing a real tweak off an upright approach. Sleeves down, demeanour keen and unafraid, he gives a shine of the ball on his left buttock then transfers it in the middle of a jauntily busy three-pace walk and then one springy bound and it is whirring down at the bat.

'His aim is more middle-and-leg than off-stump for, though his flipper can hurry through, the wrong 'un is less well disguised. Gatting and Hick especially will be the two detailed to dismantle Warne's cocksure confidence at Old Trafford. It could be an intriguing passage when Border first tosses him the ball.'

I have (I assure you) very seldom been so prescient.

Two days later, the first Test at Manchester began well for England. Australia were bowled out for 289 in their first innings and, in reply, Gooch and Atherton reached an untroubled and promising 71 for the first wicket before Hughes had the latter caught behind the wicket. In strode England's acknowledged champion against spin, Mike Gatting – tubby, truculent, bearded and, as ever, bristling with intent to get on with it like a young-ish Henry VIII on first spotting Anne Boleyn. Immediately the Australian captain threw down the gauntlet and summoned Warne into the attack. An expectant stirring, a frisson, stimulated the packed throng. It was Gatting's first ball, and also Warne's very first in an Ashes series. Captain Graham Gooch was the batsman at the other end and he remembers:

'You just presumed Warne would begin with a loosener, most bowlers do. No chance. He just walked up and I heard it *flick* from his hand. The delivery hovered down on the line of Mike's pads and then it seemed to hang and dip in the air even further towards the leg side. Now if Mike had been well set, and not just arrived at the crease, I'm still convinced at that stage the ball would have been meat-and-drink to him and he'd have treated it just like it looked – an overpitched leg-side cheese roll to be whacked without ceremony over deep midwicket and into the crowd. But quite rightly, in a Test when you're a new bat and he's a new bowler, you just want to have a look-see, get a feel yourself and also check what the bowler's about. So as the ball floated down, now looking as if it would pitch almost outside the width of the crease, Mike was content enough just to push out, cover up if it happened to turn a bit, or let it continue floating innocuously down leg side to the keeper.

'Then the ball pitched. It gripped the turf, and it turned a good foot, possibly more, almost at right-angles. In a fizzing blur it ripped past his bat and across Mike's body – and plucked away the off-bail as crisp and sweet as a nut. Bloody hell, I could hardly believe it. Certainly Mike couldn't. He just stood there in half-forward defensive mode, totally transfixed, sort of half-whistling through his beard at such an ambush.

Delivery of the Century
GATTING b WARNE 0

The difference between an amateur and a professional athlete is the latter is paid by cheque. *Jack Kelly Jr, US Olympic committee member, 1983*

The fast money attracts the boxers and the schemers. But the boxers bleed, the schemers smirk. The boxers depart, the schemers survive. It has always been that way in boxing, and it always will be. *Dave Anderson, US sportswriter, 1977*

Fielder of the Century

The skill and the joy

As the century made plans to gather for its millennium celebrations, the consensus in modern cricket allowed the springheeled, slightly built South African Jonty Rhodes to be hailed as the game's finest outfieldsman. Good as he was, those longer in the tooth knew Rhodes still had some way to go to match even a couple of his fellow countrymen, namely Colin Bland, the Rhodesian Springbok of some three decades before, and Tony Harris from the 1940s.

It was on the Saturday afternoon of the 1965 Lord's Test, a glorious high-summer English day, when we in the old carousing Tavern crowd, in convivial fettle and good voice, were stunned into two successive and awestruck eruptions of unbiased acclaim when Colin Bland, from midwicket, announced himself with two breathtaking direct-hit run-outs of England's Ken Barrington and Jim Parks. In two blinks, those swooping throws on the run changed the course of the match and the series. One-day cricket was in its infancy then and that sort of run-out was a revelation. Mind you, Bland's strikes were no revelation to me – living briefly in what used to be called Salisbury (now Harare) a few years earlier, I had watched Bland practising obsessively for hours at the local sports club by throwing at a single stump placed inside a hockey goal-net. Afterwards you'd say 'Wow!' and Colin would mutter, sheepishly, something akin to golfer Gary Player's 'The more I practise, the luckier I get.'

On that 1965 tour, when the South Africans played at Canterbury a wet wicket held up play and Kent's Colin Cowdrey asked Bland if he'd give the restless crowd a fielding exhibition. A set of stumps was placed on the outfield, the ball driven to Bland at different speeds and angles and, from around twenty to thirty yards, of fifteen tries he demolished the stumps a phenomenal twelve times. In fact (apart from little me) on that earlier thrilling full-house Saturday afternoon at Lord's, it was the English batsmen who should have been fore-warned about Bland – for only the winter before, on that same club ground at Salisbury, the tall, athletic, dead-eyed fieldsman had simil-arly and dramatically thrown out with direct hits two England bats-men, Brearley and Dexter, on MJK Smith's MCC tour.

For all, say, the brilliant Jonty Rhodes's electric run-out of the Pakistani Inzamam-ul-Haq in the 1992 World Cup – he seemed still in horizontal dive when the stumps were broken by the ball – memory insists without a shadow of a doubt that while Rhodes might have matched his compatriot as a ball predator, Bland's throwing was far more killingly accurate. Rhodes has pocketed some thrilling 'goal-keeper's' catches, but those who were there say Bland's blinding catch of the New Zealander John Reid in Johannesburg on the Kiwis' 1961–62 tour must take the palm for the century's best.

Eighteen years before Bland, the South Africans had brought to England the dashing Tony Harris, who was thrilling out in the country or on the fringes of the sanctum. Like Bland, he was a free hitter at the crease but, as John Arlott noted with warmth in his clas-sic book on that 1947 series, 'Harris preferred his fielding, gay as a cricket and fast as a rabbit, to the cares of Test match batting.' Around the shires, English urchins, freed from the gloomy restric-tions of war and now eating the odd banana even, relished Harris's dare and gaiety, knowing he had been an RAF Spitfire ace (bailing out from his blazing plane to be taken prisoner-of-war), and also his general all-round oomph – he too was a Springbok rugby cap and had back home in the bush, we were told, shot his first man-eating lion at five, wrestled (and won) against a crocodile at ten and, even before he left school at Kimberley, starred for his province not only at cricket and rugby but at soccer, squash, golf and tennis. He was tops at fielding.

A quarter of a century after Harris had entranced the 1947 Trent Bridge Test field with his outcricket, there came to the same place, to play for Nottinghamshire, a Retford boy, Derek Randall, who, for speed and keenness and irrepressible charms, was to go on to warm all the world's Test cricket with his fielding. Once he had perfected, by constant practice, an unerring underarm – his quicksilver run-out of McCosker on the Ashes-clinching day at Headingley in 1977 remains unforgettable – as ally to his anticipation and bounding acrobatics, the man they called 'Arkle' (after the racehorse) was deservedly acknowledged as the finest outfielder of his generation. What serenely golden days in the sun they were for England when the Retford imp was patrolling one side of the square and the sleek young (before his arm 'went') David Gower the other.

Paul Parker, of Sussex and, just once, England, was another cover-point of sublime and swooping certainty. But possibly nearest to Bland's attacking ferocity in the field during my lifetime was Clive Lloyd, of Guyana and Old Trafford, in his gangling, loose-limbed prime. Bland better looked the part, handsome and very 'officer-class' and bristling with command as he almost willed the ball to come to him or the batsman literally to chance his arm. In contrast, and on the face of it, Lloyd seemed far less prepossessing to watch; as John Arlott observed once, when not in urgent action Lloyd tends to shamble about like some amiable Paddington Bear; but threaten to take him on from cover-point and young Clive was capable of exploding into action like a roused panther.

Lloyd's successor as West Indian captain, mighty brooding emperor at the crease Vivian Richards, was in his more supple gymnast's youth just as beady-eyed a threat to batsmen chancers from short cover or midwicket. Don't forget, the first time cricketing England (apart from Somerset's Taunton and Bath) realized one of the game's all-time monarchs had come among them was in the 1975 World Cup final at Lord's when young Isaac Vivian Alexander ran out with merciless direct throws first the Australian opener Turner and then Greg Chappell to set West Indies on the way.

Collie Smith and (anywhere) the onliest Garfield Sobers were remarkable West Indian fieldsmen. And there were plenty more where they came from – for instance, when he wasn't gloved and keeping wicket, the young Rohan Kanhai was a demon in the covers. And if any one man in the century's penultimate decade could make a case to be worth his place in one of the strongest of all Test XIs purely because of the value of his outfielding, it was Guyana's Roger Harper. Tall, even coltishly gangly, in the lower-middle order he could hit high and hard and as an off-spinner he was no shakes at all as a successor to Lance Gibbs – but as a fieldsman, no watcher dared take their eyes off him. The mandarin who picked the Rest of the World XI to play MCC at Lord's on the occasion of the club's memorable bicentenary match in 1987 almost deserves a knighthood for picking Harper for the 'Universe'. For MCC, Graham Gooch had scored a booming hundred. Harper came on to bowl. With lordly stride, Gooch took a step down the pitch looking to dent once again the freshly painted white pavilion pickets. In the same split-second bat hit ball, the tall bowler following through, bent, fielded the leathered flash in his prehensile left hand, transferred it to his right and threw down the batsman's stumps before Gooch could even have sensed danger. The batsman did turn and dive back, sprawling. But the square-leg umpire had no need to raise his finger. In a full-house and sun-blessed setting of grandeur, it had been a grand innings. But nothing was as grand as the bolt of lightning which ended it.

I was told at my father's knee that Learie Constantine was the grandest all-round fieldsman of all. My uncle asked if he'd forgotten Patsy Hendren and his footballer's gallop in the deep, or Jack Hobbs in the covers and, after him, Cyril Washbrook in his cream Blackburn-flannel shirt – and anyway, what about Alan Rees of Glamorgan? Every generation, everywhere, has its talisman in the field. 'Nip' Pellew, sprinter's dash and baseball throw, was long considered Australia's best through the first half of the century – till Neil Harvey collared the second half. Paul Sheehan came later, a true great. The smooth and athletically swooping Kiwi Martin Donnelly, who played rugby for England, electrified Oxford's gentle Parks at cover-point as did at Lord's, differently, the Middlesex captain Robbie Robins, as hyperactive as a Retford Randall. Much later, Middlesex's Roland Butcher was a coruscating joy in the field, close-up at the end but in his youth a shining beacon out in the country.

Later still, another Neil Harvey (both Christian names after the great Australian), Old Trafford's Fairbrother, became just about the best of his bunch. Every county delighted in its best and boasted of them – my own, down the century's generations, began with Jessop and Hammond, through Monks and Milton to the wing-heeled Foat. Glamorgan had Wooller and his fly-paper close catchers (and Peter Walker too) and then preened themselves with Matthew Maynard; while Surrey basked on for summer upon summer about their snap-happy leg trap of Surridge, Stewart, Lock and Co. Until the safe-as-houses, utter brilliance of Graham Roope came along. At The Oval next century, reminiscent talk will be about Chris Lewis's swallow-like exploits at backward gully – and, same position a hundred miles away, Warwickshire will be murmuring the same sort of awe about Trevor Penney. Men of Kent still sigh with pleasure when Alan Ealham's fielding is mentioned, just as Kentish men exclaim 'Ah, yes!' in a reverie at the name of Asif Iqbal. And who can ever forget seventeen-year-old Sachin Tendulkar's running catch at Lord's – or Aussie Matthew Hayden's backwards somersaulter come to that – and name me a county which hasn't always claimed to have the best unsung slip-catcher on the circuit?

That catch of Hayden's was, in fact, in a one-day international, and there is no remote doubt that the limited-overs game and its run-saving frenzies have improved fielding quite beyond old-timers' imagination. To be sure, those ancient sepia-washed, wide-angled photographs of the Test match scene in the first half of the century show a batsman playing a shot with half the out fieldsmen standing bolt upright and unready, some with *their hands in their pockets*. In MA Noble's book, one of the first decent tour chronicles (*Gilligan's Men: A Critical Review*) of MCC's trip to Australia in 1924–25, he lists in passing no fewer than forty-five 'catchable' catches dropped in the five-match series, twenty-four by Australia, twenty-one by Englishmen. That is appalling, nine per match: think, with all that inept spilling, what fun today the compilers of TV boobs and gaffes would have had. Yet, obviously, it allowed the good fieldsmen to stand out. CB Fry watched cricket till the 1950s and although he would never not give an acclaiming nod to the colourful Percy Chapman as a supreme cover-point for Cambridge, always he rated Gilbert Jessop the finest outfielder of all. So did Dr WG, predecessor of 'the Croucher' as captain of Gloucestershire.

In the midsummer of 1905, Gloucestershire were playing Middlesex at Lord's at the same time as, across the river, Surrey were hosting the Australians at The Oval. The Prince of Wales, as Surrey's president and landlord, attended the latter match on its final afternoon, and asked Dr Grace to accompany him. They sat on the committee-room balcony. Towards the evening, Surrey's champion Tom Hayward, batting at the Pavilion End, hit Trumble a massive blow which carried into the crowd at the Harleyford Road-Vauxhall corner. From the throng, the ball was suddenly returned in a fizzing flat, low arc straight into the wicketkeeper's gloves. 'Good God, Gloucester must have won,' exclaimed WG, 'only my Jessopus could have thrown that ball.' He was right: Gloucestershire had won at Lord's and Jessop had cabbed across the river to take a look at the Aussies. He had walked into the ground just as Hayward's hit had landed and 'tossed' back the ball as only he could.

Reading of such a throw, and imagining it – *thwack!* – slapping the stumper's gloves as hard and arrow-flat as it had left the fieldsman's hand some seventy or eighty yards away made me think of just one man – the Barbadian Keith Boyce who played (and enjoyed) such glorious cricket for Essex and, often, the West Indies for a dozen years in the 1960s and 1970s. He could hit with a languid power and could bowl fast to mean it. But as an all-round fieldsman, athletically feline in the country or menacing on the cover fringes or closer for startling and telescopic catches which no other man would dream to go for, Boyce was a breathtaking fulmination.

One afternoon at Chelmsford, around 1972 I suppose and certainly before the county ground had assumed its stadium-like enclosure, Boyce had enacted an electric series of *tours de force* in the field when, on the seats of the popular side, I came across an aged, grey-haired West Indian. He was weeping softly. I asked him, 'What's up, friend?'

'Sorry,' he said, and as he turned I saw they were tears of happiness. 'This boy of ours, Boyce,' he said, 'he reminds me so of Learie – the anticipation, the reflexes, the skill, the joy, the *fielding*. He can never be as good as Learie – no fielder ever could, or would, be that – but, I promise you, he is the nearest thing to Learie in his prime that I have ever seen.'

Lord Constantine, of Maraval and Nelson, had died only two years before. I was perfectly content to take that old man's word for it. He had seen the great man in his pomp. So had my dad – and it was one of the first immutable certainties he had ever drummed into me:

Fielder of the Century
LEARIE CONSTANTINE

> Dempsey hit me hardest, 'cos Dempsey hit me two hundred eleven thousand dollars' worth, while Louis only hit me thirty-six thousand dollars' worth. *Jack Sharkey, US heavyweight*

> The important thing in the Olympic Games is not winning, but taking part, for the essential thing in life is not so much conquering, as fighting well. *Bishop of Pennsylvania, 1908*

> If young men are active and in good health, incited by the instinct of emulation, they will desire to contend, in the name of their country, against men of other lands. *Baron de Coubertin (Pierre de Fredi) (1863–1937), founder of the modern Olympics*

Openers of the Century

In this case, only two

Any sensible man would nominate the glittering and diminutive Indian Sunil Gavaskar as the opening batsman of the century. His footwork was as impeccable as his courage and serenity. Of the thirty-four Test hundreds he scored, an astonishing thirteen were against the West Indians' merciless and unrelenting pace barrage in the latter third of the century. Moreover, from series to series – sometimes from Test to Test – Gavaskar never had the comfort, nor relief, of a regular opening partner filially to share the strike, bear the responsiblities.

The century's most long-standing opening partnerships – happily married couples, you might say – have been England's three duos Hobbs and Sutcliffe (who went forth to bat together 38 times), Hutton and Washbrook (54), Gooch and Boycott (49); the enduring Australian mateships of Simpson and Lawry (62) and Taylor and Slater; and the West Indians Greenidge and Haynes, who took guard together at the top of an innings a phenomenal 148 times. They had sixteen opening partnerships of three figures.

These happy couples went together like Morecambe and Wise, Marshall and Snellgrove, Matthews and Mortensen. With far less Test cricket, Hobbs and Sutcliffe posted first-wicket stands of 100 or more fifteen times in only twenty-five Tests together to lead easily the partnership averages. Hobbs was Surrey, celebrated, and modest, and he was the whole cricket world's magus on either side of the first War. Before it, the player-writer who bowled at him, Robertson-Glasgow, said, 'Hobbs may have had all the brilliance and daring, but it would be a rash man who denied that his meridian of skill was shown about the years 1919–26.' By all accounts, his stupendous partnership with the disciplined, more self-made Yorkshireman Sutcliffe drove Australians to distraction and, one reckons, it was hard to discern which predominated, the sheer pleasure of batting or their unshakeably confident trick of staying in.

After Hobbs and Sutcliffe last opened an innings together, for the Players XI at Lord's in 1932, another writer, Ronald Mason, acclaimed 'a legendary technique and repute unequalled by any other pair; the lean, active, quizzical Hobbs and the neat, wiry, imperturbable Sutcliffe, who together set a standard that can serve as a guide, but defied all attempts at emulation'. In 1994, the nonogenarian RES Wyatt, who also rewardingly opened with Sutcliffe in the 1930s, told me, 'Of all the great players Herbert was the least selfish, he was a grandly inspiring partner and absolutely fearless.'

Around the same time, Cyril Washbrook, himself in his eighties, said that his partnership with Len Hutton – which embodies England's highest opening stand, 359 against South Africa in 1948–49 – was, 'and like any worth its salt should be, based on technique, composure, mutual encouragement, and firm friendship'. An attraction of opposites? 'I suppose so. Perhaps I was in more of a hurry to take off the shine. I was a hooker, you see. I was the pugnacious one, if you like, to Leonard's calm. But all based on a perfect understanding between the wickets. Which made for a real partnership, didn't it?' Before his death, in 1990, Hutton had agreed: 'Cyril was my best and favourite partner, the ideal: technique, composure, staunchness; a firm friend, too.' Washbrook recalled their partnership record in Johannesburg 'as if it was yesterday', and going out together after the tea interval, 'onto the ground with Len; vast crowd, and this fellow comes out of it and says, "Only thirty more for the record, boys." Len looks at me and mutters, "What's he on about?"

' "Blow me," I say, "not a clue."

' "Well," says Len, "we'd better get thirty more and see what record it is, eh?" '

No one has better described the arts and science of opening the batting than one of its most stupendous practitioners, Bobby

Simpson, who walked out, and in, with his friend Bill Lawry, a gum-chewing crag with a nose almost as large as his concentrating powers. For thirty years, Simpson and Lawry headed Australia's opening aggregates with 3,956 runs, and on the world stage they were only overtaken by Haynes and Greenidge in the late 1980s. Again the partnership was built on affection and trust. Simpson told me: 'Bill was a remarkable man; hard as nails, ruthless, detached and determined at the crease – but wonderfully, immensely generous to bat with. Off the field he had a marvellous jokey, hilarious nature, but on the field he was grim and grinding and obviously never able to project his real personality on the crowd. But we had a tremendous opening partnership because, even if it didn't look it to you, we both knew the secret of relaxing totally between deliveries . . . As a definite plan and policy we would rotate the singles, share the strike as near to fifty-fifty as we could, to keep giving the bowler a different target, give him as few chances as possible even to bowl a full over at you, so he could never work out his game plan with any consistency, never get a prolonged shot at you. The singles and threes are the vital scoring shots in cricket, not the twos and fours.'

Australia's next heirs to the green-capped line begun by Ponsford and Woodfull were Mark Taylor and Michael Slater, again two attracting opposites – the former methodical, defiantly patient, the latter all vim and get-up-and-go. Said Slater: 'Our differing styles are good for each other. We feed off each other, lift the other's game. There were always little trigger-points, perhaps pointing out something halfway through an over, or agreeing to try to swap bowlers if someone is giving one of you a problem. When it is tough going, it is good to know that the person at the other end is right behind you.'

The 'opposites' theory down the century has endured as tried and, literally, tested. Before setting up home with Gooch, for instance, Boycott had fruitful partnerships with Bob Barber and John Edrich. Boycott much preferred the former – Barber fluently, even languidly, got on with it and the scoreboard was always on a hum. Edrich was a fine player but too much like Boycott himself – gritty, patient, a porer. Thus the tyro recruit, plodding Gooch, was ideal for Boycott; the poring scholar and the lusty blacksmith. Gooch, of course, went on batting for Essex almost to the end of the century. Once Boycott had gone he had sixteen other opening partners for England (the same as Hutton before and after Washbrook), including his long-time Essex partner John Stephenson, who played one Test only for England. Stephenson said that when he first went in with Gooch, 'the great man would score so quickly that it would sap the bowlers' hearts and confidence. When he was on 50 and I was on 8, it felt like batting on another planet. In the first seasons of our partnership, if Graham wasn't hitting the ball for four all the time he would get annoyed with himself, but as we went on he became increasingly keen on quick singles and fast threes. He says strike rotation is crucial. Not much calling goes on, he just looks up and we go.'

The very best were chalk and cheese all right.

Desmond Haynes had a broad smile and a carefree kind of comradeship which charmed the shires and warmed the Middlesex dressing-room when he played for them in the 1980s. In contrast, picture researchers were on a bonus to find photographic evidence that a grin had ever creased Gordon Greenidge's cheeks; he was as solemn in manner as his treatment of a new ball was savage.

Haynes wore a gold pendant on his necklace inscribed with his philosophy, 'Live, Love, Laugh.' Greenidge wore a perpetual frown out there, his coiled, muscular, boxer's shoulders seeming burdened, like those of Atlas, with the troubles of the world. No batsman can have played more blazingly resplendent innings than Greenidge and yet been profiled and praised in print so skimpily. Hale fellows and small-talkers steered well clear of him. Haynes's area of the dressing-room was a cheery space; Greenidge invariably bagged the darkest corner, where he brooded and quietly, obsessively, rearranged his kit into ever more neat and meticulous order.

Haynes and Greenidge first donned their crimson-cherry caps and passed through the wicket-gate together at Port-of-Spain in 1978. After which bowlers the world over would wake in the night, calling feverishly for long draughts of cold water and telling their wives of the routine nightmare they had just relived: Greenidge and Haynes at the crease. If the one did not get you the other would – but very often they would do so in tandem. When they split they held West Indies' record opening partnerships against England (298), Australia (250), New Zealand (255) and India (296). And with his previous partner, the dazzler Roy Fredericks, Greenidge held the record against Pakistan, a comparatively modest 182.

The previous West Indian opening partnership of enduring quality was that of Allan Rae and Jeffrey Stollmeyer. They opened on twenty-one occasions in thirteen Tests in the 1940s and 1950s, putting on 1,262 runs for an average partnership of 72, topped with 239 against India in 1948–49 and exceeding 100 on five occasions, or twenty-five per cent of the time.

Haynes, they say, has much of the upright elegance and unflurried charms of the late Stollmeyer's batsmanship. But there is a description by the grand Trinidadian philosopher CLR James of the very first of the black West Indian opening batsmen, Clifford Roach – who, alas, could find no regular first-wicket partner – in the early part of the century.

It reads: 'Roach is not unworthy to be mentioned in the same rank as Macartney. Glover, the fast bowler, sends down a short ball on the off-stump. Let any cricketer who wishes to understand what happened take a bat or walking stick and assume position. Then let him move his right foot back and across as far as it will go, and then let him lift his bat as high as he possibly can, and from that position let it go like a piston at the unfortunate ball. Third man on the boundary might as well be in the slips for all the use he was.'

Greenidge to a T – a fierce eye and the vengeful swipe of a Moghul warrior with a scimitar.

They were together for thirteen years. When Greenidge retired, Haynes paid tribute: 'Gordon was a marvellous influence on me. He didn't have to say much. Just watching him from the other end was a lesson in itself. He was so organized in everything about the job. You had only to look at his corner of the dressing-room to see how he approached his batting. Everything was so neat and tidy, prepared and laid out. Like his batting. You went with him and you knew he was ready to stay out there a long, long time. Gordon taught me an enormous amount about batting as well as professionalism. You just looked across at Gordon and said, "Man, that's a true pro." I was perfectly happy, and proud, to be second fiddle to him.'

Robertson-Glasgow once wrote of George Headley: 'Great batting often has the beauty of the blast or the grandeur of the gale ... As he walks down the pavilion steps you expect, in hope or fear. Only three or four can do this for you always.' Or, in this case, only two.

Openers of the Century
GREENIDGE and HAYNES

The biggest problem today is that the Olympic Games have become so important that political people want to take control of them. Our only salvation is to keep free from politics. *Avery Brundage (1887–1975), US President of the IOC*

Pressure does crazy things to athletes. Some love it, thrive on it. Others choke on it. Most learn to live with it. A few go nuts! *Herman L Masin, US sportswriter, 1980*

You have not lived in the world of competitive sport until you have fought a battle that is not against an opponent, but against yourself. *Peter Pollock*

Catch of the Century

Ten minus one

At Brisbane in November 1985, New Zealand beat Australia by an innings and 41 runs. It was Hadlee's match. The superb Kiwi opening bowler was in his pomp and, in all, took 15 wickets for 123 runs, the best match figures ever by a New Zealand Test bowler. In Australia's first innings, Hadlee's return of 23–4–52–9 had been bettered in all the century only by Laker at Manchester in 1956. On the first day, Australia were reeling at 175 for 8, Hadlee having taken all eight, when the tail-ender Lawson desperately flailed at a delivery from the Kiwis' tyro change-bowler Brown. The ball skewed from the bat high and skywards towards deep third-man and the vicinity of Hadlee's fielding position. The great bowler hared around to get beneath the steepler. He could have half-tripped, pretended to lose sight of it in the sun, fallen over or, dammit, just let the thing pop out of his hands after a gallant try. But Hadlee made ground and, on the run, dashingly held the catch to give Brown his first Test wicket – and also, in that one act, to deny himself all ten. Next over, Hadlee dismissed Holland (c Brown!) to take his ninth wicket and wrap up the Australian innings. So he finished with nine for 52 when, but for that wonderful and unselfish catch, it would have been all-ten for 52, one run better than Jim Laker's all-ten for 53 world record of 1956.

Catch of the Century
RICHARD HADLEE

Sixer of the Century

Simply, a soaring trust

It looked like an unbreakable world record, set in stone for immortality. In 1935, Somerset and England's Arthur Wellard smote 66 sixes in one season of first-class cricket to smash Arthur Carr's previous record of 48. With less county cricket being played as the century continued, surely no batsman would play enough innings in a summer and Wellard's big-hitting record looked increasingly distant and inviolate, although John Edrich (48) and Vivian Richards (49) had each once narrowly failed to post at least the half-century in bold but vain attempts to reach Wellard's faraway target. Till Ian Botham's astonishing blitzkrieg in 1985. Such had been the sustained power of the Botham assault that when he went out to bat for Somerset against Northamptonshire at the Weston-super-Mare festival, it was only 10 August and already Botham was just two sixers short of equalling his county compatriot's fifty-year-old record.

That afternoon, on a still racy-fresh wicket, Somerset were 144 for 4 and Northamptonshire's two opening bowlers who had shared the early spoils, Griffiths and Mallender, were back for a pre-tea spell in harness. Facing his second over, Botham announced his bonny intent, opened his barndoor shoulders and hit Griffiths out of the ground for six. In Griffiths's next, a second sixer followed, even higher, wider and more handsome. Had the tide been in, you fancied it might have landed in the sea. Botham had equalled Wellard's record, though few of the excited holiday crowd realized it for Weston boasted no PA announcement system. Next over, Botham took aim against the quicker, craftier and sometime England bowler Mallender. After three 'sighters' Botham clocked Mallender long, high and straight, and into a distant clump of parkland trees to establish a new record. Next ball – just for laughing luck and celebration – he repeated the mighty blow into the same faraway coppice. Botham's innings ended before the close of play, at 134 – off 147 balls, with eight fours and ten sixes.

The final monstrous hit of that innings had, in fact, posted Botham's almost incredible ninety-ninth sixer of the summer – if you included the no-less serious, but deemed by Lord's as 'second-class', one-day competitive matches for the NatWest Trophy, Benson & Hedges Cup and Sunday League. With defensive bowling the priority in these games, the truth is, paradoxically, that sixes in limited-over games are probably better earned.

After Weston, Botham's next innings was not till the following week – for England in the Test match against Australia on the far wider pasture at Edgbaston, a ground where, earlier that season, Botham had hit twelve sixes in an innings, just one short of the all-time county championship record held jointly by Greenidge of Hampshire and Humpage of Warwickshire. Now, in this fifth Test, the England top order, led by Gower, made hay and the score stood at 572 for 4 when Botham arrived at the wicket and took guard. The Australian pace bowler McDermott had just dismissed Lamb and, sensing a breakthrough to England's tail-enders, snorted in from the Pavilion End off his gathering gallop of a twenty-yard run . . . Botham took a half-stride chase from his crease and hit this first delivery a rapturously thrilling blow onto the top deck of the packed hospitality boxes over long-on to the left of the pavilion: 100 up! The next ball, too, went back over McDermott's head for a one-bounce four, and the next but one was another hooraying six which scattered again the cowering (and cheering) hospitality diners: 101 up!

If Charles Thornton was the nineteenth century's most compelling hitter of a cricket ball, Gilbert Jessop gaily carried his whirring cane-handled bat into the twentieth. But their actual tally of what we score now as sixes is not logged, for not till 1918 was the law changed which scored six runs if the ball was hit full-pitch over the boundary rope – hitherto it had to be hit clean out of the ground itself! The historian Gerald Broadribb has, however, conjectured that using the modern scoring method, in Jessop's twenty seasons which spanned the two centuries 'he probably averaged thirty-five sixes a season.' Some extended strike-rate, to be sure. A spectacular, although much shorter display of batting pyrotechnics came towards the end of the century, in another and unsuspecting county match between Glamorgan and Gloucestershire at the small border town of Abergavenny in July 1995 when the latter's twenty-year-old Anglo-Australian bat Andrew Symonds hit the sometime England bowler Watkin into an adjoining tennis court to ensure the sixteenth six of his innings (ultimately of 254 not out) was inked into the scorebook. The shot overtook the world record set by the New Zealander John Reid, playing for Wellington in 1962–63 – and with four more sixes in his second innings, Symonds also passed the record of seventeen in a match, set by Jim Stewart of Warwickshire in 1959. Bowlers' compliance – encouraging an early declaration, perhaps – has often meant first-class sixes have not been overearned by batsmen, although there was no suggestion of such easy gains in any of the above chronicles. Nor on the two occasions a batsman hit six sixes in one six-ball over – Garfield Sobers at Swansea in 1968, or Ravi Shastri at Bombay in 1984.

But context is all, and the spotlight of a tense Test match makes for a searching examination of nerve and verve. What was to become one of the finest and most warmly rewarding Tests in the latter third of the century was turned on its head by a fulminating fusillade of hitting. It took the breath away at a packed-house Lord's in July 1990. England needed to take the last Indian wicket to make the tourists follow on. India, in turn, needed 24 to make England bat again, and not only that. If they did not do so, the ignominy would be doubly and gloweringly heavy for unaccountably, and against all sensible augury, the Indian captain Azharuddin had given England first innings after winning the toss. So the Indian last wicket was also batting to save its captain's face. This is a crucial, and spiritual, matter for Indian lieutenant-warriors.

On the dismissal by Fraser of their number ten batsman Sharma, the callow young Indian slow bowler and genuine number eleven rabbit Hirwani was at once called on to survive the sixth and last ball of Fraser's over. More by good fortune than skill he did so, but his attempt made it look likely that just one more delivery would do for him.

India's nonpareil all-rounder Kapil Dev had meanwhile been fretting at the other end. Now he would face the experienced England offspinner, the shrewd and roly-poly Hemmings, who had already challengingly ringed the perimeter of his outfield with catchers. Ones or twos, who cared? All England needed was just one more delivery to Hirwani. Just one.

Kapil, at the Pavilion End crease, extravagantly blocked the first two balls of Hemmings's over. Then he took stock, walking at a stroll around the square to settle himself, it seemed, as Hemmings fretted to get on with it. Kapil discussed it with himself: twenty-four were needed; should he go ape for them at an almost certainly suicidal gulp against this wide-spread perimeter field, or should he cautiously attempt with ones and twos and the occasional boundary to nurse the colt Hirwani from the need to face just one ball? The latter was still the sensible bet. Kapil took fresh guard. He had made his decision. He narrowed his eyes and, the adrenalin now cascading in his breast, he settled to receive Hemmings's remaining deliveries. Gooch, the captain, held up play a moment – to move deep midwicket, Allan Lamb, just two paces squarer on the boundary rope. Hemmings then signalled, with a flap of his hand, for Fraser to move, just-so, finer at deep third-man. Then the veteran off-spinner (who thought he had seen it all) waddled three paces and, with an optimistic little skip, bowled.

Off the four successive balls, Kapil hit catches all right – but only great bludgeoning skiers of utter grandeur. The building workers in hard hats, who were erecting the Compton and Edrich stands at the Nursery End, ducked and took cover. In the four balls, 1–2–3–4 gigantic sixers sailed into the blue English-heatwave sky and cleared the field one after the other: 1–2–3–4. Well, 4 x 6 = 24. The deed was done. Thanks to Kapil's astonishing eye, the glory of his daring, and the (well, literally) soaring trust in his own ability, India had saved their captain's face – and also the follow-on. Off the very first ball of Fraser's next over, Hirwani was lbw. It did not matter a jot.

Sixer of the Century
KAPIL DEV

Over of the Century

Six – and out

Bridgetown, March 1981. England's opening batsmen, Boycott and Gooch, stride forth to open the reply to West Indies' all-out 265. 'In less than five minutes, Michael Holding's opening over to me had entered the annals of Test history,' remembers Geoffrey Boycott. 'It was a tailor-made pitch for pace. The first delivery was hostile and fast, and as it reared up at my face I was just able to turn my wrist to glove it downward, short of second slip. The second ball again spat straight at my chin; I attempted to play it, then snapped my head back at the last split-second. The third was more on a length, darted back into me and struck me a rottenly painful blow inside my unprotected left thigh, but too high for any lbw shout. The fourth was short and nasty and bouncing, but I played it and kept it down as I fended it off somehow and squirted it straight into the ground towards gully. The fifth was again as rapid as a gunshot and as I jerked my head back to avoid it I could hear the angry buzz of the ball. Sixth ball, I played a fraction inside the line, missed it, and it plucked out my off stump like a crazy thing. Ah well, you can't win 'em all.'

From the tour book, *Another Bloody Day in Paradise* (André Deutsch, 1981): '. . . the third, fourth and fifth deliveries each time made you fear for Sir Geoffrey's gallant life, and the sixth and last – as though the hateful half-dozen had been orchestrated into one gigantic crescendo – tore the off stump from the ground and had it spearing some twenty yards as if for the very heart of the wicketkeeper Murray. In the momentarily stunned silence of the vast throng which followed this public execution, Boycott looked round and palely down at the remains of his wicket and then, as the din assailed his ears, his mouth gaped and he tottered as if he'd been visited by the Devil himself; and then, slowly, he walked away, erect and brave, and beaten. That single over, magnificent and cruel at the same time, had, as it soon turned out, won the Test match and, indeed, the series.'

Over of the Century
MICHAEL HOLDING

Everywhere in England and America statesmen were already preparing their triumphs of 1914 and '39, by spending long days on the golf course and long nights at the bridge table. *Sir Osbert Sitwell (1892–1969), poet and writer*

Canada is a country whose main exports are ice hockey players and cold fronts. Our two main imports are baseball players and acid rain. *Pierre Trudeau, Canadian Prime Minister*

I never eat fish. They're my friends. *Johnny Weismüller*

Catcher of the Century

Reeling them in

Allan Border held the most Test match catches in the twentieth century. The Australian captain averaged exactly one per match, and Vivian Richards has an almost identical ratio. Border's predecessor Greg Chappell has the best average of the leading catchers, followed by Ian Botham.

	Catches	*Matches*
Border	156	156
Chappell	122	87
Richards	122	121
Botham	120	102
Cowdrey	120	114

As occasional up-and-down change bowlers, Border took 39 Test wickets, Chappell 47, Richards 32 and Cowdrey none. Apart from a very occasional caught-and-bowled, Botham could only reel in his 120 catches when he was not bowling at the other end. In other words, while he was bowling his 5,200 Test overs (which included 383 wickets) Botham was in no position to take a catch – which makes him, phenomenally and unquestionably, and 31,200 balls' worth, the supreme

Catcher of the Century
IAN BOTHAM

Leg-bye of the Century

Cometh the gaffer

At teatime on the fifth and last day of the first Test in Durban, South Africa, in 1948, England needed to score 128 in 135 minutes. One-day cricket had not yet versed players in the crafts or sciences of pacing an easy enough run-chase, and England's upper order panicked into collapse as the sun began to drop over the yard-arm and the southern ocean. And when the sun sets in Africa, it is dark in no time.

At a desperate 115 for 8, with eleven still needed, the burly Derbyshire miner and pace bowler Cliff Gladwin walked determinedly through the murk from the pavilion to join Alec Bedser at the wicket. He might have thought he was back home, down the Doe Lea pit, with a miner's lamp strapped to his cap. As he reached the crease, the South African captain Nourse enquired of Gladwin, 'What are you looking so cheerful about?' Replied the Englishman: 'Well, cometh the hour, cometh the man.' There were two balls left of the penultimate over. Bedser at once snicked a single; then Gladwin's cow-shot fell harmlessly and they ran two.

The final over would be bowled by the home side's leading seamer, Lance Tuckett. They were eight-ball overs then in the southern hemisphere. Eight to win. A run a ball. 'Just bowl straight and let them get themselves out,' muttered captain Nourse to Tuckett. The huge crowd was rapt in silent concentration. First ball, Bedser missed, but they scrambled a bye to the wicketkeeper Wade who was standing back, more nervous of letting through four byes at one gulp. Second ball – cometh the man, all right – Gladwin's nerveless heave carried high into the gloom and, with deep midwicket Eric Rowan misjudging the flight, one bounce over the ropes. The scattily brave blow meant just three were needed to win, two to level. Gladwin's bat whirred again, he missed, but they scampered another bye to Wade. Bedser gravely played two dot balls. Still any of four results was possible. Bedser poked the sixth delivery towards cover point and the two big strapping men hared for a single. The scores were level. Two balls to go. Gladwin wound up for glory, swung – and missed. Wade the stumper took it at a run and non-striker Bedser, looking for a bye to win the match, had to cram on all brakes, turn, and dive back into the bowler's-end crease. One ball left; still one to win. Tuckett brought in his field, then pondered it more. Gladwin shouted down the pitch to his partner, 'Don't worry, my young champion, we're going to get 'em, just leave it to your Derbyshire gaffer.' Tuckett fiddled again with his field. Eventually, ominously, the bowler moved in towards Gladwin through the gloaming. It was dead straight on middle-and-leg, a good-length, nasty riser. Gladwin swung in a great heavy-footed pirouette, missed again, and the ball whacked him painfully inside his right thigh. As the ball dropped, the close fieldsmen frantically converged on it; equally, from the other end, Bedser frantically converged on Gladwin at speed, hollering 'Run!'

Bedser made it by a whisker as the stumps were broken – by which time Gladwin had galumphingly made the other crease as if the hounds of hell were after him, and he was now dancing a victory jig, his bat flailing the air, as thousands raced onto the field, in celebrating sportsmanship, to carry Gladwin back to the pavilion on their shoulders.

After that tour, Gladwin never played for England again. Many years later, asked what he was thinking about as he ran that famous Durban twenty-two-yarder, the old miner said, 'That the boys back home in the pit were never going to believe that it was "the gaffer's" leg-bye that did it!'

Leg-bye of the Century
CLIFF GLADWIN

Season of the Century

Unrationed delights

In the English summer of 1947, Denis Compton illuminated the grey, still frightened post-war drabness and smithereened records for a single season, scoring 3,816 runs at an average of 90 each innings, and hitting eighteen centuries. Wrote Neville Cardus in the *Manchester Guardian* that autumn: 'Never have I been so deeply touched on a cricket ground as I was in this heavenly summer when I went to Lord's to see a pale-faced crowd, existing on rations, the rocket-bomb still in the ears of most folks – and there was this worn, dowdy crowd raptly watching Compton. The strain of long years of anxiety and affliction passed from all hearts and shoulders at the sight of Compton in full sail, sending the ball here, there and everywhere, each stroke a flick of delight, a propulsion of happy, sane, healthy life. There were no rations in an innings by Compton.'

Season of the Century
DENIS COMPTON

Test Innings of the Century

Ultimate valour and audacity

I was brought up in the certain knowledge that Gilbert Jessop's match-winning innings of 104 in seventy-five minutes in the Ashes Test of 1902 was the greatest ever played. Till I saw for myself the two bonfires lit by Ian Botham's pyrotechnics in the summer of 1981. Which was better? How do you gauge them? For 'comparisons are oderous' as Mrs Malaprop said.

Before he died, that grand cricket histo-statistician Derek Lodge attempted to evaluate all the truly great innings on a formula of his own devising in which he scrupulously took into account six determining factors – size of innings, speed of scoring, state of the game, state of the pitch, quality of the opposition (based on their ultimate career performances in Tests) and value of 'support' received in the innings from other batsmen in the team.

Lodge's meticulous 'slide-rule and context' calculations made Jessop's 104 (England needed 215, he had come in at 48 for 5) the clear winner – followed, in no particular order, by a half-dozen knocks of accepted and imperishable glory: Dudley Nourse's 231 in Johannesburg; Don Bradman's 334 (309 of them in a day) at Leeds; Stan McCabe's 232 at Nottingham; Tuppy Owen Smith's 129 at Leeds; Asif Iqbal's 146 at The Oval, and Ian Botham's 149 at Leeds.

But where does that leave us? For instance, although the legend says, to bear out Lodge's calculations, that once Stanley McCabe got his eye in, captain Bradman ordered his whole side onto that squat, romantic Trent Bridge players' balcony in 1938 and said, 'Watch this innings, boys, you'll never see another like it,' the facts are that Bradman himself later wrote that two earlier Test match innings by the wondrous McCabe had been, on the whole, much better – namely, 187 against England in 1932 at Sydney, and 189 against South Africa in Johannesburg three weeks later. So which was the best?

Lodge's criteria logged Botham's unforgettable, almost riotous turbulence at Headingley. A calculator might miss the truth, which is that it was a carefree, what-the-hell-we've-lost-let's-give-them-a-game-at-least sort of innings. While Botham's other Test century in that memorably zany summer – 118 at Manchester when the match was very much tingling and up for grabs – was far more the genuine article, indeed was acclaimed next day on the front page of no less than *The Times*, by its unexcitable cricket correspondent of long memory, John Woodcock: 'Botham's innings at Old Trafford was, of its kind, perhaps the greatest innings ever played.'

But again, where does that 'of its kind' by Woodcock leave us? Anyway, why does it have to be a three-figure score which embraced the grandest of all innings? What about Trumper's 74 (out of 122) in 1904? Or Dexter's 70 in 1963? Or Gower's 72 in Perth in 1982? Or Eddie Paynter's 83 at Brisbane in 1933, getting out of his sick-bed to make them? Or, come to that, how would Dean Jones at Madras 1986 rate for courage? Or Saneth Jayasuriya's 340 in 1997 for sheer boldness of spirit – or his Sri Lankan compatriot, Aravinda de Silva, for utter enchantment.

Perhaps one should be done with it and simply state that sheer weight of runs is totally conclusive in this discussion, and hand over the silverware to the luminous Brian Lara for his Test record 375 against England in Antigua in 1994, plus the tin-lid also for his all-time, any-place, bill-topping 501 at Edgbaston just a few weeks afterwards?

Both were unquestionably 'great' innings. But just what grade of 'great' for this almost mystical deliberation for the pantheon of grandeur over quantity? Never mind the width, feel the quality. Would Michael Atherton's 185 at Johannesburg have been a greater innings had England won, not 'merely' drawn? Likewise good strong-armed Dennis Amiss against the West Indians, twice? I think so. In this context, nominating the greatest of all innings, I reckon your team has to win at the end of it.

Or does it?

Derek Randall's enchanting 174, played for all history's sake in Melbourne's Centenary Test of 1977, was deemed a far more relevant knock than the same Retford ragamuffin's ('C'mon, Rags, c'mon!') heroic 150 at Sydney a year later – because the 174 had driven the seething maestros Lillee and Thomson to distraction, and twelve months later Randall was playing against what amounted to an Australian second XI, Kerry Packer's 'revolution' having taken place in the interim.

So context is all. Good point. Yet both those innings by Randall must be allowed to stand for election as the century's grandest of all. Because Mr Packer was nothing to do with him. You can only play against the best on offer at the time. We don't say Jack Hobbs was better, do we, before the first War than after it, because so many possibly outstanding bowlers had been slain in that conflict? You can only take guard and face up to the bowler who bowls. Would Jessop's innings at The Oval have been diluted in history if that resplendent bowler Trumble had announced on his deathbed in 1938 that he had, on that very 13 August 1902, developed a carbuncle on his spinning finger? I think not.

Mohammad Azharuddin of India, atwitch with finesse and dare, counter-attacked to score 'only' 121 at Lord's in 1990 but the quite majestic charms of the show easily had as much to offer as, in the same glorious match, Gooch's mammoth and, obviously, match-winning 333. So where does that place those two different knocks in the search for a 'finest' innings?

While we're at it, was Aza's even richer glory in one innings, half a dozen years later in Cape Town (in company with the even more 'great' Tendulkar), a finer election address for his place in the all-time log? Perhaps it was. It is a devilish decision to make. Similarly, was 'old' Emperor Viv mightier than Clive Lloyd's heir-apparent 'young Vivian', when he hit his callow but callously merciless 291 in 1976 – if only in the context of giving an intimidating warning to more than a generation of bowlers to come? Is the first announcement of grandeur the best? Or the mature last richness of it? Lloyd, too – wasn't his upstanding debutant's curtsey, 118 at Port-of-Spain, one of the innings of the century, despite everything he would later achieve?

You bet it was. But which of them all was Lloyd's best? Exactly the same with the 'unknown' Lara's voluptuously precocious 277 at Sydney, fully two years before his records began to fall. However many more records he breaks, might that first innings of Lara's always remain his best?

If Jack Hobbs was, all agree, just about the very best of all batsmen, then which was his single greatest innings? Nobody nominates the same one. Take your pick, from 126 at Melbourne in 1911–12 to 142, same place, 1928–29. His exact 100 on a sticky at The Oval in 1926 gets quite a few agreeing nominations – till you look it up and see his blood-brother Sutcliffe got 161 that day. Some sticky! And was Kennington really ever unplayably sticky?

Was Hutton's 364 on Surrey's same featherbed anywhere near as good as Hammond's comparatively 'paltry' 240 in the same year at Lord's? Which should be nominated here? Only one answer. And if the *real* truth were known, didn't the mighty Wally play a likely Innings of the Century about every other year between the mid-1920s and late 1930s – but, alas, they came but commonplace when matched in the following innings by Bradman's relentless, fierce totting-up of wonder? Then again, for all the ultimate splendour of Hammond – and Hobbs as well – was Hutton's apparently sublime 37 at Sydney on his first tour Down Under in 1946 actually better, in its time, than any century by him or the two preceding mighty 'H's? Who knows, really? And which supporters of Hobbs and Hammond could say, hand on heart, that their heroes would readily have bettered Hutton's 202 out of 344 under those familiar south London gasometers in 1950? Or his undefeated 156 out of 272 at Adelaide only seven months later? Likewise, which was grander in 1948 – Compton's 145, injured, or 184 in the Trent Bridge gloom? Or any number of his sparkling match-turning 'cameos' for lots and lots of runs and happiness.

Did any of those innings by the dashing DCS produce as utterly memorable a technicolored display as that single brief (in Test terms) evanescence of the precocious and, for history's sakes thanks to his benighted country's apartheid, very precious RGP – namely Graeme Pollock and his 125 at Trent Bridge in 1965? That splendour was marvelled at, by the way, by the schoolboy David Gower. Did the often sublime Gower ever play a left-hander's innings better than that by Pollock? Or Barry Richards a right-handed one? Barry was another Test cricketer we will never evaluate fairly. He might have been the best ever. Or he might not have been.

Did the Martins, Donnelly or Crowe, or Turner or Bert Sutcliffe (or Herbert Sutcliffe, come to that) play *the* one truly greatest Test innings, but nobody recognized it at the time? Or Zaheer Abbas, or Javed Miandad? Or Colonel Nayudu, or little glitterbug Vishy or, already, Sachin Tendulkar? Or one of the three 'W's? The glorious triumvirate of Weekes, Worrell and wicketkeeper Walcott each logged magically appealing innings for this particular manifesto. Nevertheless, will their predecessor swing the vote, because the West Indian maestro George Headley's two innings (106 out of 277, and 107 out of 225) against England at Lord's in 1939 were probably the two greatest *successive* Test innings ever played? Or were they the hundreds in each innings *against* the West Indies by Greg Chappell at Brisbane in 1975–76? Then again, was Martin Crowe's 188 and youthful genius at Georgetown in 1984 really a better innings than his 115 as (almost) a cripple at Old Trafford ten years later?

Had Gavaskar's 221 at The Oval in 1979 won the match (as it so nearly did), would that have made it a greater knock than Jessop's match-winner on the same paddock seventy-seven years before? It must have. But Greenidge's blistering 214 – on one leg – at Lord's, five years after Gavaskar's valiant try, *did* win, against all morning bets, the match for the West Indies in 1984. So why not give it to Gordon? Perhaps because Garfield Sobers's counter-attacking 132 which set up the tie at Brisbane in 1961 was better. Was it? Who's to judge? Me? Better than Viv in his smouldering pomp when he hit his fifty-six-ball century at Antigua in 1986? So is it Richards wreathed in laurels? For sure, we could not garland a more genuine all-time true great.

Knowing the valorous Viv, he would probably know full well who did actually play the Innings of the Century. He witnessed it, close-to in the slips; he crouched for every ball delivered by his West Indian battery to Graham Gooch of England at Headingley in 1991. Viv knew the stark facts – certainly his opposing captain Gooch did. He made 154; England's next highest score was 27. And England won.

Simply, even pathetically, England had not beaten the West Indies in a home match for more than two decades, not since 1969, in fact, when the West Indians had a far less lethal attack. Now they had the malevolently searching Ambrose, the Antiguan of the skyscraper arm, steep bouncer and terminal yorker; the two Jamaicans, Patterson the epitome of the slogan 'pace like fire', and the fast, mean, accurate and diligently scrutinizing Walsh; and the Bajan Marshall, snakily lethal, unrelenting and considered by most at the time to be the very best of the best in the world.

When they came to Headingley, in four of their last eight innings – that is, once a match – England had failed to reach even 200 against the West Indies. Here they did again, making 198 all out in the first innings, but the bowlers responded manfully and bowled out the tourists for 173; so, to all intents, even-stevens on the first innings. Some hopes – on the third morning, Ambrose, with avenging fury, wiped out Gooch's opening partner Atherton, and then at once Hick and Lamb. England were 38 for 3, bleeding badly and only 63 ahead; it looked as if the match would be over by teatime. Gooch stood four-square, defiant. He found two younger squires with grit and guts enough for him to nurse, first Ramprakash, then Pringle. The intense vigil was to last more than seven and a half hours.

Turn and turnabout, the West Indians attacked. Under the pewtery sky, the pitch was flat enough but damp and difficult. It was a day for bowlers all right – as well there were three short breaks for rain, which fudged the batsmen's concentration, jarred their 'groove', and were long enough for the platoon of bowlers to change, refresh themselves, and put their feet up for ten minutes.

It could not be purely a dead-bat 'burning-deck' innings; runs were crucial, lots of them. Gooch knew he could not simply defend, cower behind the sandbags. He knew he had to bat first for pride, then for safety, and then long and far enough to leave the West Indies a last-innings target which would, simply, scare even their batting strength in these conditions. In batting for a day and a half, Gooch achieved all that – and England's all-out total of 252 (Gooch 154 not out) set the West Indies 278 to win. They folded to 162 all out to give victory by 115 runs to England, and to Gooch.

The Innings of the Century: fortitude and concentration, applied technique and placement; the sharpest single never spurned, ones daringly turned into crucial twos. The knowing throng rapt, admiring, pent-up, mostly silent . . . a smatter of applause for a well-run two, even for a ball watchfully 'well left'; certainly for a fizzing yorker skilfully dug out; eruptive relief which could be heard down in the city square to celebrate a boundary. Against this attack 'boundary balls' come rarely, yet Gooch was never too locked-in to the defensive mode to miss one; in all he was to hit eighteen fours. With bat held high, head turned, as if squinting down a gun-barrel at the enemy, and hands cocked, Gooch repeats to himself, 'Don't give it away.'

For once he bats in a long-sleeved sweater, testament to the grim weather and, in a way, the grimness of the vigil. A crown and three lions for England. White T-shirt undervest at his collar. Unbadged white helmet. Moustache bushy, black. White gloves, piped in red and blue and, aptly, bearing the legend 'ULTIMATE' across the knuckles – and at every single, or over's end, he is biting at the velcro at his left wrist and tearing off that single glove, which he either carries in his hand or hangs on his bat-handle, a limp flag on a pole on an airless day. Once, in mid afternoon, the twelfth man comes out with two or three left-hand gloves from which to choose, and Gooch pokes and prods at the selection on offer like a housewife at a fruit stall . . . Then he settles back to his audacious task, two feet four-square at the crease, and heart of oak.

To carry his bat was historic feat enough. To do so in fashioning, almost single-handedly, a victory was unique for an Englishman. In the century, only Len Hutton twice, Geoffrey Boycott and Michael Atherton have carried their bat from beginning to end of a Test innings, but in doing so none of them had made it count to secure victory. Twenty-five Test openers carried in their bat in the century, but at a percentage of 66.11 Gooch's score was the highest by far of a side's total of any bat-carrier. In seven and a half hours, from first to undefeated last, Gooch's runs made up exactly two-thirds of those made from the bat – 154 out of 231 – against one of the most potent attacks in history; in poor light, and interruptions for rain, with 27 the next highest score. In the whole match only five of the twenty-two players passed 30 runs, but Gooch did so twice.

Test Innings of the Century
GRAHAM GOOCH 154 NOT OUT, Headingley

Stumper's Match of the Century

Thanks to the bowlers

Ed Pooley, of Surrey, was England's celebrated gloved livewire of the nineteenth century – and even though he was jailed for a pub-brawl assault and missed the rest of MCC's first tour of New Zealand and died, destitute, in a Lambeth workhouse early in the new century, *Wisden* logged him in posthumous glory at the top of their record list of Most Dismissals in a Match almost till the end of the twentieth, when James of Matabeleland snaffled thirteen Mashonaland victims at Bulawayo in 1996.

Behind the stumps for England, Pooley was followed by Dick Lilley from 1896 till 1909. He 'stood up' to every style of bowling, till Dr WG told him, 'Why stand up to all of us, Dick, why try to kill y'self? You'll get more catches standing back.' He did, too. In the gauntlet-wearing pantheon, Lilley was followed by 'Tiger' Smith. Then came the great impervious 'Struddy', Herbert Strudwick – who once while on tour Down Under was delivered a letter from home addressed simply 'Struddy, 'Stralia.' George Duckworth was Lancashire hotpot-warm, and raucous of appeal. Les Ames of Kent was much more dignified Home Counties Tory, and the first truly grand wicket-keeper batsman picked (just as the free-driving, competitive Stewart would be over half a century later) particularly for his batting. Ames's compatriot Alan Knott, however, was a rare genius behind the stumps and the best of the century's wicketkeeper-batsmen. Ames scored eight Test centuries, and Knott five. Between them came yet another from Kent, genial Godfrey Evans, not as steady-as-she-goes as Ames, nor as inventive an improviser with the bat as Knott's Mr Punch – but just as much a chivvying Master Puck talisman to his team.

Sir Neville Cardus defined and divided the two distinct types of English summer stumper – 'the one indignant and shrill, the other calm, polite and enquiring'. And all down the years the division has held good: Dick and the Tiger, Struddy and Duckworth and Ames, Godders and Parks, Taylor and Knott, Russell and Stewart ... The one appealing to the Gods, a ravenous presence behind the sticks: 'Hey, ump? Out! Out, I say? On y'way! Hop it!' The other gentlemanly and apologetically firm: 'Sorry about that, ol' fellow. Only nipped the leg bail. Good afternoon, ol' man, the pav's to your left, over there past fine leg. Mind the step, and have a decent shower.'

For instance, Knott could not have been more different in nature or style to the two England keepers who came before and after him, John Murray and Bob Taylor. For all Knott's impish batting for England, at no time was his sixth-wicket originality more valuable than at Bridgetown in March 1974 when, with the team fighting a desperate rearguard, Knott put on, in the first innings, 163 with white knight Tony Greig and, in the second, 142 with Keith Fletcher. Knott's two knocks were epic; and he had also let through only three byes in West Indies' massive total of 596. With the gloves, John Murray was as tidy-trim and cool as he could be with the willow. In a vein of form he could look a classic bat. During his record stand of 217 for the eighth wicket with maestro Tom Graveney at The Oval in 1966, also against the West Indies – upright, officer-class off-driving and identical blue England caps – oftentimes down there you could not tell John from Tom. Some tribute to a number nine stumper.

Like Knott's two at Bridgetown, that Oval innings very nearly took the palm here. So, come to that and in contrast, might have Murray's dead-bat score of 3 not out in the Ashes Test at Sydney on England's 1962–63 tour. Different days, different epics and, somehow, a wicket-keeper's knock *demands* back-to-the-wall defiance. Never more so than on Godfrey Evans's first tour of Australia in 1946–47. On it, Evans set two imperishable records – for defensive batting and for, well, defensive wicketkeeping, so no wonder the cheery tub of fun had his feet up as the train carrying the England party left Sydney for

Newcastle on Christmas Eve, 1946. The day before at the SCG, England had lost the second Test match by an innings, just as they had done the first at Brisbane. In Australia's innings of 659 for 8 at Sydney, Evans as wicketkeeper had set an all-time record for such a total by not conceding a single bye. Nor was he to let through a bye in Australia's first innings of 365 in the next Test at Melbourne.

The Sydney match was only his second Test. On his début for England, at The Oval in August 1946 against India, he had let through one bye. Which, till the New Year, was the only one he was to concede among 1,355 runs.

Half a century on, the ever-genial ancient with the grin through the mutton-chop whiskers still vividly recalls that 'wretched and idiotic' solitary bye: 'Jim Langridge of Sussex tossed down this silly little blighter outside off stump; it might have kept a bit low and I took my eye off it for a fraction. I didn't half swear at myself when it got through.'

In the Australian innings of 659 at Sydney, Evans stood up to the wicket throughout the forty-six overs delivered by England's new-ball bowler Alec Bedser: 'He needed me to; he bowled so much better for it. But it made for a heck of a lot of bruises on my chest and arms.'

It was not the only (still inviolate) world record set in that series by England's tyro stumper from Kent. In the fourth Test at Adelaide he batted for ninety-seven minutes (and ninety-eight balls) before scoring his first run: 'We were in big trouble on the penultimate evening. The first innings had been even-stevens, but when I went in at number ten we were 255 for 8 and if I'd got out, the merciless Braddles would probably have knocked the winning runs off all by himself next day. I'd been clean bowled for a duck by Ray Lindwall in the first innings, when Denis (Compton) hit a wonderful big hundred. Now Denis was forty-odd not out with only me and Doug (Wright) to come. I survived that night, runless, for forty-five minutes. Next morning we went on as before, against Lindwall and Miller with the ball still new and then against Toshack, McCool, Johnson and Dooland. Not a bad attack, eh?

'They were eight-ball overs then. Denis would take the first five balls, then we'd contrive to scramble a single for me to hold out for the remainder. And so it went on ... Denis was magnificent. We got him to his second hundred of the match, and we declared one ball after lunch. The Aussies were never going to get 340, so it was a draw. I had gone runless another fifty-odd minutes that morning – and then I began thrashing them all round the ground, didn't I, and ended on 10 not out.'

The partnership had rattled Bradman. 'Early prehistoric sledging if you like,' remembers Evans. 'With Denis facing, Bradman put all his fielders on the boundary so Denis could only attempt to get through with fours, or we could hare impossible twos. Denis got cheesed off.

' "C'mon, Don, this isn't cricket, set a proper field," he said.

'The Don retorted, "You're meant to be the great young batsman. I'm not giving you runs, you've got to work for them."

' "Set a proper field and I will," snapped Denis. It was an eye-opener for this greenhorn to be in the middle of the verbals between these two of the game's immortals.'

Verbals, too, almost half a century later in South Africa. 'Go on, scaredy-cat, give it a go, I thought you were meant to be a brave little rabbit,' ribbed the South African captain Hansie Cronje as he saw Jack Russell eye up a fielding change which invited him to be tempted into the sweep shot with no deep-fine or square leg in catching positions. 'Go on, Jack, I dare you,' Cronje kept teasing – and each time he was answered by a loud bellowing raspberry in a Gloucestershire accent – 'GET LOST!' And the little man settled back into his, by then, almost trance-like defiance.

It was the third Test match at Johannesburg in December 1996. South Africa had been in the driving seat all through and now, having been asked to survive more than five sessions, England had a pretty clear view of defeat. The winning target had already become laughably theoretical once England had lost Stewart, Ramprakash, Thorpe and Hick before even the final day's play had begun. In the morning, the fifth wicket (Smith) fell immediately after Atherton had posted his century – so Russell, his dark glasses, helmet and Kitchener-moustache making him resemble a California traffic cop, joined his captain with five full hours to bat out for a draw. Their country needed them, so they screwed their courage to the crease and when, after 277 minutes of the partnership, Cronje threw in the towel and declined to bowl the last few overs, the two marched off to English jubilation. Atherton's undefeated 185 was possibly the finest match-saving captain's innings of the century and, in a drawn Test rearguard by any other English bat, equal to Dennis Amiss's 262 not out at Kingston in 1973–74.

But for Russell, a 277-minute unbeaten innings of 29 to save the game was only a crowning glory to what was already the wicket-keeper's match of matches. For immediately before England had embarked on their so-nearly fateful second innings at Johannesburg, Russell had taken the penultimate South African wicket to fall – Eksteen c Russell b Cork 2. It gave him his eleventh stumper's wicket in the match and the all-time world record for Test dismissals set by one of his predecessors, Bob Taylor. 'I was euphoric, I just whizzed up to Dominic (Cork) and jumped into his embrace,' said Russell. 'Batting records are all their own work, a stumper cannot do a thing without bowlers.' In the pavilion, the first man to congratulate Russell was Taylor himself.

Stumper's Match of the Century
JACK RUSSELL

> The present state of English rugby is serious, but not hopeless; the present state of Irish rugby is hopeless but not serious. *Noel Henderson*

> Say mister, a good jockey don't need no orders from an owner before a race – and a bad jockey couldn't carry them out. *Jack Leach, former jockey*

County Match of the Century

Train takes the strain

Warwickshire v Hampshire at Edgbaston from 14–16 June 1922. The home side was captained by the Hon FS 'Freddie' Gough-Calthorpe, the visitors by Lionel Hallam, third Baron Tennyson and grandson of Victoria's Poet Laureate.

Lord Tennyson had captained England in the Ashes series only the year before. Calthorpe was to captain them on two upcoming West Indian tours. Both men had an Edwardian flamboyance and conviviality. Tennyson perhaps leaning even more towards the Regency. He captained Hampshire from 1919 till 1933, and throughout his chauffeur-butler Walter Livsey was the county's wicketkeeper. Calthorpe won three blues at Cambridge but was said never to have so much as met his tutor.

Tennyson won the toss and asked Warwickshire to bat although there was nothing much in the pitch. Batting in his Repton cap, Calthorpe (70) and his fellow amateur Reggie Santall (84) contributed to the bulk of Warwickshire's 223, Santall breaking two tiles on the new pavilion roof and Calthorpe easily clearing its turret with a six into what were then farming meadows. No matter, his family owned them, and all the vast acreage that is now the Edgbaston Golf Club.

Hampshire's reply began in mid-afternoon. Forty minutes and 53 balls later they were all out for 15 – with the four byes Tiger Smith let through making up more than a quarter of the score. There were eight ducks. Tennyson hit a four, and the No 4 Phil Mead was six not out. Calthorpe took four for four and Howell six for seven.

Hampshire followed on and at close of play were 98 for three, still needing 110 to avoid an innings defeat on the Thursday. Calthorpe commiserated with Tennyson in the amateurs' bar. 'Don't worry, ol' sport. If it finishes early enough tomorrow I'll lay on a late lunch for us amateurs, and what about a decent day's golf on Friday, what?'

'Lunch party?' roared Tennyson, lispingly affronted. 'Gowf on Fwiday? I'll tell you what, my good thir, Hampthire will be wining thith damned game by Fwiday!'

'Don't be ridiculous, Lordship,' said Calthorpe, using Tennyson's familiar nickname.

'Plathe your betth, thir,' snorted Lordship.

Tennyson was a famous gambler (as his unputdownably ripe memoir *Sticky Wicket* testifies) and even then, doubtless, Livsey was behind the pavilion polishing the new black-and-white Rolls-Royce said to have been paid for with £7,000 winnings from a bet on which of two flies would defenestrate first.

The late John Arlott, student of all things and Hants in particular, told me of this cricketing wager: 'Calthorpe shook on it at once, and though reports of the stake and the undoubted huge odds vary in telling, undoubtedly the win, however unlikely, was set to be a mighty one for Tennyson.' Arlott added it was probably the first early night of Tennyson's adult life.

However, there was to be no good start next morning. Howell bowled Mead at once – Hampshire 127 for four. Tennyson strode to the wicket in his trilby followed at a short distance by Livsey; as ever, Lordship took a last puff at his briar, then tossed it back towards Livsey who retrieved it and retreated, leaving his boss to take guard.

Tennyson only knew to pile into the bowling for all his determination. He made 45, caught off Calthorpe. At lunch, Hampshire were 177 for six, still needing 31 to make Calthorpe's openers pad up again. George Brown was at No 6. The straight-backed, strong countryman left-hander – uninhibited, combative, belligerent – willed the match to turn for his captain. With WR Shirley, Brown put on 85 for the seventh wicket and then, from 274 for eight (still only 66 ahead) added 177 with the gallant and faithful Livsey for the ninth. The butler had already made two 'pairs' that early summer, and the county committee were muttering about his dual roles.

Brown was bowled just before the close, and Tennyson had a glass of champagne for him at the pavilion gate. Brown 172, Hampshire 475 for nine – 267 ahead. Livsey, unbeaten on 90, drove his boss to Stratford in the Rolls for supper, and completed his century next morning to leave Warwickshire to score 314.

Calthorpe made 30, Tiger Smith 41 and WG Quaife 40. They were all out for 158. Hampshire had won by 155 runs, and 1923's *Wisden* noted: 'The victory taken as a whole must surely be without precedent in cricket.'

Tennyson pocketed his cheque from Calthorpe, then told Livsey to drive home alone in the Rolls. Lordship would travel with the team by train.

Years later, the amateur No 3 bat HLV 'Harry' Day (who had contributed 0 and 15) recalled: 'His Lordship led us to the train for Northampton. We all settled down until it was realized his ordered menu had not been heard of, so at a rush we ran for the Southampton train. Bottles popped and the carriage rocked all through southern England.'

County Match of the Century
WARWICKSHIRE v HAMPSHIRE, 1922

> Mere participation in sport can cast a woman's sexual preference into question, just as participation in ballet can for men. *The Sporting Woman, 1982*

> If members of the Jockey Club were ever to appear on *Mastermind* it would be in their best interest not to choose racing as their specialized subject. *Alistair Down*, Sporting Life

County Innings of the Century

Improvising defiance

It was difficult to ignore the all-rounders – those who played obviously fine innings on the back of superb bowling – like the three in the century who scored a hundred in both innings of a match and also took 11 wickets: BJT Bosanquet for Middlesex (1905), George Hirst for Yorkshire (1906), and Franklyn Stephenson for Nottinghamshire in 1988. Or what about Kevan James of Hampshire, a century against India followed by four wickets in four successive deliveries in 1996? Or the one and only Walter Hammond for Gloucestershire against Surrey at Cheltenham in 1928 – a hundred in both innings and 10 catches in the match?

But one single innings it is, and of the tens of thousands played the shortlist has been pared to three:

Ted Alletson, for Nottinghamshire against Sussex at Hove, 11 May 1911. Alletson was a strapping and popular 6-footer, but not much more than a bits-and-pieces all-rounder, playing intermittently for the county between 1904 and 1914, taking 33 wickets and averaging only 18 with the bat. He was the son of a wheelwright on the Duke of Portland's estate. At Hove that day, he went in at No 9 when Nottinghamshire were 185 for seven in their second innings and only nine runs ahead of Sussex. There remained 50 minutes before lunch, by which time the match would surely be over. The Sussex attack included the high-class Relf brothers and EH Killick. Nevertheless, the 27-year-old tail-ender Alletson, who had made only seven in the first innings (c Killick b Albert Relf), had made a breezy 47 not out by lunch, with last man Bill Riley yet to break his duck. They resumed after the interval at 2.15 pm. Alletson was dismissed 35 minutes later, at 2.55 – during which time he scored a further 142 out of 152, the most astonishing fusillade of sustained hitting in the history of the first-class game, before or since. In one five over spell, Nottingham added 100 (Alletson 97, Riley 3), and in one over he hit Killick for 34 runs, a record which survived till 1968 when Gary Sobers hit the maximum 36 off Glamorgan's Malcolm Nash at Swansea. Alletson was finally caught on the boundary off George Cox for 189. It remained his only century in first-class cricket. Sussex needed 237 to win and ended playing for a draw 34 short and with only two wickets left, so Alletson's innings did not quite win the match. Half a century later, Sussex's Bob Relf recalled, 'The shower of cricket balls just kept going over the boundary.' Facing 51 balls after lunch, Alletson had failed to score off 12 of them, the rest went for eight 6s, eighteen 4s, two 3s, six 2s and four singles.

Returning home a hero, the Duke of Portland presented him with an inscribed gold watch and, many years later, John Arlott wrote a whole book about the innings. Tel Alletson went through the First World War in the Royal Garrison Artillery, and later became a coal miner at the Manton Colliery near Worksop. He died in 1963, aged 79.

Harold Gimblet for Somerset against Essex at Frome, 18 May 1935. Gimblett was a 20-year-old farmer's son from Bicknoller in the blissful Quantocks, who played village cricket for Watchet. The afternoon before, out of the blue, he had been told to report to play his first match for Somerset at Frome, a town on the other side of the county. Get a dawn bus to Bridgewater and wicketkeeper Wally Luckes would pick him up in his car, was the order. He missed the bus, and hitched a lift in the back of a lorry. Somerset batted. The distinctly handy Essex attack included the England bowlers, Maurice Nicholls (fast) and Peter Smith (leg-spin). Gimblett was put in at No 8. At lunch, Somerset were glum at 105 for five, and the Bath amateur HD Burrough was dismissed immediately after the interval. Gimblett walked out at 2.20 pm, having been lent a spare bat by the kindly England all-rounder and big hitter, Arthur Wellard, whom he now joined at the wicket – and proceeded to outscore. In nine overs, Somerset added 69 runs, 48 to Gimblett. He posted his half-century with a six, having faced 33 balls. His next 50 came in 35 minutes. The century had been scored out of 130 in only 63 minutes, and was to win him the celebrated Lawrence Trophy for the season's fastest century. The shy young farmer was ultimtely c-&-b Laurie Eastman for 123 in 79 minutes. Gimblett to all intents had handsomely won the match for Somerset, for Essex were at once bowled out for 141 and 147. The farmer's boy became famed overnight. The following week even the London magazine *Punch* immortalized him thus:

> *How comes it that his agricultural youth*
> *Can meet the wiliest ball and freely scotch it?*
> *Simple and elementary is the truth,*
> *His Gimblett eye enables him to Watchet.*

With almost as much blistering trenchancy as he had displayed that day at Frome, Gimblett went on to score 23,000 runs for the county, with 50 centuries. He played three times for England; it should have been more. Unlike his batting, however, Gimblett's demeanour away from the crease was that of a worrypot, a victimized melancholic; he took his own life in his caravan in Hampshire in 1978.

Javed Miandad for Glamorgan against Essex at Colchester, 1 September 1981. Javed was, and was to continue to be, a celebrated Pakistan batsman. He ended his career in 1994 with nearly 9,000 Test runs and 23 centuries. Javed possessed a glittering array of strokes and a cussed, and technically near flawless, stickability – and never was this full hand of remarkable talents better displayed than at Colchester in the dying days of the County Championship season of 1981.

Outstanding batting by the Essex openers Graham Gooch and Brian Hardie had enabled Essex to set Glamorgan to score 325 to win in 323 minutes on the final day, a target presumed by all as ludicrously out of the question on a broken and crumbling 'park' pitch. By all except Javed, that is. To Essex's strong attack of John Lever, Norbert Phillip, Stuart Turner and the two high-class spin bowlers, David Acfield and Ray East, the bespoke pitch looked finger-licking good:

325 at a run a minute, the target was a joke. When the 24-year-old Javed took guard, Glamorgan were already 7 for two. In no time that became 44 for four. Only two other batsmen in the innings scored double figures, one of them, the experienced Alan Jones, making 36. For Essex, England's Gooch watched the innings closely as he fielded at slip: 'It was truly miraculous, I have never ever seen an innings like it. The ball was turning square and we were crowded round the bat looking to get home early. Javed played every conceivable stroke known to man, and then some more, all with astonishing improvization. His batting partners hardly needed to play a ball, so precisely did he nurse them and so mischievous was his farming of the bowling.'

When the seventh wicket fell at 227, Glamorgan needed only 98 to win. Continued the still awestruck Gooch: 'Then came the most fantastic and unbelievable passage of all. The Glamorgan captain Robin Hobbs was next man in – only to be out first ball. But he had come in at 227, and was out for a first-ball duck at 270. Utterly amazing. For eight full overs Javed had contrived to face every single one of those 48 balls.'

When the last man, Daniels, came in, 34 runs were needed for victory. Javed unflappably organized 20 of them before the No 11 was lbw to Lever. So Essex won by just 13 runs, with Glamorgan all out for 311 – Javed carrying in his bat with exactly 200. 'It was an utterly one-off and breathtaking show,' said Gooch.

Alletson's Match in 1911 was drawn. Gimblett's Match in 1935, remarkably his debutant's curtsey in first-cricket, was won by Somerset. Javed's Match in 1981 was lost by Glamorgan. But because heroic defiance is allowed to be, in cricket win or lose, such an illuminating positive, the palm goes to the magical Pakistani.

County Innings of the Century
JAVED MIANDAD

Traffic Jam of the Century

Frantic fraternalism

In the late afternoon of Tuesday 4 June 1994, a Birmingham businessman, Mushtaq Mohammad, was hard at work in his office in the centre of the city. As usual at that time and before she knocked off, his secretary delivered the Birmingham local evening newspaper to her boss who would, as usual, be working on into the evening.

She put the newspaper on his desk and mouthed 'goodnight'. Mr Mohammed was on the telephone. Of a sudden he made his excuses and hung up. He ran into the outer office and put on the local radio station. The newspaper banner headline had announced 'Lara 400 and Still Going'. The radio told him more – down the road at the Edgbaston cricket ground Warwickshire's magical young West Indian batsman Brian Lara was now 479 and still going.

Shouting to a colleague to 'lock up' Mr Mohammad danced down the stairs, two at a time, and into the office car-park, the city centre's evening rush hour was just beginning. No matter, he would surely make the journey of, what? two miles, in time. For sure, unless Lara went absolutely potty in the last couple of overs before close-of-play, he would see the deed done, or not.

It was 5.25 pm now and the traffic clammed up around him. He fumed and fretted, revved and hooted . . . Finally, tyres shrieking to a halt behind the Edgbaston pavilion, he leapt out and raced through the Members' entrance to the famous field . . .

He had missed the one decisive stroke by no more than half a minute . . . Lara was walking shyly off to acclaim, acknowledging it with a serenely tired smile, his upraised bat in his left hand and a souvenir stump and his helmet in the other. Mr Mohammad saw the scoreboard. It read Batsman No 3 – 501 not out. An applauding man told him what had happened: 'He was on 497 and there was only one ball to go in the match. Durham's John Morris bowled it and the little genius whacked it skimmingly through the covers for a perfect boundary – 501 up and that was that, he'd got the world record score,' the only individual score in first-class cricket ever to exceed 500.

Mr Mohammad had missed seeing it by half a minute, if that. His thoughts in a rush spooled back 35 years. There had been one delivery left as well on that famous day in Karachi. His beloved brother Hanif had been 499 not out when (ah me, if only he'd gone for a boundary) he pushed the final ball from the Bahawalpur bowler for a single to post the 500. His batting partner, wicketkeeper Abdul Aziz, had hesitated; so momentarily had Hanif. He was run out for 499. So what, it was still the world record and *Wisden* reported in awe, 'Hanif batted superbly, rarely putting the ball in the air and never offering one chance.'

And but for Birmingham's terrible rush-hour traffic Mushtaq Mohammad (for it was he) would have been the only man in history (surely) to have been witness to both these twentieth-century innings of enduring immortality. For the nearly-as-great a cricketer Mushtaq had on that Parsee Institute ground in Karachi on 9 and 11 January 1959, even shared a partnership (he scored 21) with his brother Hanif. So had another brother Wazir, who had made 31 that day. In fact, another brother of their five, Sadiq, was also a famous Test cricketer (between them they scored 11,000 Test runs with 190 first-class 100s) and another, Raees, was twice Pakistan's 12th man.

Ah well, sighed Mushtaq to himself, all great records have to be broken. He was only sorry he had not arrived at Edgbaston a minute earlier. He would wait a while, then go in and congratulate the wonderful young West Indian on behalf of his brother – and, to be sure, on behalf of the whole family – and then he'd drive back to the office.

Traffic Jam of the Century
BIRMINGHAM, 6 JUNE 1994

Rugby

Try Scorer of the Century

Classification changed

They come in different shapes and sizes – the tries, that is. And so do the try scorers – and from every segment of the speedometer. In the 1995 World Cup in South Africa, the New Zealand winger Jonah Lomu was built like a JCB but still ran as if powered by turbo-charged engines. In a handful of matches he became, universally, a household name. In the twenty-first century, the strapping build and sheer souped-up dynamic of the phenomenon Lomu may be the norm for wingers. Meanwhile, in the twentieth, the glorious variety of them has been spice to relish. There have been explosive, straight-track sprinters with delicate frames and ankles, such as Ken Jones, Pat Lagisquet, JJ Williams, or those olde-tyme revivalists Archibald Gracie and Eric Liddell. Or thunderous, scary ground-rumblers like Doug Smith, Ted Woodward, BG Williams or John Bevan. Or full-shouldered, full-pelt, wings-on-their-heels 'spheroids' such as Grant Batty and Rory Underwood. Or red-hot all-rounders with rugby 'brains', like Mike Slemen, Stu Wilson, Ieuan Evans or John Kirwan. There have been solid, speedy enough toughies like all those recent Scots, or Western Samoans, or Ireland's teaky Trevor Ringland. And a handful of unclassifiable one-offers like Chris Oti, Roger Baird, Simon Geoghegan or Rodney Webb, and good Mandela's Chester Williams. I never saw, of course, those two famed rockets of the 1950s on the veld – Tom Vollenhoven and Theunis Briers, both bullet-heads and bullet-speed – but I did see their successor, Gerry Germishuys, scorch the Lions' tail in 1980 with endless tries.

Vollenhoven came north to rugby league in England and there, generations later, was still being spoken of in awed reverence. As is, from an even earlier decade, the bald and bandy-legged Australian stepper Brian Bevan who scored an incredible 796 tries in his league career, a lorry-load which only Wigan's Welshman Billy Boston, with 571, could remotely make a dart at matching. As the century neared its end, Martin Offiah was the rugby leaguer on the wing who most stirred the adrenalin in either hemisphere. Get the ball to Offiah in a glint of space and a colleague had earned his win-bonus much more often than not. Further south, for England, times without number, we waited and sighed for David Duckham to be given a decent pass. So did David. But the Lions understood his famine – and he must have pinched himself for dreaming when he scored those six in a game for the 1971 Lions or that scintillating try against North Auckland on the same scintillating tour. I remember Duckham's first vivid score at Twickenham. Another daring pass and loop in his first Calcutta Cup game. In the next season came his, mine and everyone's favourite of all – that coruscating sprint against the dreaded Springboks at Twickenham, fair hair streaming like a pre-Raphaelite angel, winged boots never more than an inch from the left Royal Box touchline till he ducked inside the murderous tackler De Villiers with no more than a shrug of a hip. From ten yards away, Mervyn Davies once told me, 'David's sidestep looked obvious and predictable, but when you were confronted with it in close-up it had you stranded and leaden-footed.' Mervyn complimented very few Englishmen. And then the Nijinskys – the darters, the dancers, the sidesteppers, the intricate top-lick weavers of spells: Peter Jackson and Gerald Davies ... Ah, Gerald, frail-looking, pale and lonely on his touchline, scarlet shirt buttoned to the neck, fingers picking at his 'tash, or arms crossed as he warmed both hands in his armpits, till the ball was delivered and he'd pin his ears back and go at and through the slithering, cursing cover like an electric eel with brand new batteries.

Gerald of Wales was the best of the very best. Then David of Australia came along – David Campese of the Universe. His game had the flamboyance of the Latin-Celt. Which he was. His mother was a Murphy, whose family sailed from Kinsale to New South Wales at the turn of the century. His father, a carpenter, was born at Montecchio, a village between Venice and 'fair Padua, nursery of the arts', and left for Australia the day after his twenty-first birthday. David was born in Queanbeyan, New South Wales. The schoolboy's hero was Gerald Davies of faraway Wales. Gerald was, at the time, truly the genius of the touchline, of the streak and the strike at the corner flag – or, come to that, any part of the line you suggested. Beauty and balance with a feline awareness of all around him, and the scalpel slash of claw when it was time for the kill. It was, we were soon to suss, this new Campese's credo.

Campo, *Campissimo!* He smithereened every try-scoring record in the union game. In that respect he was, to rugby, almost what his compatriot Sir Donald Bradman had been to cricket. His acceleration allowed him to burst through the tiniest chink, sure, but what ghosted him past most defences was his sense, his 'nose', that a gap would appear if, instead of *that* way, he went *this* way. Campese opened up whole new thought processes about lock-picking. No player of rugby football can ever have 'read' a game better, or better assessed the split-second option (and chosen the right one) than Campese. He was utterly daring. His was a one-man tale of the unexpected. He was operatic in his strut and his swagger, his twig of the whole context, and the rich possibilities of the precise moment. He could defend as well, and hoof it, too. He was a prodigal son, sure, but a prodigiously vaunted and quite glorious one.

As the natures of both his family forebears traditionally testified, Campo's style was theatrically chock-full of blarney. Music by wonderful Verdi; libretto by wonderful Brendan Behan. Campese revelled in being downstage in the light of the lime. Like another famed Australian, Dame Nellie Melba of the concert stage, to the end of the century Campese continued coming back for one final-final tour – or match – or try. I was at the old Arms Park in Cardiff for one of those final-finales. The legendary star saved the best till last.

Tony O'Reilly, no mean touchline trampler himself, once spoke of rugby's joy in the wing-threequarter – 'for there is hardly a more stirring sight than the lonely foray of a solitary figure striding to death or glory into the gathering gloom of a winter's evening'. Such was the sight of Campese in Cardiff that Saturday against Wales – a sixty-yarder in the final minute to pipe the cake with icing. It had the vast throng in the old stadium on their feet, to a man, garlanding the Australian with a din of acclamation throughout his almost knock-kneed little trot back to the halfway line. An hour later I gawped, like the groupie I am, with a jostle of Welsh autograph urchins as the Australian squad embarked on their hotel coach. All but one of them were dressed in badged green regulation blazers and free-issue outback brogues. Campo carried his blazer, as well as a beautifully cut Italian raincoat; his shoes, slacks and haircut obviously bespoke Milan. He liked to chew a toothpick, as young Italian dandies did. Campo was the dandy of sport.

Between Campese scoring his try and signing my programme, I had telephoned my copy to the *Guardian*. In the press box, I had sat next to Gerald Davies himself. He was filing to *The Times* thus: 'At this crowning moment, the crowd stood to hail the conquering hero with the accolade of a standing ovation. And as he sauntered back, they saw in him what they had known all along – that he was the rugby player all Wales had wished themselves to be somehow: the greatest player in the world, ever and bar none.'

Quite so. There was Adrian Stoop. There was Percy Bush. There were the Cliffs, Jones and Morgan. There was Jack Kyle and Mike Gibson and two other Michaels, Jones and Lynagh. There was Bob Scott and Zinzan Brooke and Graham Mourie. There was Barry and Phil and Mervyn. And just think of all those Springboks. At one time or another during the century, the whole rugby world acknowledged as incomparably the greatest Gareth Edwards, Mark Ella, and Serge Blanco . . . But in the very scribbling of this chapter, it was obvious its classification screamed out to be changed from 'Try Scorer of the Century' to the undisputed greatest

Rugby Player of the Century
DAVID CAMPESE

Try of the Century

One minute and forty-five seconds

In the closed freemasonry of British rugby union, comparatively introverted and happy to play amongst itself for nine of the century's ten decades, there can only be two candidates to be Try of the Century. Can't there? The general consensus is that only the toss of a coin could separate 'Obolensky's try' on 4 January 1936 at Twickenham, and Gareth Edwards's 'Barbarians try' on 27 January 1973 at Cardiff. Both were scored against the always mighty All Blacks of New Zealand.

Alexander Obolensky was more dramatic than most history. He was a Russian prince, born in 1916 and sent from St Petersburg by his father Prince Alexis for an English education and for his 'safety'. From Brasenose College he played for Oxford, still in his teens, in the University matches of 1935 and 1937. He had corn-stoop hair and could run like a hare. Oxbridge contemporaries continue to revere his spirit. 'A carefree White Russian Parisian type, full of gaiety, who'd train on champagne and a dozen oysters,' remembers Vivian Jenkins. He was still only nineteen when England picked him against the All Blacks for his first international match, and his fellow England backs were almost as callow. At fly-half England fielded a Bart's medical student, the twenty-year-old Peter Candler; at centre were Peter Cranmer, twenty-one, Warwickshire cricketer and later journalist, and Ronald Gerrard, twenty-two, from the West country also a dashing cricketer and soon to be posthumous war hero.

Studying the fuzzy monochrome footage (shot from high in the

West Stand) you see England heeling from a set scrum on the halfway line. Candler passes to Cranmer, who slips his marker and runs straight before linking again, inside, with Candler on the ten–yard line. The fly then veers right and at speed towards Gerrard and Obolensky's wing. The All Black cover closes, but it is here that the Russian boldly defenestrates English public school orthodoxy and nervelessly steps inside his centre, Gerrard, and looks for Candler's pass, which is perfectly presented. Obolensky takes the pass about eight yards from the twenty-five-yard line. The New Zealanders, hopelessly wrong-footed, screechingly pull up and change direction like cartoon cats. The Russian continues to lance full-pelt and untouched to the line, which he crosses midway between the posts and corner. 'The try of tries?' Certainly the score was begun from deeper in midfield, but there was a tang about it of David Campese's right-to-left wrong-footer against New Zealand in the 1991 World Cup semi-final in Dublin.

Later that year, the RFU selected Obolensky for a 'missionary' tour to South America and, against 'a Brazil XV' in July 1936, he ran in a (still) record seventeen tries. In 1939, Obo signed for the RAF. His friend, Welsh international Arthur Rees, learned to fly with him. A smiling Obo fretted: 'What I can't quite get the hang of is the land-ing.' On 29 March 1940, Obolensky's Hawker Hurricane crashed as he attempted to land at Martlesham, Norfolk. It was a fortnight after his twenty-fourth birthday. He was the first of 111 rugby internation-als to die in the following five years.

The Barbarians try of 1973 in Cardiff was altogether more a 'collect-ive' voluptuary. Who cannot still recite Cliff Morgan's running commentary on BBC TV?

. . . Kirkpatrick . . . to Bryan Williams . . This is great stuff . . . Phil Bennett covering . . . Chased by Alistair Scown . . . Brilliant . . . Oh, that's brilliant . . . John Williams . . . Pullin . . . John Dawes, great dummy . . . David, Tom David, the halfway line . . . Brilliant, by Quinnell . . . This is Gareth Edwards . . . a dramatic start . . . What a score!

It was a try by a magnificent seven – and a quarter of a century later I sat each of them down in turn and asked, 'What really happened?'

Certainly nothing at all would have happened if Phil Bennett had not fielded Bryan Williams's bobbling kick under his own posts and then, instead of kicking for touch, played a startling game of hopscotch as a furious wave of adrenalin-charged All Blacks bore down on him. In the very act of turning, Bennett drove his right foot into not one, not two, but three riveting sidesteps.

... Brilliant, oh, that's brilliant ...

'At the time, I was intent only on getting out of trouble. I sensed they were right on top of me. Perhaps the whole beautiful, amazing thing wouldn't have happened if I hadn't heard Alistair Scown's menacing footsteps bearing down on me. As it was, I gave a bit of a hospital pass to JPR, didn't I?'

... John Williams ...

'Well, certainly I nearly lost my head as Bryan Williams lunged at me. But what utter brilliance by Phil. I remained convinced that the whole thing was really Carwyn James's try. Unique to the Barbarians, who disapproved of coaching, they asked him to give us a talk before the game. There was a lot of needle in the match; both us and the All Blacks were treating it as an unofficial fifth Test decider after we (the Lions) had beaten them, coached by Carwyn, Down Under eighteen months before. Now, preparing to go out, Carwyn soothed us, calming and relaxed, told us to enjoy it; and I'll never forget his last words, to insist to Phil, who was full of trepidation as he hadn't played long for Wales and certainly not for the Lions, to go out and play just like he did for Llanelli. So he does – then he gives it to me, and as I'm almost scalped I see John (Pullin) outside me and pop it to him. And do you know I still think to myself sometimes, "Where the heck did he come from? What's John, our trusty old hooker, doing there?" '

... Pullin ...

'Tell him I was there because speedy running forwards are not a new phenomenon. I'd been doing it all my career, but nobody seemed to notice. The try is still vivid in my memory? Well, has to be, they seem to replay it every week on TV, can't escape it. Seriously, there *was* a real needle to the game. "Exhibition match" was our last thought. A 3–0 win would have been enough for me. I suppose, looking back, it would honestly have been normal for me to have kicked for touch when I got the ball, but at the time it never entered my mind – I was back in New Zealand playing for Carwyn and the Lions and he drilled us all tour that if someone else had a bit of space then you pass it on to him. And John Dawes was moving quite nicely, wasn't he?'

... John Dawes, great dummy ...

'Ah me, the dummy that never was! But I'm eternally grateful to Cliff, telling the world I was a purveyor of great dummies. And I'm not going to argue with thirty-five million viewers, am I? In fact I was already looking to put John (Bevan) off down the wing, but the "dummy" was more eyeing the opposition as if I intended to pass. Anyway, suddenly they weren't there any more, I was through the gap and now looking for support inside. The fascinating things are: would Benny, who was pretty much a novice in international terms then, have dreamed of opening up if Carwyn's last words hadn't been to "sidestep this lot off the park, like you do at Stradey"? And that Gareth, if you study the TV replay, had covered right back from the halfway to our own line and when John passed to me, Gareth was actually well behind us, so he covered a heck of a lot of ground in that single minute. And incidentally, tell old Pullin that if the "mismove" had been invented in 1973, he wouldn't have got his pass and been world famous now.'

... David, Tom David, the halfway line ...

'Is that really me, taking the ball at such a helter-skelter in every one of those million TV replays? I wish the BBC would stop them. Well, the world and his wife thinks I'm still twenty-three and an electric athlete of under fourteen stone, and then they see my middle-aged spread coming through the door and say: "That's never him, the guy in the Baa-Baas try – can't be, impossible." To be honest, whenever I see it I think of two blokes from Gloucester way. Well, of course, I had only been told I was replacing the injured Mervyn (Davies) on the day of the match. Hadn't played for three weeks seriously because of my knee, see. The Saturday before, I thought I needed a run-out to get a bit fit, so I asked some pals up at Cilfynydd for a game. They were playing a little club at Gloucester called Hucclecote. No problem, they say, so off we go to Gloucester and I turn out in the centre. Foggy, I remember, which is perhaps the reason I seem to score a try every time I get the ball. Tons of them, haring through the centre like a knife through butter. Great. Knee great too, so no worries by the end of the week when I'm called up for the Baa-Baas. Except little me's surrounded by all these all-time rugby greats. The only sadness is, my name's not in the programme, being such a late call-up. It also worried two blokes in that great crowd, too. They were from Hucclecote. It said "Mervyn Davies" in the programme. They must have thought they'd either had too many beers or were in the middle of a bad dream: "Stone me, if that's not the bugger who played in the centre for Cilfynydd against us last Saturday." That evening they sought me out to settle their argument. "Hello, boys," I said. "Sure, I'm the local valley boy from the centre for Cilfynydd who made good in a week, and gave the pass for Derek Quinnell's magnificent catch this very afternoon." '

... Brilliant, by Quinnell ...

'Funny you describe it as a slip-catch on the run. That very thing, ridiculously, was going through my mind as I held it. That there I was on the Arms Park, and I'm thinking about a boyhood triumph all those years ago at Coleshill Sec Mod when my Form 2A played the big boys from 4A in the school cricket cup final and I took a truly wonderful catch at silly mid-on, just like this one I had just taken off Tom. (And I'm pretty certain that childhood winning catch was off the bowling of Form 2A's little Phil Bennett himself.) When I got back with the cup that afternoon our form master, Mr Brace, said, "Quinnell, a truly magnificent catch, but remember you only field at silly mid-on because you're built for comfort, not speed." That's what I was thinking as I scooped up Tom's pass at my bootlaces – till I was soon enough exploded out of my reverie by this series of banshee shouts behind me. "Here! Here!" I knew Gareth was coming like a train, screaming like a raving idiot – so recalling Mr Brace again and my lack of speed, I just pop the ball out to the left and let John (Bevan) and Gareth sort out who takes the pass.'

... This is Gareth Edwards ... a dramatic start ...

'Don't forget the match was less than five minutes old. Everyone was still so pumped up, the context was demanding someone bang it into touch, settle everything down. Phil should have put the ball in the stand. Phil, brilliant Phil ... I had charged back, following Bryan Williams's cross-kick to get behind Phil, and I remember thinking, as clear as if it was last Saturday, "What's the little blighter trying to do now?" as he began that series of sidesteps. Now I had to turn around and start motoring again. So I saw most of it unfold from behind, like a jockey who's last in the Derby. Every tiny facet of the jigsaw had to be in place – on another day any of those passes would have gone to ground. As I raced to catch up with the move, I suddenly heard the cadence change in the din of the crowd – it can always sense something is "on", often quicker than the players. I was at full lick now, and instinctively sensed that their fullback Joe Karam had eyes only for John Bevan, who was squeezed tight on the touchline. If I "intercepted" Derek's pass at speed, I could be through Karam before he realized. So I just screeched "Here!" to Derek – and then just went like a nut for the corner flag.'

... **What a score!** ...

What other scores, too, down the century . . .

How, for instance, would Barry John, the man they called 'the King', have responded to that bouncing ball at Cardiff which Phil Bennett retrieved with such spectacular results? Barry would have been playing instead of Phil that day, had he not retired from rugby the year before. But in try-scoring, Barry's moment of truth had come at Wellington on 6 July 1971, for the British Lions against the Combined New Zealand Universities. After about half an hour, there was a set scrum, midfield, on the Universities' twenty-two. The Lions heeled. The reserve scrum-half, the popular Chico Hopkins, shovelled it out to Barry, who caught the ball, stood stock still for a split-second, then feinted to drop the goal – the obvious thing. The loose forwards moved in desperately to charge down the 'pot'. Instead, John glided outside their desperate lunges by an inch or two and made as if to link up with his centres, Dawes and Gibson. He 'showed' the next defender the ball, which gave him time to come strongly off his left foot and leave the fellow crash-tackling thin air. Every man jack of the cover was now either on his heels or on precisely the wrong foot, and as four or five of them braked either to stop, turn or alter gear, John tiptoed delicately through to pop the ball down over the line.

The *Sunday Telegraph* rugby correspondent John Reason, who had seen no end of 'special' tries in his long experience, told his readers the following weekend how every man on either team – not only the mesmerized defenders who had been turned to stone – had been transfixed in wonder:

'The try on Tuesday left the crowd at Athletic Park absolutely dumbfounded. John had touched the ball down between the posts and was trotting back to take the conversion himself before the realization of what had happened sent the applause crashing round the ground. John confessed afterwards that he thought there must have been an infringement. "I thought Chico must have put the ball in crooked, or something," he said. "I couldn't understand why the crowd was so quiet." '

Many years later, the moment was still vivid for its dazzling perpetrator. 'Looking back, I know that try owes a lot to that first feint to drop the goal. To this day I don't know why I didn't go for it, I had enough room to pop it over. But from then on I could just sense intuitively that not one of the opposition around or ahead of me was balanced and sort of ready for me. So I just continued on – outside one, inside the other – all the way to the posts. I know it's funny, but it was all as if it was in a dream, that I had "placed" the defenders exactly where I wanted them, like poles in the garden to practise swerving. I don't know what you call it. Transcendental? Metaphysical? I don't really know the exact definition of those words, but it was just marvellously weird, like I was down there re-enacting the slow-motion replay before the actuality itself had happened. As if I was in a dreamy state of *déjà vu*, that I was in a game, and doing something that had already taken place at another time.'

To be sure, another place, another time, and in 1953 another Welsh legend, the Olympic sprinter Ken Jones, was famed as well for a lifetime after his score – from Clem Thomas's cross-kick – against Bob Scott's 1954 All Blacks (scores against great sides are trebly valued). Welshmen have a litany of tries to log off for history. A few, just off the top of my head and without looking up chapter and verse ... Cliff Morgan's for the Lions at Ellis Park in 1955 (for victory by 23–22) when he put in his place his wing-forward tormentor of four years before, Basie van Wyk ... A dozen years later, another young Welshman, Keith Jarrett, making a similar monkey of the staunch English fullback Roger Hosen ... And utterly great tries too, as memory's rewind-button spools back, from the likes of Dewi Bebb and JJ Williams, and Gareth and Phil (both against Scotland), and Gerald (the most palpitating of his, a bewildering hopscotch of full-lick sidesteps, was delivered by Davies in the Sam Doble memorial match in 1977). For (and against) the British Lions down the century, no end of glittering scores – well, scores of them, from the dashing Percy Bush in New Zealand in 1904 right up to the darting Jeremy Guscott in Australia in 1989, and Matt Dawson eight years later in South Africa when his almost tongue-in-cheek deception on the Springboks '22' probably qualified for the Dummy of the Century but certainly altered the course of a whole Test series in a single stroke.

Each to their own: if it was a wholly English jury, it would demand counsel, having lauded the Russian prince at length, recite at the drop of a red rose three more acknowledged super-duper solo tries indelible in their lore – each at Twickenham: Peter Jackson's against Australia in 1958; and, both against Scotland. Richard Sharp's in 1963 and Andy Hancock's two years later. Applause, applause, and for all three *Te Deums* will be sung. But just across the Channel, a French rugby fan as likely as not will think simply of Jackson, Sharp and Hancock as possibly an English firm of solicitors. Frenchmen would say (to a blank stare from any Brit) that far and away the greatest solo try ever scored was against New Zealand and a 90mph gale at Wellington in 1961 by Jean Dupuy. Or Jean Prat against these same Blacks at Colombes in 1954. And then claim that the three grandest *collectif* tries in all the game's long history were each scored by French teams. *Et voilà!* And he wouldn't be far wrong in that, either. In 'the score from the ends of the earth' in 1994 in New Zealand, France scored a break-out try of utter resplendence to rock the All Blacks terminally. They did the same, against Australia, in the semi-final of the first World Cup in 1987. And in between was Twickenham 1991 and the grandeur of England's Slam, but the even greater grandeur of France and Serge Blanco.

Scots, too, have their long shortlist, any amount by their generations of glistening wingers. But what about Gregor Townsend's reverse pass to Gavin Hastings in 1995? Or almost a half-century before, was Wilson Shaw's the most regal in the royal blue – as the *Scotsman* described the auld Twickenham enemy being made 'tae think again' in the winter of 1938: 'It was still anybody's game right up until two minutes from the end. Referee Ivor David of Wales, having charge of his first representative match, looked at his watch.

There were just two minutes – surely one side or the other would score again?

'It was Shaw who got the vital score, for he gathered in the loose before any Englishman could kill the ball and went away to the right, dodging and swerving, and no one could lay a hand on him. English defenders dived and fell in his weaving path, but none could stop him and eventually he raced round Parker to cross the English line and score the try of the century. Thousands of Scots in the large crowd threw their hats into the air, and they were satisfied now that England could not overhaul Scotland.'

But did that match KG MacLeod's against the first touring Springboks at Hampden Park in a quagmire on 17 November 1906, when he picked up a crossfield kick, said the grand London reporter EHD Sewell, and 'set off like lightning and took the slimy, greasy ball cleanly while going at absolutely terrific speed on boggy ground, which must have made such speed seem miraculous. As he went on to ground a triumphant try, the volume of applause that arose would have challenged comparison with Hampden's own authentic soccer roar.'

In between, for the Blues, there was AL Gracie's humdinger against Wales on 3 February 1923 – an overhead pass, a diagonal sprint, a third and final dummy, and a perilous run back inside the dead-ball line to get the ball under the posts – during which one of his boots struck the mouth of a watching schoolboy who, as the reports said, 'unhappily lost a number of teeth'.

Ireland, too, any amount of them: was Jack Kyle's a better try at Belfast against France in 1953, or the one for the British Lions at Dunedin in 1950? Who really knows, and Dr Jack's so modest he'd never voice an opinion. Likewise, which was the best of Alan Duggan's hatful on the wing in the 1960s? Or do you have to go back to Basil Maclear, the Dublin fusilier stationed at Cork's Fermoy, against those same first doughty Springboks in 1906? 'Dromio' of the *South Wales Argus* was there: '. . . with a flying leap he took the ball, and then going straight on, he had very nearly 100 yards to go. But, with a combination of force and swiftness, he passed man after man until he reached the halfway line. As the whole South African side had been up in the attack, there was nobody between him and a try but the fullback, Steven Joubert, and, of course, the second half of the field. The back made to tackle his man and was half bowled over. Maclear went on and the back came after him; there was a second tackle, courageous but only half-successful. For the next few yards Maclear staggered along, carrying the fullback draped around him like a cloak. Then, with a hand-off that was a gesture of royal dismissal, he broke away and scored.'

In spite of the great Basil's effort, however, Ireland lost 15–12. The bonny boys in green also lost, by a whisker, 19–18, all of seventy-four years later at the Parc des Princes in Paris. That amphitheatre of grandeur was first opened in 1970 and French rugby moved in from splintery, darling old Colombes (where the 'Chariots of Fire' actual Olympics had been held). So from 1971, every second New Year, Ireland played 'Les Allez Cats' in Le Parc (till French rugby moved to its spanking new World Cup stadium in 1997). Ireland scored just one solitary single try there. More than a quarter of a century, and only one five-pointer – so much so that when the Parc was opened, a try was worth only three! How's that quarter-century job for the Try of the Century?

Freddie McLennan, the bold Leinster winger, holds this bizarre and very Irish record, crossing the line during that palpitating defeat by 19–18. McLennan, an architect, is now settled in Cape Town. Did he remember his one-off slice of history? 'I'm glad you asked me that,' he answers twenty-five years later with his still-breezy Celtic charm on the telephone. 'Funny thing was that the day before the match we went out for a walk on the pitch. It was blowing a gale. A wee paper sweet-wrapping dislodges itself from my blazer pocket and flies way over the try-line and lands under the posts. I tell the boys, "It's an omen, lads. I'll score a try tomorrow on that very spot."

'So along comes the game next day and we're playing towards that end. Sure enough, after a bit of messing around midfield, the French scrum-half Jerome Gallion loses the ball and our centre Paul McNaughton breaks clear and then hands on to me. I fly down the touch and over the try-line and then cut in towards the posts, for one thing to give Ollie (Campbell) an easier conversion. By which time Gallion has covered back like a train and he almost scrags me as I touch down in haste. "Jesus, Mac, what the heck were you trying to do?" say the lads frantically. "I was trying to dap it down where that sweet-paper landed yesterday," says I. "It was pre-ordained, you see." '

Celtic romantics, and rightly, must mark down Freddie's shining and *solitaire* winking emerald as so glinting a thing as to be Try of the Century. But let them just continue to sing thankful songs in its homage. As the century ran to its end, television bombarded us with Tries of the Century most weeks of a month. Sky TV does five 'Obolenskys' a season, four Wilson Shaws, and might not even bother putting that once-memorable olde English firm of Jackson, Sharp and Hancock on the Try of the Weekend voting caption.

So if Freddie Mac, being Freddie, gets the women's vote, a serious jury has to demand collectivism in a team game such as this one, where eight heads-down heavers and hewers win the ball for the seven show-off and strutting fancy-dans to mess about with: the old division, if you like, of piano-shifters and piano-players. In this case, too, the southern hemisphere, with so much breathtaking rugby to choose from, can summon their own one-man judge and jury and write their own book . . .

Thus is our blinkered EU shortlist shrunken to two – each communal, joint-stock (and profit-sharing) tries. Might 14 March 1991, in all truth, be best of best? It was inspired by greatness, Serge Blanco, and was run in during the intensity of a Grand Slam finale. Grandeur, it was. England missed a long penalty and all eyes and senses, certainly those of the England XV for a fatal moment, relaxed and prepared for a twenty-two drop-out. Suddenly all hell broke loose – or rather, the incomparable, dusky warrior-captain of France did. '*Moi, moi!*' shouted Blanco to Berbizier, who had fielded the ball. Blanco has always put his trust in his Gods who favour the foolhardy. He was now across his line but still ten yards short of his own twenty-two. In a trice the ball was with Lafond outside him, and the wing's left hip took out Andrew, first to spot the danger; an instantaneous finger-tip pass inside allowed Sella, at speed, to round his own despairing white marker.

Sella was now over the twenty-two and momentarily clear as England regrouped and frantically funnelled back. The stalwart Probyn had tanked across to confront him on France's ten-metre line. Sella feinted to knife inside him, so stopping the prop in his tracks and as he did so, he turned in a dummy-scissors loop and fed, decisively on the outside again, the delicate Camberabero. The pit-a-pat fly-half could now snipe across the halfway mark. With dainty exactness, he chipped the ball over the head of the retreating Hodgkinson, caught it full-pelt in his stride and was now up to England's twenty-two. Though England's bold general Carling had, remarkably, made it across the field, he could only fling himself at Camberabero a split-second after the Frenchman had dapped the most perfectly weighted cross-kick to within five metres of the posts.

It took out the corner-flagging Hill and left Saint-Andre to compose himself, collect, and triumphantly launch his body and the ball at the line as Guscott's all-in, last-gasp dive lassoed his ankles. The palpitating thing was done. *Applaudissements et acclamations*. And how . . .

That try had 'context' all right. Well, it was a Grand Slam decider. Had it won the match, it would take the palm. There was, however, even more 'context' weighing down the British Lions when they played the South Africa Select XV on the tour of 1980. It was seven days before the first Test at Newlands and many in the team were playing for their place in that match. More, much more – the previous British Lions, in 1974, had blazingly set fire to the veld and laid to waste the 'invincible' Springbok boast. So they were playing for their peers, their predecessors, and their own place in history. Also, that very week had been reported in the Johannesburg township press the news that the rugby-playing political prisoners incarcerated in Robben Island, the likes of Nelson Mandela, Steve Tshwete and good Joe Slovo, would be supporting the British side in the upcoming Test match against the pride of their oppressors, the Springboks. So they were playing for them, too. That news item had meant an awful, awesome lot to a number of these rugby tourists far from home. I know, 'cos I was there... And now they were on the point of losing to the Springboks Select in their own Voortrekker high-ground homeland.

It was 21 May 1980, and they were packed into Potchefstroom's quaint low-slung grandstands high on the rock-hard veld. This time, the estimable Quinnell himself was producer-director. The sun was dropping and time was fast running out for the beleaguered British: 16–19, and it was going to be the Lions' first defeat outside Tests in

South Africa in twelve years and twenty-six matches. The referee, as the football commentator once put it, was 'looking at his whistle and preparing to blow his watch.' The frantic counter-attacking wave came and came again as the ball went through thirty-three pairs of hands in a move lasting one minute and forty-five seconds – an unbelievable amount of time, if you think about it. On and on it went, from hand to hand, from left to right, forwards and backwards, forwards and backwards and forwards again . . . Quinnell always there, rucking and running alongside his tiny West Walian lieutenant, Richards. It was almost touch rugby. O'Driscoll, Williams, Rees and Phillips; Patterson, with the fast fingers, kept switching the options; cool-hand Renwick was always there, and the prancing Woodward. What started as a rather forlorn gesture of defiance – the referee could not blow the final whistle till the ball was dead – rolled on and on to a crescendo of heroic proportions, as the doughty Scot called Hay turned into a tackle on the touchline only a few feet away from me, to show the spring-heeled Slemen a gap, through which he drove the killing, thrilling thrust and ended the prolonged whirr of determined pride. It was done. The Lions had won.

Pandemonium – and 50,000 South African hands smacked palm-to-palm in generosity and wonder, as the old Empire of friends came together in good sportsmanship and chivalry for just a moment or two of unimaginable worth.

Try of the Century
BRITISH LIONS, Potchefstroom, 1980

> Us Scots do not believe in our football team in spite of its failures, but because of them. Because we have never reached the top we can allow ourselves to feel we are always about to do so. *Willie Allan, Scots FA secretary*

Tackle of the Century

Arms and the man

On the last British Lions' tour of the century, in 1997, there was such a plethora of shudderingly scary 'dump-truck' tackles put in that this category became suddenly oversubscribed. Many of these were made, on the British side, by recent Union recruits from the weight-trained and more one-on-one physical League players, such as Scott Gibbs, John Bentley, and Allan Bateman. Hitherto, in the comparatively less gruesome defences of the Union, one recalls being winded oneself, by association as it were – for instance up in the Parc des Princes grandstand towards the end of England's World Cup quarter final on 19 October 1991, when Michael Skinner's exocet midriff job made Marc Cecillon shriek with ambushed anguish when France's giant No 8 drove back from the back of a 5-yard scrum on England's line and Skinner dropped him as if he was a rampaging buffalo stun-gunned in the slaughterhouse.

Thirteen years before, also near the right cornerflag but this time at Cardiff, another Frenchman was just as terminally stopped in his tracks by the audacious and incomparably defiant Welsh full-back John Williams, JPR or 'Japes', of immortal memory. This was on 6 March 1967, and to all intents a Grand Slam decider on a razor's edge – Wales only six points up with six minutes to go. Right wing Jean-François Gourdon was big as a galleon and fast with it. The wind was in his sails and he would surely score – till JPR holed him and sank him (with the cornerflag too) with an obliterating body charge of operatic thunder. It shuddered the famous field as the tackles of yore had, many of them put in by those two most uncompromising legends of the Arms Park lore, Claude Davey, Wilf Wooller, Clem Thomas and Jack Matthews. Likewise every historic stadium the world over has its full-moon ghosts rampaging around the dead-of-night paddocks joyfully putting in their crash-tackles again.

Down the years, too, father handed down to son wondrous tales of different sorts of tackles, lassoing rodeo things round the ankles, or clean-cut pruning-shears' jobs around the shins – like Tom Kiernan's on Gordon Waddell at Murrayfield in 1959, or Jon Webb's on Jonathan Davies at Twickenham, or Scott Hastings on Rory Underwood a year later in Edinburgh in 1990. Ankle-tap of the century may well have been the above Jonathan D on Jeremy Guscott at Cardiff in 1997.

The most famously cruel sandbagging collision of the first half of the century came in its 49th year – the University Match of 1949 when one England player, quicksilver wing JV Smith, was in the dying minutes on the point of winning the match for Cambridge after a 70-yard length of the field dash in the December gloaming. He was pursued and caught by all four of his dark blue international confrère, namely John McGregor Kendall-Carpenter, and outrageously ransacked into touch a ruler-length from the line. Remembered Kendall-Carpenter all of 40 years later, 'JV should have dived like a bullet for the score. Instead, in his last stride, he turned and glanced at me. I could see fear in his eyes, a hunted look – I knew I had captured my prey and, instead, it was me who dived, and I dive-bombed him mercilessly into the ground.'

That remained this terminal buffers' gem for a dozen years. In 1961, the mighty Springboks in myrtle-green in their turn and en bloc collectively ransacked British rugby, winning 29 matches out of 29. Not even the All Blacks of New Zealand had so terrorized and laid to waste the northern hemisphere. The narrow-eyed South Africans' thirtieth and final match was against the 'pick-up' Barbarians, at Cardiff on 4 February 1961. The home side were given no chance, especially when last-line defender and one of the grandest of all Welsh full-backs, Terry Davies, cried off at the eleventh hour. They replaced him with a sailor, Haydn Mainwaring, stationed at Swansea and playing for the local All-Whites.

The Arms Park in those days was inevitably a bog of porridge after rain, but remarkably the lightweight Barbarians ran in two early and unconverted tries (scored by the Morgans, Derek of England and Haydn of Wales). Then they dug in behind their ramparts to await tremulously the non-stop blitzkrieg from the undisputed world champions. The tourists remorselessly threw the lot at the scratch side who, in turn, tackled like devils possessed. Six-nil it remained. The dreaded 'Boks surged again and again, in waves. Still the line held. As no-side approached, the unconsidered Mainwaring, who was playing an all-round blinder anyway, put in two tackles, both of which deserve chronicling in this century's best anyway – the first a crunching straightjacket body-wrapper on the world-famed attacker Jannie Engelbrecht, the next a full-stretch dive convulsively to cut off at the knees the full-lick and seeingly in-the-clear Springbok wing Michael Antelme.

Mainwaring was a burly enough, and balding, 14-stoner. The Afrikaaners' captain was almost from another planet, a mighty 16-stone scrummager of packed muscle, and rampagingly fast with it. Now, at the last, Avril Malan took things into his own massive mitts and burst with avenging fulmination from a lineout on the Barbarians' 10-yard line and, bouncing off one then two desperate tackles, got up a hooting head of steam as he saw the try-line open up for him. Another tackling Welsh full-back of grandeur, Vivian Jenkins (he had famously stopped Prince Obolensky in his tracks more than a few times in the 1930s), was now rugby correspondent of the *Sunday Times*. Within a quarter of an hour of the event, the great Viv had picked up his pressbox telephone to dictate this paragraph to his London newspaper:

'At full pelt now, full 30-yards Malan covered the ground like a galloping Goliath. Then a full-back appeared and, you might say, a resounding crash occurred. When Mainwaring met Malan there was a thud like a comet burying itself into the earth and following the incredible explosion it was Malan, hit first with the full heroic force of Mainwaring's right shoulder, who was hurtling up and backwards and then sideways into touch. The South African captain remained floored, semi-conscious and spreadeagled, for at least a couple of minutes.'

As St John's disciples, little men with buckets and miraculous sponges, rushed to form a huddle round this stricken carcase on the touchline's cinder-track, Mainwaring trotted back, unconcerned, to his position. He might not have noticed the sheer and utter silence that had fallen over the vast amphitheatre – like poor Malan's, its collective breath had also been taken away with the wonder of such a defiantly courageous acceptance of a challenge. And after that momentary evanescence of pin-drop silent 'sound' which any sports lover knows, the arena let rip with acclaiming tumult for what it had witnessed.

To all intents, Mainwaring's tackle on Malan ended the match. Barbarians 6, South Africa 0. Groggy still, and on legs of old rope, Malan reassumed his place for the game's final rites. As captain of a now only 'almost' 100 per cent record-breaking team (P30, W29, L1), Malan was at once sought out, hoisted and chaired from the field. The arena, it seemed to a man, woman and child, gave full voice with 'Bread of Heaven' and 'Cwm Rhondda'. The two on whose shoulders Malan was carried off were the Baa-baas centre Brian Jones and – the full-back Haydn Mainwaring. When they gently put him down to the ground in the 'tunnel', Malan collapsed again. It had been some tackle.

A post-match banquet followed within a couple of hours at the adjoining Angel Hotel. A lifetime Barbarians' club membership was announced for the mighty Avril Malan by the club president, Glyn Hughes. Malan did not appear to receive it. A doctor – or rather sailor Mainwaring – had consigned him to bed.

Tackle of the Century
HAYDN MAINWARING

Prophet of the Century

Callow revolutionary

If David Campese was the rugby player of the century, his young Oz compatriot Mark Ella was by a mile the most refreshing John-the-Baptist ball games can have known. He was there, enlightening the world in the early 1980s; by the mid 1980s he was gone, leaving his goodness and honour signed down the skies of the whole century. In the 1990s, he was manager of the Aborigine cricket team which toured the world. As a rugby player he had been an original, an immense presence – and, you could argue, even the very best of all. In 1984, while he was, at fly-half, conducting a whitewash of all British rugby as utter luminary of the Australian touring team, I witnessed the young man give a seminar to Irish coaches in Belfast.

There are more things in the philosophy of young Mark Ella than are dreamed of by the majority of grey-beard, clipboard-screaming coaches in Britain. For almost an hour, the twenty-five-year-old sat on a table in the Malone RFC clubroom and talked without a note to an entranced group of sixty or so of Ulster's leading coaches, schoolmasters and players.

'What I'm about to tell,' he began, 'is not meant to degrade your British style of play at all: I just think it is worth it to compare it with my own attitude towards rugby . . .'

He was received in awed silence, except for the odd scratching of a pen as a coach scribbled notes. Talk about the infant preaching to the wise men in the temple.

His arms were folded across his green national sweater as he extemporized, with insight and no little wit, his brown leather lace-up shoes gently rocking from the table. Behind him the usual clubhouse plaques in signwriter's gilt named the captains and the cups and the caps. The legendary Ernie Crawford played for Malone in the 1920s, Jimmy Nelson in the 1940s ... those old-timers would have been awestruck at the aplomb of this young man – even more so by the content of his tutorial.

May and Gordon Ella brought up their twelve children in a shanty hut, which a nailed-up plyboard partition turned into a two-roomed job. The family slept on shared mattresses on the floor; no privacy, no sewerage; there was one cold tap; a bath was a communal trough in the yard; a shower was when it rained, for the roof was a sieve. Yet it was, the boy will tell you, a home with a lot of love and laughter. May was the adored, feared matriach; Gordon, whose white grandfather had married an aboriginal girl, was the romantic who loved to catch mullet off the cliffs when he had time away from the factory night shift. But at least – as ghettoes go – the compensation was the sea down the lane and the sun on their backs. And 'La Pa' had a junior rugby and cricket team, so the children knew more than the rudiments when they were admitted to Matraville HS – since when Mark's brothers, the twins Glen and Gary, first inspired the Australian Schools XV to a thrilling walkabout round the world before graduating, each one, to the full national side.

Mark won his first cap for Australia in 1980. He was twenty. The torch he carried became brighter with every appearance. In 1983 he was elected Young Australian of the Year. I sat there in Belfast, listening to him, and musing ... I had seen the languid, outside body swerve of Richard Sharp; the carefree, waiflike, insouciance of Barry John; the hopscotch of Bennett; the vim, dash and control of young Gibson; the dozy skill and awareness of Porta ... This boy here is in that classic line. But he is a revolutionary within it.

He scarcely fits into the canon. An original. It is worth rereading the description of the old-time Australian player and visionary coach, Cyril Towers. He had written in the Twickenham programme a week before: 'Ella runs from the shoulders down, with the fingers, hands and arms completely relaxed; he takes the ball on one side and passes before the foot comes down again; his concept of the fly-half position is that it is semi-restricted – the attack must begin further out; he is very difficult to think against – if you think ahead of him, he will slip inside, and it's no good thinking four or five moves ahead, because he hasn't invented them yet.'

Ella sits on the clubhouse table. No side, no swank. Only his soft voice, and the coaches' pencils frantically scratching at their notebooks. Many of them must have been coaching rugby for over twenty years. They were not going to miss these revelations from the twenty-five-old prophet: 'You Irish have particularly impressed me that you are trying at least. But it's still dull football. You have got out of the habit of entertaining and running the ball – it's an attitude which has evolved over the years. In Australia, we have been playing running football for a long time. I grew up playing that way. But here, the natural ability has been coached out of the players. You are playing too basic a game, concentrating on the physical aspect rather than moving the ball. Everybody says Britain has potentially the best backs but they only turn it on for five minutes in an entire match. That's no good. We have already lost count of the number of occasions teams started to run the ball against us when we are out of sight and the match won. Only then would you Brits move it.' And so on. He spoke as he played. True genius. And then he moved on to bigger things.

Prophet of the Century
MARK ELLA

Money is how we keep the score in motor racing. *Colin Chapman, 1928–82*

While some championships are won, most of them are lost. What I've really done is failed a little less than others who have had the chance to win. *Jack Nicklaus*

Tennis

Wimbledon Final of the Century

Envenomed points everywhere

From the 1920s when Wimbledon moved to, well, another part of Wimbledon, you can reel off the classics: Borotra–Lacoste, Cochet–Borotra, Crawford–Vines, Falkenburg–Bromwich, Drobny–Rosewall, Newcombe–Rosewall, Smith–Nastase, Borg–McEnroe, Connors–McEnroe, Becker–Edberg or, come to that, Edberg–Becker.

Old time histories, and old-timers' memories, insist Jack Crawford's winning five-setter against Ellsworth Vines in 1933 was simply unsurpassable. 'This had excitement, tension, and beauty, with every one of its fifty-six games a gem,' wrote the *Observer* next day. There was a temptation also to jump forty-seven years and go for the final of 1980, and Bjorn Borg's astonishing fifth title in a row, an epic match in its own right irrespective of the winking neon asterisk, a tie-break, which closed down its fourth set. Eight summers before, in Wimbledon's first Sunday final, was played a match which another generation of Centre Court spectators would claim as 'unsurpassable', when good, solid, staunch soldier Stan Smith prevailed after no end of alarms against the sprite-ogre and touch player of beguiling talents, Ilie Nastase. Trailing 2–4 and 0–40 in the fifth, Smith frantically scrambled a volley off the wooden frame of his racket and thereafter, riding that luck, his officer's resolution under fire corralled the increasingly hyper and ammo-wasting Romanian. The perception of 'goodie v baddie', like in boxing, has always heightened Centre Court tensions – Tilden needed his Johnston to rage against, and Nastase his Smith, just as Frazier did his Ali.

On 5 July 1975, you could not exactly say Jimmy Brash needed his Arthur Ashe. Well, not around teatime anyway. Ashe v Connors it simply has to be. It was more of a mind game than an athletic final. Connors was the champion, a pugnacious strutter who at twenty-two seemed destined to hold this title for the rest of the decade. Bookmakers made him 6–1 on to win, the hottest favourite in the championships' history. Ashe was thirty-two and it had been seven long years since he had been the first black player to reach a Wimbledon semi-final. Theirs was the first final in which chairs were provided for the contestants beside the umpire's ladder. This magnified viewers' thrall as the television cameras moved into sharp close-up at every change of end. Ashe, his head turbaned in a green towel, maintained a trance of concentration. Alongside him, Connors's brazen confidence was visibly draining away into fidget and fret and fuming despair.

On the Friday evening before Saturday's final, Ashe was the only one of his friends not flinching. At his favourite Westbury Hotel in Mayfair, he announced softly that if Jimmy wanted to work with speed on the morrow, he would be matched by slowness and stealth. If Jimmy was looking to be fed his exuberant 'running angles', he would be disappointed, Ashe announced. All he was going to get was short, low mid-court balls at his ankles: 'I'll mix it up to mix him up. I'll serve sliced and wide to the deuce court, otherwise straight at his body. I'll keep him bemused and behind the baseline, and when he comes in, I'll lob him.'

Sure you will, Arthur, we said doubtfully as Ashe took us off for an early nightcap at the Playboy Club, where his final blackjack call won him £100. Connors, after a physio session at nearby Chelsea Hospital, was having a room-service supper at his hotel in the Gloucester Road with his mother Gloria. In those days they were as frugal as they were close and shared their twin-bedded suite.

Arthur was up early in the Westbury. Over two helpings of eggs benedict he read *The Times* and the *Guardian*, remarking that their tennis writers, Rex Bellamy and David Gray respectively, would be eating their doom-laden words by teatime. He took a stroll up Bond Street and by mid-morning was knocking up on the grounds at SW19 with his Australian friend 'Nails' Carmichael, who was belting each ball for Ashe to return with dinks, angles, flighted swervers and lobs. Nearby on an outside court, Connors turned up around noon to hit with his pal Nastase. A crowd had gathered to watch. Nastase aped Ashe's mannerisms, at one point donning steel-rimmed spectacles. Connors was convulsed at his friend's antics.

Connors had announced himself with awesome power the previous year, cruelly obliterating Ken Rosewall in the final. The veteran favourite managed to win four games in the third set after being blown away 6–1 , 6–1 by a venomously youthful gale in the opening sets. Now, twelve months later on that unforgettable Saturday afternoon, it was also 6–1, 6–1 after two sets – to Ashe. Connors was reeling like a drunken matelot as he was lobbed, dinked, teased, passed, out-rallied and frustrated. At one stage, someone in the crowd hollered, 'C'mon, Jimmy, start trying.' Connors spat back, 'F'Chrissakes, I *am* trying!'

That was in the third set. It lasted only one more. As Gray apologized in his newspaper report, 'The tennis thinker was by then in total intellectual control.' It closed at 6–1, 6–1, 5–7, 6–4 (it could so easily have been just three sets) and no more strutting champion and monarch had been so resonantly put to death since Hamlet was 'thrusting the poisoned cup down the King's throat and winning envenomed points everywhere'.

Wimbledon Final of the Century
ASHE v CONNORS, 1975

Women in sport? Who wants straight-legged, narrow-hipped, big-shouldered, powerful Sheilas, aggressive and ferocious in mind and body? *Percy Cerrutty, coach*

Sudden-Death of the Century

Sums better than summary

On the first Saturday of July 1980, the Swede Bjorn Borg reached a place no other man who played tennis had ever been. He won his thirty-fifth match on the trot at the championships and thus an unparalleled fifth successive Wimbledon singles title. In doing so he beat the American left-hander John McEnroe by 1–6, 7–5, 6–3, 6–7 (16–18), 8–6. The match took three hours and fifty-three minutes. That bunch of figures you've just read includes a seemingly discordant parenthesis (16–18) which is, in fact, the whole point – or rather, the whole thirty-four points. The astounding, fulminating, excruciating thing lasted twenty-two minutes, longer than many sets. You can safely say that Wimbledon had never seen anything like it, because it was the first sudden-death tie-break – winner first to seven or more points with a clear two-point lead – ever to be played in a Wimbledon final.

Borg, fridge-cool, impassionate, ruthless, whipcord-strong, a champion's vast experience; McEnroe, passionate, Celtic, timebomb-tense, just twenty-one but with a deft, featherlight touch which made for an instrument of genius in his left hand. It was McEnroe's first Wimbledon final (he was to reach the next four finals, and win three of them).

As forewarning to the riveting opera, Borg should have closed out the fourth set and been accepting the trophy from the Duchess by the time the tie-break was called. At two sets to one and 5–4 in the fourth, he rolled to 40–15 and two match points. He served with an imperious swish and you could sense the coronation robe already on his shoulders. With utter courage, McEnroe saved the two match points, then broke the serve, held his own, and in no time it was 6–6 and tie-break. Borg only had to win it to ensure his place in history as best of the very best, the 'unbeatable' – but now he was staring down the beady eye of that same history, for the only other man in fifty years to lose a Wimbledon final after squandering a match point in his favour was the Australian John Bromwich in 1948 who, they said, was never the same player thereafter and scarcely won another match. That one point did for him. Now Borg had already tossed away two. Would omens be prophetic here?

As the century ran to its end, big servers would decide tie-breaks by just a tedious series of staccato, one-shot unreturnable ejaculation-aces. When skilful rallies were still allowed in men's tennis, the tensions of a tie-break were heightened by the crowd's almost football-style partisanship. The quietude as the rally evolved shape and strategy would be almost palpable, in a way you could 'hear' the throng holding its breath; then, the point won or lost and the acclaiming release of pent-up noise would be unrestrained. It was heady stuff, and it began here in lawn tennis's cabbagey-green colosseum this Saturday in July 1980, when the partisanship on the shrill-ometer was exactly as it should be, about sixty/forty. Most for the posterity-seeking, sallow ice-box champion with his girl's swirl of blond hair cascading behind him; the rest for the undaunted, freckled new challenger, his Celtic curls busbied into a top-knot with a blood-red bandeau.

PLAY! In a way it remains indescribable in words and adjectives, and, oddly, cold figures better do the job ... Two, three, four, five times in this twenty-two-minute eternity, Borg had match-point, just one stroke away from immortality ... unimaginably, two, three, four, five times McEnroe defied him with his stinging, often sensational retorts. In his turn, McEnroe six times held set-point to level the sets at 2–2 – and six times Borg empirically wrenched it back. It was cannon's mouth stuff of quite frightening splendour. In one continuous sequence, turn and turnabout, nine consecutive and rasping first-serves were in; simply, it out-superlatived superlatives. In between these laced and furiously rasping serves, there were dinks and topspinners, swervers both ways, passes, down-the-liners, crosscourt out-of-this-worlders, lobs, volleys, stop-volleys, half-volleys, baseline clippers, feathered backhands, pistol-shot backhands, ditto forehands . . .

It was a dazzling McEnroe forehand return of service, hit whistling-hard and with topspin on the run, which ended it in the twenty-second minute and on the thirty-fourth point. As Borg followed in to cover the net, and kill at it, such a fizzing return surprised him for an instant and he readjusted and bent for a defensive stop-volley. He had not accounted for the fierceness of the left-hander's topspin. The ball fell heavy on his racket, and dribbled off it and into the net like it was punctured. It was done.

McEnroe had levelled to 2–2. Borg won the fifth.

Sudden-death of the Century
JOHN McENROE v BJORN BORG, 1980

I often surprise myself. You can't plan some shots that go in, not unless you're on marijuana, and the only grass I'm partial to is Wimbledon's. *Rod Laver*

What do you think on the last tee before winning an Open championship? Does your life flash through your mind? Do you think of your parents, your wife, your schoolteacher, your first job? No, you just think of hitting your last drive straight. *Tony Jacklin*

Player of the Century

Carouser's contempt of caution

When HL Doherty and AF Wilding won their stack of Wimbledon titles early in the century, the final was called the challenge round – i.e., last year's winner just had to turn up on the day to play the guy who had won through the draw for the honour of 'challenging' the champion. Made it kinda easy to retain your crown, what? Since when, in little pockets of years, a continuing series of players have stood apart, acknowledged by peers as the best – Bill Tilden, Henri Cochet, Fred Perry, Donald Budge, Pancho Gonzales, Frank Sedgman, Rod Laver, Roy Emerson, John Newcombe . . . right up to, at century's end, such as Boris Becker, Stefan Edberg and Pete Sampras, who could well win more than anyone.

But one man not only illuminated his own drab, still scared post-war era, he lit up with warmth the whole century. He was the very best player in the world at tennis as well as, simultaneously, the very best sportsman in the world at sportsmanship. He was Lewis Alan Hoad, known to the world and his wife and their charlady simply as 'Lew'.

From 1953 to 1956 Hoad won an astonishing thirteen grand slam titles. In 1956 he was Australian, French and Wimbledon champion, and only defeat at the US championships by his buddy from the Sydney suburbs, Ken Rosewall, ruined the glorious clean sweep.

In that same sublime four-year stretch, Hoad won ten out of twelve Davis Cup singles for Australia and seven out of nine doubles. Then, his always suspect back beginning to worsen, he joined the professional tour organized by Jack Kramer, the American former champ and entrepreneur who did not break the 'shamateur' hypocrisies of the establishment game till the late 1960s.

The first Wimbledon singles victory of Hoad's – against Rosewall in 1956 – also represented David Gray's debut as a reporter for the *Manchester Guardian* at London's strawberry fields. Gray, who was to develop a famed and knowingly graphic canvas of the literature of tennis, outlined that first final in a handful of sentences: 'When Hoad is on court, there is always a sense of drama. The mind cannot sleep, because the unexpected always must be expected. With Rosewall, the movement of the ball comes to an anticipated end and the workings of his mind are plain; but when Hoad is in command, the result is amazing and one has to work back from the end to see the means by which it is achieved, for Hoad's play moves in a world of high imagination. Rosewall is the neater strategist, but Hoad's range of ambition is greater.'

The following year, the smiling Hoad became the first man in yonks to retain the Wimbledon title – in a quick-fire victory over another of the glittering band of Australian youngsters, Ashley Cooper. Gray this time called it 'majestic . . . a complete demonstration of power and purpose, strength and speed'.

Hoad's contemporaries loved him as much as they were in awe of him on the court. The South African Davis Cupper and author, Gordon Forbes, played with and against Hoad on numerous occasions. Once, in a pre-Wimbledon tournament at Bristol, Forbes beat Hoad: 'To defeat Hoad was a thing which took place in a dream – uneasy, ecstatic, triumphant in bringing down an idol. He was just off-form really, for he was a majestic player with a superb and flawless selection of strokes and a court presence as arresting and fearless as that of a handsome god. I worshipped him then as only the young can worship.'

Hoad in his prime was contemptuous of caution, nervousness or any mannerisms remotely connected with gamesmanship, meanness or tricky endeavour. He had the wolfish grin of a Miller or a Botham and although when in the mood, and in trim, he also had a wolfish competitiveness, losing seldom hurt if it happened dead on opening time. As the always colourfully apt Rex Bellamy of *The Times*, who was the closest to the players of his time, remarked one day, 'When it came to hitting the grog, Lew was also a world champion, even by Australian champion's standards. He drank enough beer to irrigate the Nullarbor Plain. The night before he won the French championship, he reduced himself to a condition that would have wrecked most men for a week.'

When Hoad turned pro, the wily Kramer prudently gave him extra money – but also a clause demanding that any bonuses would be for winning. Kramer knew his carefree superstar would be inclined just to play for fun and the love of life and the next hangover. When he won his first Wimbledon in 1956, everyone in the game presumed Hoad would sign for Kramer there and then – but he gave the 'amateurs' another twelve months of his glory, won it again and so trebled his Kramer's down-payment.

At the Wimbledon Ball, immediately after Hoad's victory, the game was fully expecting that during his winner's speech he would announce his defection. It was in the chandeliered Great Ballroom of the Park Lane Hotel. Various lords and wing-commanders went through their speeches and then Lew was called upon for his (presumed) dramatic announcement. He got to his feet and straightened the knot of his unfamiliar tie, and then in his most laconic Aussie drawl, he began, 'Lay-deez 'n' gennlemen, you know you are very lucky to have me here among you tonight . . .' He paused over the bated breath before continuing, a mischievous smile playing on his lips . . . 'Because right up to 7.30 tonight, my only suit hadn't come back from the clayners.' There was a din of relieved applause; Wimbledon had their beloved Lew for one more year.

When tennis was done, Hoad retired to Spain with his riches. He kept generous house – the only entry qualification: you had to be a laugher. When Arthur Ashe was on the way to ambushing Jimmy Connors in Wimbledon's 1975 final, with the fourth and final set at 4–4, the telephone rang in the men's locker-room: 'Mr Ashe? I'm afraid he's on court, sir.' It was Hoad, watching the match on Spanish television, who was on the line. 'I know he's on court,' he said, 'but just leave that telephone dangling off the hook till he comes in, because I want to be the very first to congratulate him.' It was left dangling, and he was.

I last met him at Wimbledon perhaps a half-dozen years before his death, after a long illness, in 1994 aged fifty-nine. He was still relishing life (and it was mutual): 'We had fun. These millionaire players now don't know the meaning of the word "fun", do they? When I played Davis Cup for the first time – and we won in front of 25,000 people – I was given £5 for the week's expenses. But I had a fantastic life. I was only sorry in a way I had to turn pro – but you cannot eat silver cups, can you?' And he laughed, and the fair hair bobbed around just like it used to three decades before when the wrist-whip and topspin not only hit tennis balls, but hurt them. The only things, mark you, that Lew Hoad ever hurt in his life. His generosity was genial and so was his immense talent. And his sportsmanship.

Player of the Century
LEW HOAD

> It's easy to beat Brazil. You just stop them getting twenty yards from your goal. *Bobby Charlton*

> No one wins the Open. It wins you. *Doug Sanders, losing Open golfer*

> I did not really need to spend a penny. But I went down to the Lord's toilet, went through all the motions, even pulling the chain. The trick, the deception worked. When I came to the surface and looked at the game again, Asif was out and Lancashire were on their way. *Sir Neville Cardus*

Match of the Century

The condensed anthology

The two-day, 112-game, five-and-a-quarter-hour blockbuster on Wimbledon's Centre Court in 1969, in which forty-one-year-old eminence Pancho Gonzales beat Charlie Pasarell in pre-tie-break days by the now unbelievable 22–24, 1–6, 16–14, 6–3, 11–9, was the undoubted best of the century for a little short of three years. Tennis's Frazier–Ali, Coe–Ovett – that is, the world championship to decide it once and for all, the very best against the very best – took place on 15 May 1972 at the Moody Colosseum in Dallas, Texas. Some nineteen members of the two professional groups of lawn tennis writers on each side of the Atlantic were there; fourteen of them survived till 1989 when eleven of the fourteen voted it the match of the century in a sports journalists' poll. Being specialists devoted globally to the game day in, day out and year after year, they had all seen many more tennis matches than I had. That for a great majority of them it transcended anything in their recollection before or since made me squeeze myself at my good fortune at having been up there in the press tribune with them that momentous evening.

Rod Laver, left-handed, powerful, a venomous hitter – they called him 'Rocket', in awe – versus Ken Rosewall, diminutive stylist and bespoke shot-maker, whom they called 'Muscles', with irony. Two immense, awesomely experienced champions at the very peak and pinnacle of their game. Both Australian, they had almost been brought up together, friends and razor-sharp rivals. This last shoot-out in Texas would decide it for posterity. The first four sets took a fraction over three hours at a point-counterpoint zig and zag, and when Laver levelled the match in the fourth (6–4, 0–6, 3–6, 7–6) it looked as if the younger man would prevail. Those thirty-eight games, even in that second-set whitewash Laver aberration, were packed, left-hand-right-hand, with the whole century's thesaurus of tennis skills and strategies as well as, also for history's sake, a savagery of commitment. Every rally somehow became an anthology of the finest shots ever played.

The one difference was that Rosewall had a first service with such a dinky-slow parabola it looked like it was an urchin ballboy who had been summoned to start proceedings. Laver's serve, on the other hand, had groundsmen all over the world stitching double-mesh to their stop-net behind the baseline. This inability of Rosewall's to set in motion a rally with a challengingly strong and spitting defiance made his game so compelling, because his all-court strokeplay had at once to make amends, to reseize the initiative.

Doubtless because television schedules demanded, American rules allowed a tie-break to settle a final. And inevitably, 6–6 was called in the final palpitating set that night in Dallas. Sudden-death.

Here was the condensed anthology, if you like. The sumptuous shots were utterly breathtaking, so were the returns thereof. Also the intensity and, yes, the desire – for £50,000 would go to the winner, at the time the biggest prize ever offered in the sport. Laver went 4–2 up, then 5–4 and two serves. It was surely done. Then of a sudden, miraculously, Rosewall rolled back all his years to frisky boyhood again and with two backhand strokes of fulminating defiance and rare and daring beauty – both on the run, one flat and mercilessly unplayable down the line, the other ravishingly whipped crosscourt – took the lead at 6–5, and served for the match. Laver, in shock and disbelief, could only return limply into the net, the ball splodging sadly on the catgut like a broken egg.

Not only Laver was in shock. No one moved. Not a sound. Then a great wall of sound and acclamation enveloped the vast Colosseum – everybody standing. And the two emperors embracing.

Match of the Century
KEN ROSEWALL v ROD LAVER, 1972

Lady of the Century

Portrait in motion

She lost more Wimbledon finals than she won – respectively three and two. She was the first mother to win the great gilt biscuit since Dorothea Lambert-Chambers in 1914 when Wimbers was still a garden-party jolly in the suburbs.

She was Evonne Goolagong, and she was nineteen in 1971 when she beat, with a smile on her face, two legends, Billie Jean King in the semis and Margaret Court in the final. She was an enchanting faun, too feminine in grace and carriage and nature even to be called a tomboy; she was obviously a competitor, that's for sure, but, crucially, she was happy to display always and in her every gesture what sheer fun she was having while she competed; this apparent joy suffused any court she trod. Or rather, not 'trod' – Evonne had no 'tread', nor did she 'run'. She flowed.

What was to come after her in the ladies' game underlined her glory a hundredfold. Well, simply let us say the earth would have stopped turning on its axis if Evonne Goolagong had been heard to grunt in a tennis match.

Nine full years after winning Wimbledon, in 1980 she returned, unpractised, to London's strawberry fields for one last go for old times' sakes – and, of course, for fun. She had been injured, and she had been ill. A week before Wimbledon and she had not hit a ball for eleven weeks. In no time, the fluid, unfrilled majesty of stroke was re-summoned, but it was her heart and fortitude which were tested first: in the third round she was down a set and won; in the fourth she was down a set and a break, and won. Always with a smile of delight, and it carried her to the semi-final and a meeting with the new, unsmiling, teenage sensation with the scarlet-painted fingernails and the make-up cake on her face to hide the freckles. Tracey Austin had lost only once in her previous thirty-six matches. Now it was twice, for again Goolagong, now Mrs Roger Cawley, came from behind to pin the fraught, programmed, one-track American to the net-stop. In the final, Evonne met a Christine Evert-Lloyd on an unbeaten roll of twenty-six matches and who had just dispatched the champion with the muscular left-arm of a Popeye, Martina Navratilova.

Someone once said that because her dusky outback beauty was even more appealing than her liquid and beguiling backhand, Miss Goolagong's opponents considered her not so much a player as a portrait. Well, that afternoon the runaway favourite on the hot streak, Mrs Evert-Lloyd, was probably still making up her mind about that one when the end raced towards her – and she was blown away in two.

Gloriously won and, it goes without saying, with smiling chivalry too; and graciously lost. Instinctive touch had overcome taught precision; gaiety overcome taut strategy; athleticism overcome strict discipline . . . In two words, 'happy naturalness' had won Wimbledon. As it probably never would again.

Lady of the Century
EVONNE GOOLAGONG

> For the Davis Cup you have to have separate bedrooms from your husband while he is in training. You spend the whole of the year living with him then all of a sudden they say, 'No, no, naughty, not the night before the Davis Cup.' I suppose it's because they are representing England. *Mrs Mark Cox*

Brat of the Century

G'day, Wing-Commander

'Man, you cannot be serious . . . You guys are the pits of the world.' was my personal favourite in 1981, the year of his first Wimbledon title. In an early round, playing a Rod Frawley ranked 119 in the world, he snapped within minutes of the start when he muffed an iffy ball near the chalk. He implored the heavens with this screech: *'You're a disgrace to mankind!'* The umpire (it would be) Wing-Commander George Grime announced an official warning for 'rudeness to officials'. At which Mac retorted with another wailing, plaintive holler: *'But Umpire, I was talking to myself!'* He was fined £10,000 (later revoked).

When he wasn't playing beguiling tennis (correction, often when he was), the steam poured from his ears at Wimbledon from his first appearance in 1978 to his last, at singles, in 1991 when, going down to defeat against Stefan Edberg, he swore at a linesman six times in six seconds in an exchange which one newspaper rendered as follows: 'McEnroe, you stupid McEnroe-er. Good McEnroe-ing call, you son of a McEnroe-ing bitch. You McEnroe-ing report me after the McEnroe-ing match is over and I'll McEnroe you . . .' The linesman sat impassive. Nor did he report him. But an errant ITN microphone picked up the rant loud and clear. Fined £10,000. Cheap at the price.

Brat of the Century
JOHN McENROE

Siamese Twins of the Century

The head and the hat

The middle third of the century was tennis's bequest for the grandeur of doubles – that stupendous team game between sets of telepathic and elasticated Siamese twins. Perm any two from France's 'Four Musketeers' of the 1920s and '30s – Borotra, Lacoste, Brugnon and Cochet – for they seemed to play (and usually win) with each other, turn and turnabout, on any whim of *confraternité* which took their fancy, as did the originals of their collective nickname, 'One for all and all for one.' And certainly, in turn, they each won Wimbledon doubles titles partnering one of the brotherhood – although, of course, the Davis Cup was their most successful battlefield. They popularized doubles all right – and the fun of it. After all, doubles should really be considered *the* senior tennis discipline, for it is the one played and enjoyed far more regularly on the world's public-park courts.

The Doubles *Match* of the Century was undoubtedly that between. Ilie Nastase/Ion Tiriac of Romania and Stan Smith/Eric van Dillen of the United States in Bucharest in 1972. But the Doubles Team – the Siamese Twins – of the Century is another matter. On results alone, the Australian 'Woodies' – Mark Woodforde and Todd Woodbridge – should take the prize; eschewing singles, they made themselves millionaires times over in the last decade of the century with ruthless, dedicated and metronomic performances which had you gaping at their discipline, teamwork and blocking of angles. But only gaping, not necessarily enjoying. Their immediate predecessors, those they saw off, were each similarly slick and unsmiling – such teams as (no christian names needed in doubles, the great pairs trip off the tongue like Marks & Spencer, Haynes & Greenidge) Taroczy & Gunthardt, Jarryd & Simonsson, Curren & Denton . . . To me, somehow, that trio of duos doesn't at all seem as endurably set in a romantic's dictionary as such old firms as, offhand, Budge & Mako, Perry & Hughes, McGregor & Sedgman, Mulloy & Patty, Hoad & Rosewall, Smith & Lutz, Forbes & Segal, McEnroe & Fleming, Newcombe & Roche, Hewitt & Stolle . . . and after Hewitt & Stolle came Hewitt & McMillan, the favourites of all time: Hewitt, fierce and broad and bald as an egg, and temperamental with it, a grizzly old bear who growled; McMillan, tidy, trim, unfussy, almost faceless under his baggy white cap. Darby and Joan, they were together for almost twenty years. When they went on court of an early evening the Wimbledon players' tearoom would empty, and those late for a seat on the Centre would sit in a silent, admiring throng around the television sets.

Arthur Ashe once confided about the greatness of 'Hewmac': 'If you saw those two old guys practising on a court somewhere and didn't know who they were, you'd think anyone on your block could beat them. But you've gotta believe it, that bald guy with the paunch and the skinny kid with the cap can beat anyone. They look like a pick-up father-and-son team but they can beat anyone on the whole planet earth.'

Hewitt's right hand wielded a massive carpet-beater, but he used it with a surprising delicacy; he was a dabbing and dinking poker-work player, a swordsman at the net who would slice and nick and cut away till the far side of the court was covered in blood. McMillan did the top-lick fetching and carrying, swishing the swathes round the base-line before moving in himself for the kill. I think he was the first player I saw with the two-handed grip, certainly the first in a baggy white cap: it was because they were always put on late, at sunset-time; his forehand was like he was fishing for a big one in a choppy sea. And if Hewitt didn't get them, Mac's unflappy, inch-perfect geometry would as good as spear the opposition to death. They won – or lost occasionally – all round the world. Always they entertained. Their geometry was perfect, their chemistry pluperfect. They were

Wimbledon champions in 1967. Every match they played thereafter, usually at least to the semis, was 'standing-room only'. They were champions again in 1972. And again, an unbelievable eleven years after the first, in 1978. The Head and the Hat – Hewmac.

Siamese Twins of the Century
HEWITT and McMILLAN

What is it, being a footballer? If you take away *Match of the Day* and the Press and the fans and hangers-on, it's all very empty and lonely. *Rodney Marsh*

Try explaining cricket to an intelligent foreigner; it is far harder than explaining Chomsky's generational grammar. *CP Snow*

Trousers are now allowed to be worn by ladies on the course. But they must be removed before entering the clubhouse. *Notice in Irish golf club*

There are, they say, fools, bloody fools, and men who remount in a steeplechase. *John Oaksey*

Golf

Golfer of the Century

The wise innocent

Before professional golf became a matter of every millionaire for himself, there had been in the century three distinct periods over each of which a grand triumvirate of players ruled the game. The end of the nineteenth century and the beginning of the twentieth were dominated by the three Brits, Harry Vardon, James Braid and JH Taylor. In the second third of the century, three Americans, Bobby Jones, Walter Hagen and Ben Hogan, in their different ways took the game dramatically forward. In the 1960s, agent Mark McCormack signed up three meal-tickets for life with the grandest triumvirate of Arnold Palmer, Gary Player and Jack Nicklaus. At the end of the century, Tiger Woods prowled out of the thicket . . .

And the greatest of them all was . . .

When all is said and done and sold – and in golf an awful lot is said and done and sold – the pro game comes down to five little words: Not how, but how many? Meaning your score, because your score means victories, and victories mean money, and the bigger the victories the bigger the bundles of boodle.

Annually, for two-thirds of the century, the most prestigious victories were in four tournaments – the Open Championships of America and Britain, the US Masters (founded in 1934) and the USPGA, each of four rounds and 72 holes. Britain's annual Open first teed off in 1860. Before the turn of the century, Taylor and Vardon were already three times winners each, and both were to win it thrice more. Braid's five were all twentieth-century victories. In the next era, all the waves were being made across the Atlantic, and the match-up on the face of it was between the flamboyantly brash Hagen and the gentil, courtly Jones. Hagen did have one spectacular head-to-head exhibition match against the young Jones in 1926 and licked him 12 and 11, but in fact the colourfully brazen Hagen (who would waggle his driver on the first tee and enquire boastfully, 'Okay, who's gonna come second?') seemed to steer clear of the superbly cool and talented Jones. History's presumption is that Hagen was at Jones's throat down the eighteenth fairway by the week, but the truth is that Walter Hagen never won a single major championship that Bobby Jones played in, that Hagen won his two US Opens before Jones arrived on the scene, and that Hagen's four British opens were won, possibly by coincidence, I agree, those times Jones stayed at home. Being officially an amateur, Jones of course was not eligible for the professional PGA tournament, which Hagen won five times.

Hagen had a supreme touch with his short irons, but generally the quietly sumptuous all-round game of Jones in truth saw off his noisily appealing and thirsty extrovert compatriot. In 1930, Jones uniquely won golf's original Grand Slam – in those days the scribes called it 'The Impregnable Quadrilateral' – of, in a single year, the US and British amateur championships and the ditto two Opens. In all, till ill health literally cut his glory off at the knees and his life was confined to a wheelchair, Jones bestrode the obsessive world of hickories, hillocks and plus-fours, winning in all four US Opens, three British Opens, and respectively five and one of their corresponding amateur championships. Twenty-three years after Jones's 'impossible' 1930, Ben Hogan might have managed the grandeur of the Slam when, in 1953 in his early forties, he won the Masters and both Opens but could not compete in the USPGA because it clashed that year with the British Open.

Real historians might care to note: I fancy you can date the handover to the century's third era to an actual date, 18 June 1960, under a baking Colorado sun on the outskirts of Denver, USA, and around the elms and cottonwood trees, the lakeside willows and the sun-blinding white sandtraps of the Cherry Hills Country Club. It was lateish afternoon, the final round of the US Open, and mercifully at last the sun was dropping, spent. Hogan, forty-eight years old and long crowned one of the game's immortals, was leading. But the good old fellow was being chased and chivvied by the previous year's amateur champion, a young, plump, crew-cut college-kid blond who had dogged him for two days. With just two holes to play, if both of them finished par–par it looked certain they would tie the championship and have to play-off a full round next day – unless someone behind them went totally potty (in those days the leaders always went out after lunch). Old Ben had been here many times before and was confident he would shake off the inexperienced kid at the long seventeenth, par-5 549-yarder with a sinister pond lurking as moat to the green. A drive, a precise lay-up, an inch-perfect pitch. Each shot difficult enough for the boy to make three howlers, thought Hogan. Oh yes, the amateur tyro's name, by the way, was Jack Nicklaus.

But the twenty-year-old did not crack – it was old champ Hogan whose pitch was nine inches short of perfection and plopped into the water; he took a six. At the eighteenth, Hogan collapsed to a triple-bogey seven; he finished in a tie for ninth place. It was his last challenging throw in any major. His playing partner, the podgy kid, was deliriously applauded into the clubhouse. He had made his par–par for the last two. The crew-cut kid's four-round score of 282 that day in mid 1960 remained till century's end the lowest total ever posted by an amateur in the US Open. History: still not twenty-one, he had outmatched the matchless Bobby Jones.

WHOA! there – that day's history had more to come. Some nut way down the field did go mad. A strong-shouldered thirty-year-old pro was flavour of that summer in US golf and had, not long before, won the Masters with what the headline writers called 'a charge'. As old soldier Hogan had so calamitously played depth-charges with his Dunlop on the seventeenth in his suicidal need to get the kid off his back, this folksy new Master was way back, seven strokes and fifteen places behind. Then this open-faced fellow, who looked like John Wayne, hitched up his trousers, tossed away his chain-smoker's cigarette butt and opened his shoulders ... He was on 'the charge' again and now a vast following gallery attached itself to him: 'Whoo-aa! Go get 'em, Arnie!'

It was Arnold Palmer. He got 'em, sure enough. With a grin (and another hitch of his trousers) he hunted them down and he won. It remains probably the most thrilling last-round 'charge' in history (in the epic 1996 Masters, Nick Faldo, way back in second place, did not so much as leap at Greg Norman and get him, but the latter reversed back into him). Later that 1960 summer, Palmer was an appealing breezy second in the British Open, and the following year he won it (and the year after that) and, in so doing and for all manner of reasons, changed international golf for all time. All international sport, really.

Every television station queued up to focus on Palmer. He was a joy. He was also clearing the stage and moving the props for that twenty-year-old amateur champion who so entranced hot Cherry Hills that day. It would not be long till young Jack lost his puppy fat, swore off his severe barber and allowed his blond hair to enjoy the winds and zephyrs of golf – and began to pocket one by one and turn and turnabout (and then some more) all the major championships in the game (and then, as I say, some more).

It was lovely having Arnie hitching his trews and tucking in his shirt-tails while it lasted – it 'lasted' seven majors, too, which can't be bad. Not as long as Hagen's eleven or Jones's thirteen, including his amateur championships. But Jack's total – nearly forty years after Cherry Hills – is into the twenties and, he hopes still, rising. Only a year or two before the century ended, you could have died happy in the certainty that your generation at least had seen a golfer whose record of victories that mattered was inviolate, unapproachable. Then Tiger Woods teed off . .

If Woods (or whoever) next century overtook Nicklaus in the gold-leafed roll of all-time honour, it would be with a smile and a sporting embrace that Jack would move over on the topmost plinth of the pantheon. Around the long-ago time he overtook Hagen at twelve titles, Nicklaus said, 'In any game with "scores" being the deciding factor, you cannot measure greatness by any other method than whether it's in the record books. It's not technique or "guts" or flair that is being measured. The only yardstick is winning. You can have a classic swing, or the best competitive nature, and your shots out of sand might be miraculous by the day. But the simple fact is that if you haven't won anything, even your initials, let alone your surname, are not in those record books.'

All said matter-of-fact, of course, and no remote shred of the boast or the braggart. Like most of the few undoubted and unquestioned nonpareils of the century, Nicklaus was as much a giant of golf as he was at all life's nobilities and graces. When he gift-wrapped a faraway 'gimme' on the last – 'so old friends, as they should, can walk off level-tied after such a match, Tony ol' friend, where neither of us deserved to be loser' – Britain's fierce terrier of a competitor Tony Jacklin, could only burst into tears in the 1970 Ryder Cup. The whole world was watching, demanding a winner to acclaim – and, darker side, a loser and victim to berate. Hundreds of thousands on offer, too. On Nicklaus's gimme and say-so, they shared it.

Alistair Cooke wrote of golf's other eminence of the century, Bobby Jones:

'What we talk of here is not the hero as golfer, but that someone Americans hungered for and found – the best performer in the world who was also the hero as human being, the gentle, chivalrous, wholly self-sufficient male. Jefferson's lost paragon: the wise innocent.'

Those fine words by Cooke cloak equally as well the

Golfer of the Century
JACK NICKLAUS

If another jockey asks you for a bit of room at a fence, you bloody well give it. Next time you might be asking him. There's quite enough trouble out there without making any of our own. *Terry Biddlecombe*

Shot of the Century

Clearing a path for history

Since colour television and wall-to-wall satellite coverage, this jury has been submerged with every commentator, by the week, claiming any half-decent iron approach or sandwedge that's holed to be Shot of the Century. The *real* shortlist has been whittled down by this court to five, played by Sarazen, Jones, Watson, Lyle and Palmer.

Gene Sarazen, born 1902, was a maestro with an even longer span on the leaderboard than Jack Nicklaus. He won seven majors and played, competitively enough, in each of the century's three eras. At seventy-one, in the 1972 Open at Troon, his hole-in-one for instance was transmitted live by satellite in glorious colour all around the globe – but it was all of thirty-eight years earlier, at only the second Masters in 1935, that he helped put Augusta and its azaleas on the worldwide map with no camera in sight. Craig Wood was in the clubhouse, the presumed winner when, four holes back on the fairway of the 485-yard fifteenth, Sarazen waggled his 4-wood and let fly from 220 yards. It landed on the front of the green, sat up for a moment and then top-spun amiably straight for, and into, the hole for an albatross two. He parred the last four holes to tie with Wood – and won the play-off.

Bobby Jones always said the amateur championships gave him more trouble than the professional Opens. In the 1926 British Amateur, he went out in the sixth round and, annoyed with himself, decided to stay on and enter the Open for the first time. It was at Lytham. In spite of his putting poorly, the rest of his game on the final Saturday kept him head-to-head with his equally young compatriot

Watrous. They were still level at the 462-yard par-4 seventeenth. The *Manchester Guardian* reported: 'The decisive stroke of the week now came. Jones had driven into sand about 180 yards from the green. Jones thought a long time before he played, and then a mashie sent the ball to the heart of the green only four feet from the pin.' The birdie was decisive – and having won, Jones thought a champion should defend his title, so he returned the following year to St Andrews and was in the lead from start to finish with a new aggregate record of 285 and a glorious six-shot win. But for that mashie shot on the seventeenth at Lytham on 26 June 1926, the best player in the world might never have returned to grace the game's ancient links.

Tom Watson could be said to have led a fourth mini-great triumvirate – roughly alongside Seve Ballesteros and Nick Faldo – as the century began to think of its end. Nice fellow Tom won eight majors, till his putting let him down, and all of them in a cluster between 1975 and 1983. His all-time classic two-day shootout with Nicklaus at Turnberry in 1977 was now five years distant, but at the 1982 US Open at Pebble Beach it was again the same last-round scenario, this time with leader Tom seeming to falter at the death as big Jack roared up to his shoulder. With two holes to play, Watson needed to hold his nerve and anything less than a par 3 and a par 5 (to tie) and he'd have blown it badly. There was a doleful collective sigh from the vast gallery as he missed the green with his tee-shot on the par 3, and he was left with the trickiest of shots from semi-rough with the lightning-fast green sloping away from him. It looked impossible even to lay it up remotely near the flag. To his caddie, Watson said, 'My only chance is to hole it from here.' He did. And won the Open.

Sandy Lyle was blowing up after the turn on the last round of the 1988 Masters. He dropped three shots on the eleventh and twelfth and the American Mark Calcavecchia, playing a treat, cruised into the lead and, surely, out of sight. Then a superb putt on the sixteenth steadied the Shropshire Scot's palpitations and his momentum gathered in another shot at the seventeenth. But on the devilishly famed 405-yard par-4 last, he badly bunkered his drive – surely 'curtains'. He had four shots now to earn at least a play-off. Unlike Jones at Lytham sixty-two years earlier, Lyle did not take an age to decide his club. He grabbed his 1-iron and, as they say, went for it. It bulleted from the sand, and then kept going. A shot of a man of courage and a shot of the century – more so when it allowed him to follow with a glorious little 7-iron punch and a wondrous twelve foot putt and (what do you mean, play-off?) he was champion.

Arnold Palmer, having been a glorious runner-up to Kel Nagle the year before at his first British Open, looked mighty certain to have missed out on the old claret jug trophy in 1961 as well when, everything having gone swimmingly, he found himself way off the fifteenth fairway staring down in the direction of his ball, not only in deep undergrowth but also nestling against the substantial roots of a small bush. He and Dai Rees were each charging, nose to nose, for the title and now this damn bush had as good as tossed the jug to the Welshman, for there was no way Palmer could make the green from here. Should he just poke it away from under the bush, drop a shot, and hope for a better lie? For no lie could be more unplayable than this one. He squared up to the ball with his wedge. Then he had a change of mind, went back to his bag and took out a 7-iron. Again he addressed the ball and the bush. He was on the point of swinging . . . he stopped once more and returned to his bag. *What?* A 6-iron? No, not even this daredevil, affable Yank with the farm-boy's wrists of teak would dare go for the green with that lie? He'd have to take the whole ruddy bush with the ball. And so he did, the amazing fellow did . . .

In the *Daily Mail* one of the game's finest chroniclers, Mike McDonnell, next day memorably described what happened: 'The steel blurred into the undergrowth and there were noises. The swish of scythed grass, snapping twigs, the crack, a solid crack . . . Then it was not the sound, but the sight. A bush, airborne, grass and earth scattering around it. And somewhere the ball. But where? Suddenly the air cleared, and there it was, a black speck far away in the sky and dead on course for the green. It would reach its precise target. But some of the people did not see the ball, they were still staring in wonder at the hole in the ground where once a bush had stood. Not even a tornado could have wrenched it free so cleanly, and some would swear afterwards that the ground shook beneath them as Palmer's club cleaved that bush from his path' – and, to be sure, the phenomenal stroke cleared his route within the hour up that Open winner's coronation path, garlanded with acclaim, to the eighteenth green and the old claret jug.

That one immortal shot also cleared a brand new path for golf itself. Simply, it made it a *world* championship game again. The Open had languished since the war, played almost exclusively by Brits for Brits. Palmer's win in 1961 was seminal. He came back to retain the title in 1962, and this time he brought all his buddies from the American tour, back to the ancient home and medieval cathedrals of their game.

Arnold Palmer was a true great, and no other single shot but that one at Royal Birkdale on 17 July 1961, in which almost biblically he burned down a bush, can remotely be mentioned in the same breath as

The Shot of the Century
ARNOLD PALMER, Royal Birkdale

A distinguished professor of pathology, who recently holed out in one at the fourth at Walton Heath, thus opening the round with 4371444, asks whether he is the only man in history to have started a round of golf with his own telephone number. *Henry Longhurst*

I never liked sailing men. They yell blue murder at you all day, but then, when the boat is moored, the whisky comes out. Captain Bligh turns Casanova and is all ready to seek out your jolly erogenous zones and play deck coitus. *Jilly Cooper*

My grandfather couldn't prescribe a pill to make a greyhound run faster, but he could produce one to make the other five go slower. *Benny Green*

Choke of the Century

Five on the thirteenth

No obsessed hacker will swear he has never stood over a putt and daydreamed the commentary: 'This, from two feet, to win the US Masters.' In reality, it can fast become a nightmare if the putt is downhill, slightly left-to-right, on a green slicker and more polished than a marble mortuary-slab. At the Masters on 10 April 1989, dream certainly became nightmare for the home player Scott Hoch when he missed his winning putt from less than twenty-six inches and instead of him being robed in the historic green jacket, it was passed at once to Britain's Nick Faldo. (Poor Hoch – pronounced 'Hoak' – became forever known as Scott Choke.)

Nineteen years earlier, the popular American Doug Sanders, a colourful chap in both dress and spirit who called his autobiography *Come Swing With Me*, had a last-hole putt to win the 1970 Open – and on the High Altar at St Andrews of all places. This day he was dressed all in purple, both trews and pullover. He needed a par four up the eighteenth and the jug was his, and he'd done everything right because here he was with a cinch of a putt for his four. He settled his expensive black alligator-shoes alongside the ball and bent over his putter. He was ready for immortality.

Of a sudden, he seemed to notice something – was it an imaginary wormcast, one blade of razor-shaved grass the roller had missed, one infinitesimal grain of sand? Without changing the position of his feet, he bent to brush it away with no more than a momentary flick of his right hand. With the soles of his shoes still rooted to the exact same position, he now resettled over the ball – and as he did so, the BBC TV's doyen commentator Henry Longhurst gave a gasp and a murmured 'Oh, no' – and those in the know in the multi-million audience watching live round the world realized what Henry meant. He meant that Sanders had not reset his stance. He should have stood up, walked away, relaxed again, and then resettled.

Instead, he pulled back his putter and – gently-gently now – he jabbed at it. Oh, no . . . In the same twitch, Sanders on reflex tried to reach out with his club towards the ball to rake it back and have another go. There was no second go. The little dimpled onion, taunting him, rolled slowly four inches to the right-hand side of the hole and past it . . . 'Oh, there but for the grace of God . .' murmured the croaky Longhurst to the world.

A bogey five meant a play-off with Jack Nicklaus next day, which Sanders lost by a stroke, 73–72. But the one shot that lost it had been the day before. Sanders tied for second in four majors. He never did win one. 'No, sir,' he told me exactly twenty years later to the week, 'I don't think about St Andrews very much at all – only about every three minutes every day of my life.'

The date happened to be 13 July, the day of the

Choke of the Century
DOUG SANDERS, St Andrews

> When cricketers scowl and chew gum the result is highly unattractive. But Barry Richards completes a perfect technical picture of bland assurance unmarred by a rotating jaw. *EW Swanton*

Hole-in-one of the Century

Stamp of authority

The American pro H L Bonner holed-in-one all of fifty-seven times and said laconically, 'Each one's pretty much like the other.' Top Brit ace with thirty-one was Charles Chevalier, pro at the Heaton Moor club in Cheshire. Most dramatic, because it was so nearly a double ace in successive rounds – and in the Open, too – was Gene Sarazen's at Troon in 1973. On neither day on the short eighth, the 'Postage Stamp', did he need to use his putter. First, he clipped a little 5-iron off the tee and cupped it amid great excitement. Next day, his tee-shot was bunkered – and he holed the sandwedge! Also, the immortal little Mr Punch was seventy-one at the time.

Ace of the Century
GENE SARAZEN

> Outside a car the late Jim Clark was one of the most disorganized men I've known. He couldn't make up his mind. He hadn't a full fingernail; he ate them; he bit back to the skin on his first joint. But he drove with a certainty that was near flawless. *Jackie Stewart*

Open of the Century

Warm toast at Turnberry

Near 5pm on that second Saturday of July 1977, not a soul in that vast amphitheatre around the eighteenth green of Turnberry's ancient links would dare to say they were not witnessing the most colossal head-to-head encounter in the very history of the game. Head-to-head? But this was the British Open; well over a hundred of the world's best had entered, hadn't they? And not only that, these two Americans had been head-to-head to all intents for the past two and a half days of the four-day championship.

The numbers tell only a fraction of the point. But they are worth retelling: simply, in the last two rounds of the Open Championship of 1977, Tom Watson shot 65 and 65 to beat Jack Nicklaus by one stroke. Nicklaus shot 65 and 66; no man in the 117-year history of any Open had shot 65 and 66 in the last two rounds and lost. Watson's 72-hole total was 268, a new record by all of eight shots. In other words, had Watson not been there, the *loser* would have smithereened the Open record by a staggering seven shots.

Watson and Nicklaus had as good as destroyed the field by Thursday, and they went to bed on Friday after identical rounds of 68–70–65, the two of them a mile clear of the field. Friday had drained, it seemed, the two men dry, let alone the vast throng that followed them. But would you believe, they doubled the intensity on the Saturday and outspectaculared everything that had gone before. Stroke for stroke, shot for shot, Nicklaus ahead . . . Watson catches him . . . Nicklaus wrenches himself clear again . . . Watson hangs on . . . Nicklaus falters . . . Watson gets his hands round the big bear's throat . . . All square at the sixteenth tee. Sandy-haired challenger looks at the older blond champion. He smiles and says: 'This is what it's all about, isn't it?' And Jack smiles back: 'You bet your life it is.'

They level the sixteenth. Two to go. You could hear the deafening silence twenty miles away in Ayr. Watson throws a stupendous 3-iron to the core of the green . . . and Nicklaus is momentarily stunned, just enough to make him overplay his answering 4-iron and, consequently, miss his putt. Challenger one-up, one hole left. It is excruciating. Who will have the courage?

Watson, ahead for the first time proper, twangs his second shot to the eighteenth straight and true to the very pin. Perfection! An arrow surely that's pierced the champion's heart. But wait . . . for at the very last, Nicklaus takes an unconscionable time and then – Alleluia! – he sinks a dramatic and defiant putt of forty feet to leave Watson more to do. Watson kept his nerve . . . and ended it. They embraced.

So, with the utterly immortal HURRAH! of it, did 100,000 all around them. Old Scots wiped tears from their eyes . . . and then young men borrowed the hankie. Watson held aloft the old trophy of ancient fame and symbolism. Nicklaus at the microphone congratulated warmly the young *victor ludorum*. The man who had just broken the Open record by seven full shots – and lost! – said, 'Tom just played better.' And very soon it was suppertime at the Turnberry Hotel, the massive great folly (and glory) of Edwardiana that cranes over the links and looks far across the sea to Ailsa Craig and Arran's Isle. At the longest table sit the Nicklaus family: beloved wife Barbara, daughter of twelve Nancy Jean, son of sixteen Steve, plus sisters, cousins, aunts and friends. At the top, patriarch Jack Nicklaus tries to pretend he is not musing on the epic events just gone. Unsuccessfully.

Scarcely a forty-foot putt away sits Watson with his wife. He has angled his chair so he can look out of the window. But he has no eyes for the dusky beauty of the moment as Arran slips from view and into the sultry night. He looks steep down to the deserted village, the empty grandstands, down to Turnberry's now silent, eighteenth green where he had won the battle which will be recalled first in memories and then in words as long as a great game endures.

Nicklaus leaves the dining-room. Every diner, seventy or so, stands and applauds in a din of acclamation this loser of gallantry. Nicklaus is embarrassed and makes for the lift and bed. Five minutes later, the Watsons leave. More applause. Linda Watson goes to the lift. But her husband dallies, whispers to a waiter for one double measure, on the rocks, of his favourite MacWhatever local malt whisky. He will take it alone, out on the steps of the great hotel, in the now dark gloam of Scotland. It is brought to him. I am the only one spying, peeping round a curtain-edge from the lobby. Tom looks down at 'his' eighteenth green and raises his glass in a toast to it – and then gulps it in one, heart-warmingly satisfied.

Open of the Century
TURNBERRY 1977

Ah, cricket, the sight of bowler and players genuinely applauding a century against them. If a Rangers soccer side stood to applaud a Celtic goal I'd know the age of miracles had come. Cricket's greatness lies in the ability of players to honour a foe. It's the way life should be lived. *Professor William Barclay*

If you put monkeys on to play they'd still pack the Centre Court at Wimbledon. *Neale Fraser*

Lord Hawke probably took the same view as I do about families on tour with the MCC players. It is no more a place for them than a trench on the Somme. *John Woodcock*

Ryder of the Century

Keep your pullovers, boys

The Ryder Cup should have been dead and buried long before the century was halfway through. It was a yawner. It was begun in 1927 by one of the game's early sponsors, an English seed-merchant money-bags, Sam Ryder, a biennial United States versus British Isles. Did old Sam ever have a worse idea? Britain split the first four matches – and, quite pitifully, then won only once in the next twenty-one contests. So it was that solitary victory that made 1957 a glisteningly different year for golf all right. It was 4 October when they teed off – and there were more than omens above England's northern skies, for that morning it was announced that the Soviet Union had launched into space history's very first Sputnik.

The Lindrick course in south Yorkshire seems an unlikely pasture for the Ryder Cup. But the only sponsor who bid was the bluff Tyke businessman Sir Stuart Goodwin, who put up £10,000 for the match to be played on his doorstep. He billeted the swank stars of the Yankee team in a private commercial hotel in Sheffield. They were not best pleased. The names of the ten-man British team remain resonant of that baggy grey-trousered age – Rees (captain), Faulkner, Brown, O'Connor snr, Bousefield, Alliss, Hunt, Weetman, Bradshaw and Mills. It was a two-day event then, four foursomes on the first day then eight 36-hole singles to decide it.

On the evening of 4 October, the Brits were 3–1 down and mighty glum. From the clubhouse telephone, Leonard Crawley's rasping voice was heard dictating native gloom and doom for the next day's

Daily Telegraph: 'The golden age of 1920s American golf returned to England yesterday while the home side, particularly Faulkner and Weetman, played some lamentably poor shots.' So those two offered to stand down for the singles. Dai Rees took them at their word and dropped them, but before he could change his official order of play with his opposite number (the legendary 'bad-weather champion' Jack Burke), Weetman had a change of heart after being chided for being a drip by his wife Freda. Weetman stomped off, telling the press he would never play under Rees again. The PGA gave him a twelve–month suspension which it later halved on the intervention of Rees.

Meanwhile Rees, the endearing and diminutive Celtic gambler, knew only a bold throw could respark spirits. He put the Scottish swashbuckler Eric Brown out first against the tempestuous Oklahoman Tommy 'Thunder' Bolt, followed by the baby of the match, Peter Mills, just twenty-six, against the mighty Burke himself. If those two could put a hot streak to the morning, thought Rees, an inspirational flare just might be lit. At post-breakfast practice it was reported that animosity between Bolt and Brown had at once been joined and that 'they were already hurling clubs at each other'. Rees was content to hear it.

On the first tee, Brown drove; Bolt addressed his ball, then waggled his driver towards Brown and sneered: 'You're already beat, sucker.' Young Mills was next up. Years later he recalled: 'Eric helped calm me. He was the perfect choice to lead off against Bolt. Eric was a highly charged but almost carefree competitor. He gave it everything but at the same time didn't seem to give a damn, a one-off sort of Ian Botham of golf. Bolt loathed that type. It was a heavenly autumn morning, I remember, and all was still on the springy moorland turf. Eric at once dismantled Bolt's bravado, so as the galleries grew the applause ahead inspired me. By mid-morning there must have been about 20,000 milling about. At lunchtime, after eighteen, I was four or even five up. In the afternoon, at the eighth, a par-4 350-yarder, I knocked my second stone-dead at the flag. It was the clincher.'

Mills won 5 & 3, which squared the match, for Brown had already shot Bolt off the course by 4 & 3. 'The worst crowd ever,' said Bolt, refusing to shake hands. 'I did not enjoy that at all.'

'Of course you didn't, Tommy,' laughed Brown, 'because you were effing licked hollow.'

In the locker-room, the angry Bolt snapped his wedge across his knee and made firewood of his putter. He refused to attend the prize-giving ceremony, at which, by teatime, Rees received the Cup – for Bousfield, Hunt, O'Connor and the captain himself had followed, one by one, in kicking the Yanks when they were down. Britain won 7½ to 4½, their first victory for a quarter of a century, and their last for another eighteen years.

Brown was a typically combative non-playing captain in 1969 and 1971. Mills retired with serious back trouble two years after his round of grandeur, was reinstated as an amateur and happily ran a wine business in Jersey. 'Sir Stuart sent us £100 each and the American team gave us a little souvenir money-clip with the Cup's logo,' Mills said. 'That was the end of it.' Then he remembers something else: 'On the night of the victory, the PGA announced we could keep their specially issued grey pullover with a lion badge on it. Decent of them, eh?'

Ryder of the Century
LINDRICK, 1957

I'd give up golf like a shot. It's just that I've got so many sweaters. *Bob Hope*

I resigned as a coach because of illness and fatigue. The fans were sick and tired of me. *John Ralston, Denver Broncos*

Boxing

Fight of the Century

'A noise like a lullaby . . .'

No boxing promoter has been able to live out a happy retirement unless he had staged, let's say, at least five 'Fights of the Century'. For the hundred years, such phenomena have come thick and fast. And most of those few which did, in prospect, seem to have the necessary ingredients, in the event drowned in the sea of hype and hullabaloo that preceded them.

The century was, however, speckled with fights which entered the lore and remained there enduringly – and sometimes queryingly, as in the 'Was it a fix?' syndrome. Most schoolboys can rattle off these asterisks – the hulk Jess Willard standing over a supine Jack Johnson as the first, and great, black champion shielded (or didn't shield) his eyes from the Havana sun . . . Jack Dempsey sprawled across the ring-apron after the flailing Luis Firpo, 'the wild man of the pampas', had socked it to him . . . Dempsey again, hovering in the corner alongside the genuflecting Gene Tunney on 'the night of the long count' . . . Joe Louis skipping away to the correct neutral with the pleasure of satisfied vengeance on his face after enrolling Max Schmeling in the Flat Earth Society . . .

And so on and so forth . . . They were not necessarily 'great' fights or boxing matches but, history still insists, crucial 'occasions', signposts in the game, and the legend has duly stored them for all time. What there have been are some genuinely great 'series' of fights, that is follow-up sequels rather in the manner of the *Rocky* films. The very best of the best in this regard could well be the savagery, courage and no-love-lost of the three epics between 'Someone up there loves me' Rocky Graziano and the granite-hard, tattooed US sailor Tony Zale just before the half-century. See the fuzzy monochrome footage, filmed from long range, and, fifty years on, first you cower and then you wince. Same goes for Sugar Ray Robinson's two grudge matches against Carmen Basilio.

In retrospect and recollection, Muhammad Ali's two matches with Sonny Liston somehow allide into one saga; just as earlier did the twin-sets between Dempsey and Tunney, and Louis and Schmeling. Ali's hammer-and-sickle three-parter against Joe Frazier was a classic package of history; so in a very different way were Sugar Ray Leonard's two contests with Roberto Duran. I saw a fair number of Leonard's fights. The two Sugar Ray Leonards, from the middle of the century, were probably the very best, heavyweight Ali aside, comparative pound-for-pound fighters of the century. For me, in Las Vegas in 1980, Sugar Ray's dismantling of the tall, fierce hitter Thomas Hearns remains the 'boxer v fighter' challenge which still riddles the spine. As the rounds were tolled off under the golden orb of a desert moon, Hearns seemed increasingly sure of his destiny, for the crisp THWACK! of his punches and the smile of his white gumshield had a grotesque certainty about them. Leonard's left eye was gashed and dribbled blood and, increasingly, it looked as if he had a cricket ball embedded in his left cheekbone. But as it went on, the remarkable little fellow stayed light enough on his feet to evade the most menacing of the jackhammer rights from Hearns, and Leonard in turn was using more and more his left hand for hard and nasty little punches to the temples and nose. And by the thirteenth, Hearns's grin had gone, and now his mouth was open to gulp in the pain, for the wounded Leonard had indeed been only circling the wagon; twanging in the arrows, as he got closer and closer . . . and now of a sudden the tomahawks and burning faggots were flying and Hearns was as good as a goner, his legs old rope, his leather gloves powder-puffs . . . and the referee steps in to roll the credits.

As the millennium approached, the match-ups of horrible resplendence which had to be logged for posterity were such as Alexis Arguello and Aaron Pryor's thirteen–rounder in 1983, and the utterly brilliant Julio Cesar Chavez's nick-of-time defeat of outstanding

Meldrick Taylor in 1990.

That same rangily long-legged and hurtful hitman from Detroit, Thomas Hearns, who had been ultimately and dramatically rounded-up by the astonishing Leonard in 1980, returned to Nevada five years later where, centre-stage, he played the lead in what many knowing ringsiders consider the most epic and breathtaking punch-up that can ever, legally, have been sanctioned. Or rather, not the lead but the co-star, for he lost in eight minutes of malevolent mayhem and intensive belligerence to the brutally talented Marvin Hagler. The bell went and Hearns hit Hagler. And Hagler hit him back. 'The pattern,' as the olde-tyme sportscribe used to say, 'continued.' A hundredfold. In three minutes. 'The first round was probably the fiercest, most devouringly competitive ever seen in a major professional fight,' wrote Hugh McIlvanney. The unrestrained war continued till the third when – 'devoured' probably still the word – the two sides of Hearns's face were crunched almost simultaneously by a withering left-hook and a clubbing right-cross and then, as he fell, a final executioner's right just to make sure. The last was a wasted blow.

After such terrors, when some still-quaking soul at the ringside afterwards wondered, 'After that, who can Hagler possibly fight next?' he received the answer, 'How about Russia?' But does the laying out of a fighter's full arsenal of horrors, his whole tool-kit of terror in just eight minutes qualify as boxing's Match of the Century? If so, that was it. But I fancy we are seeking something more rounded here, a contest more meaningful than even those present, or those taking part, could possibly have imagined at the time.

If it hadn't been for the black and dignified Joe Louis, could there have been a Muhammad Ali? But would there have been a Joe Louis if Jack Johnson had not enlisted? The most seminal, by far the most resonant of all world heavyweight championship matches took place on, aptly, Boxing Day at Sydney's Rushcutters' Bay in 1908, when Jack Johnson beat Tommy Burns of Canada to become the first generally acknowledged black world champion. Or rather, the first generally acknowledged in the United States, where, being isolationist in almost all global games, they have always recognized themselves as the fount in these particular fistic matters. The first black man to win a world championship was actually the bantamweight 'Little

Chocolate' George Dixon when he KO'd Nunc Wallace in the eight-eenth at the Pelican Club, London, on 27 June 1890.

Burns was hot favourite for the Sydney fight despite being only 5ft 7in. But the white man never stood a chance. He was slashed and scis-sored to shreds, with Johnson taunting him between each razor-sharp cluster of blows. The police stewards who circled the ringside were furious at the white man's beating-up; they could stand the taunts no longer and raided the ring after Burns was put down in the thirteenth. They demanded an end to it. They allowed one more round – but that was too much and they stopped the white man's humiliation by storming the ring in the fourteenth round. Burns pocketed $30,000 for his substantial pains (the sport's first overblown purse) and the winner only $5,000.

The result appalled the white establishment around the world, particularly those two then especially hostile enclaves of racism, Australia and the United States. In fact, as soon as the match was made (the white-womanizing Johnson had already been banned from fighting for the title in his native America) the bigots began to shud-der – and bleat. The editorial in Sydney's *Illustrated Sporting & Dramatic News* was certain that 'citizens who have never prayed before are supplicating Providence to give the white man a strong right-arm with which to belt the coon into oblivion'. The *Australian Star* printed a cartoon depicting the boxing ring, one half of the watching throng cowering white men being menaced by the other half, which was black. The caption warned: 'This battle may in the future be looked upon as the first great battle of the inevitable race war. There is more in this fight to be considered than the mere title of pugilistic cham-pion of the world.'

By the by, 1908 was the very year another Sydney newspaper, the *Bulletin*, had changed its masthead banner from 'Australia for Australians' to 'Australia for the White Man'.

Filing from the ringside, round by round, back to the *New York Herald* was the justly famed Jack London. His intro read: 'The fight? There was no fight. No Armenian massacre could compare with the hopeless slaughter that took place in the Sydney Stadium today. From the opening seconds of the first round it was a fight between a colos-sus and a toy automaton, between a playful Ethiopian and a small and futile white man, between a grown man and a naughty child.'

London continued his report of the terrible one-sider through each round – 'as 20,000 horrified white supporters found their nightmared fears materialize' – but he ended a dramatic and basically unbiased sportswriter's dispatch by leaping from the fence garlanded in true colours with his final paragraph when he called on James J Jeffries, a previous champion, to come out of retirement and restore the natural order. London signed off: 'A golden smile tells the story, and a golden smile was Johnson's. Only one thing remains: our white Jeffries must emerge from his alfalfa farm and remove that golden smile from Johnson's face. Jeff, it's up to you.' (On Independence Day 1910, Johnson was to beat up the thirty-five–year-old Jeffries just as cruelly as he had done Burns.)

There was, surely, another first posted after that fight in Sydney: the longest headline ever to lead a sports page. The bold Bodoni banner over that *NY Herald* report read: 'Jack London Says Johnson Made a Noise Like a Lullaby With His Fists as He Tucked Burns in His Little Crib in Sleepy Hollow With a Laugh.'

For his time, Jack Johnson was a true great of boxing. As well, for his wretchedly bigoted times, he was a courageous pioneer. He also won

The Fight of the Century
JACK JOHNSON v TOMMY BURNS

> Why are the umpires, the only two people on a cricket field who aren't going to get grass stains on their knees, the only ones allowed to wear dark trousers. *Katherine Whitehorn*

Personality of the Century

Just hard to be humble

He was a genuine prophet. Even in that guise he was a pioneering one, for he was a prophet who talked a lot of rot. Mind you, a majority of it was appealing, amusing, enjoyable rot. One day in the 1980s, when it was already obvious that Parkinson's Syndrome was severely dulling his limbs, if not the still bright, mischievous eyes, he said with no boast and as a matter of fact, 'I am the only man in the whole history of the universe who became world famous under two different names.' And you thought about it, even considered the New Testament, and you had to believe yon Cassius Clay–Muhammad Ali.

He was more than the best boxer in the world, and the best fighter, far more than 'just' an all-time great sportsman and certainly far more than a showman celebrity famous for being famous, those limbo creatures with which the century, as it wore on, was increasingly bombarded and browned-off. Between, if you like, the Parkinson Show and Parkinson's Syndrome, there was much, much more to the epic of Muhammad Ali. And then some more again.

Apart from, possibly, family foot-races when all was hunky-dory in Eden, boxing must be the oldest sport of pre-history and the very first 'fight of the century' promotion was the night Sugar Ray Abel was tipped on his butt in the fifth by Kid Cain. In this millennium, boxing was also the first sport for humans to be 'officially' codified, in the eighteenth century, with rules and sacrosanct traditions, some of which hold good today. With them, a certain style, technique, discipline, shape and form was laid down and passed from generation to generation. One man tore up every textbook, legend, presumption and manual and then, before he was twenty-five, rewrote them. As he explained (or rather, extemporized), his tutorials took on a glow; and then he would physically demonstrate the theory with such a real effortlessness in the very cannon's mouth, and on so many occasions, that demonstrator did become prophet.

Mike Tyson, a flawed man but a meanly savage hitter who came after Ali as heavyweight champion, described his trade: 'I am in the hurting business.' As he ever did, Ali said different: 'I am in the business of not getting hurt.'

Johnson, Dempsey, Tunney, Louis, Marciano, Tyson, each at the peak of their prime? Would Ali, at his, have beaten them? Without doubt he would have. He beat Liston, Frazier and Foreman, didn't he? Whatever we know at the end of the century about the huge development of sporting man – there's a four-year graph to prove it: the Olympic Games record book – the last three names would also have beaten the earlier six. And Liston, Frazier and Foreman, perceived ogres each of them, fell to Ali. Possibly the century's best writer on boxing, Hugh McIlvanney, has no doubts: 'Compared with Ali, his predecessors are obscure figures dancing behind frosted glass.'

But the boxing was only the cause, not the effect. There is still more, much more about this prophet of honour. Another former world champion, the literate Jose Torres, tried to pin down one facet: 'If you lived in his time, lived anywhere, you *knew* him. And Muhammad for many of those people represented the best time of their lives.' Golly, can it really be over one-third of a century ago that we stayed up half the night in that Fulham Road bedsit to watch him dismantle the perceived blackguard, Sonny Liston? We could scarcely believe it was true. We presumed a fix. We knew soon enough it wasn't. He took on anyone and everyone. Here's something for *A Question of Sport*: who was the Ugly Bear, the Baby Bear, the Washerwoman, the Rabbit, the Mummy, the Beaver, the Peanut? And who, unquestionably, was the Greatest? In the mid 1960s I wangled a job with ITV, so saw a few of his fights for real in the glorious heyday before they got him and banned him for dodging the draft ('I ain't got nothing against them Viet Congs'). Some dud 'obituarist' wrote the other day that the Vietnam line was the only memorable thing Ali ever said. Well, depends how you look at it. I chortled with the best of them the first time I heard, 'I'm so mean I make medicine sick ... 'Harry, you're not as dim as you look' ... ' Get out the guns, we're settin' traps' . . 'Float like a butterfly, sting like a bee' ... 'He's got two chances – slim and none' ... 'I chop wood, so it's like I borrow all my strength from trees' ... 'If I say a mosquito can pull a plough, don't ask questions, just hitch it up.'

His being a conscientious objector at that time was the first world-wide evidence of his staunch, unflinching nobility, and stubbornness, at defending his corner. It enraged, particularly, America's white right and they made him pay for it by banning him from his profession and his livelihood for three years. His sentence over, and all America admitted that, after all, they too realized they had no right to be at war with 'them Viet Congs'. Throughout his banishment, he had continued apologetically to hold his ground and to both the intellectuals and the 'patriot' hawks in the Pentagon he would reason, 'You can't condemn me for wanting peace. If you do, you condemn peace itself. A rooster crows when it sees the light. Put him in the dark and he'll never crow. I have seen the light, and I am gonna continue crowing.'

Ali revolutionized his sport on every level as well as, to be sure, his whole race's standing in the United States and elsewhere. At boxing, as well as his fluent, unrivalled virtuosity, there was a courage and valour in him. Also a bravery outside the roped square they call a ring. Eldridge Cleaver wrote in *Soul On Ice*: 'Essentially every black champion until Muhammad Ali had been a puppet, manipulated by whites in his private life to control his public image ... With the coming of Muhammad, the puppet master was left with a handful of strings to which his dancing doll was no longer attached.' Another distinguished New York writer, a white one, Robert Lipsyte, said Ali crucially provided 'a window on a lot of social, political and religious things that were going on in America; a window into the black world that wouldn't have been available to most of his listeners in any other way.' That, alone, was enough for greatness.

So, more frivolously, was his humour. His first ticket-selling rhyme was as a young contender in 1963 when he fought Doug Jones. Pre-fight, there was a long New York newspaper strike and no big build-up. Cassius, as you might expect, did the radio and TV commercials himself. Because it was the first I'd heard, it remains my favourite:

> *Jones likes to mix*
> *So I'll let it go six.*
> *If he talks jive*
> *I'll cut it to five.*
> *And if he talks some more*
> *I'll cut it to four.*

As it happens (and happy the newspaper strike continued), the tough Jones lasted till the tenth. Ali was still at it a dozen years later alongside the lazy great sweep of the Zaire River when, fearlessly eyeballing the immense, sullen bully George Foreman before their cataclysmic 'rumble', he recited his challenge:

> *I have wrestled with a alligator,*
> *I have tussled with a whale,*
> *I have handcuffed lightning,*
> *Thrown thunder in jail.*
> *Only last week I hospitalized a brick –*
> *I'm so mean, I make medicine sick.*

Like all the finest winners, Muhammad also knew how to lose. The day after the first of his three epic contests with Joe Frazier, Ali attempted a painful smile in spite of his crushed cheekbone: 'I thought I couldn't lose, simply because I was fighting for people all over the world. If I win, people all over the world's going to think they can be winners too. You've all got to lose some to know how to win some. I feel rewarded this morning in a way, because I've been given the chance to set an example of how to lose well . . .'

Once after training, about fifty of us crowded round him on the massage table asking the usual inane questions about the state of the universe. I don't know what came over me, but I asked what the best counter was to a ramrod southpaw. The joint fell silent. Ali, with delight, said it was the first technical question he'd been asked on boxing all year. He gave orders for forty-nine hacks to be thrown out. I got a world exclusive on the secret of beating up southpaws.

Unbelievers can scoff to their hearts' content. Like the man himself said, 'I don't like to be thought of as boastin'. It's just hard to be humble when you're as great as I am.'

Personality of the Century
MUHAMMAD ALI

> I'd give my right arm to get back into the England team. *Peter Shilton, goalkeeper*

> Retire? Retire to what? I already fish and play golf. *Julius Boros, golfer*

> If a player's ball lies in a mortar shell crater he may move it without penalty. *Notice at Hillside Golf Club, Umtali*

> They're selling video cassettes of the Ali–Spinks fight for $89.95. Hell, for that money Spinks will come to your house. *Ferdie Pacheco*

Bully of the Century

Destruction of the innocents

He was a miner from Pennsylvania, with a collier's muscled, rounded shoulders and forearms as big as his thighs. But we were told he couldn't actually fight – well, he had fought nobody we had ever heard of, not even any sort of championship eliminator; he had eight defeats on his record in the small-hall American circuit, and he was only brought over to England on the *Queen Mary* to allow our two highly popular champions and, almost, folk heroes Freddie Mills and Bruce Woodcock to have a decent workout before challenging fighters with serious titles at stake. Anyway, didn't this Joe Baksi with his stubbled lantern-jaw also look like Desperate Dan, an amiable cartoon character in one of our cartoon comics? A joke.

Yet, more than half a century on, the name Joe Baksi still causes a *frisson* of chill, a shudder. What terror, still. In just five months, he demolished boyhood certainties that heroes were giants and invincible.

First up was Mills. Bonfire Night, 1946, was the first occasion this eight-year-old had been allowed to stay up in his (definitely non-combatant's) dressing-gown to listen to a ringside radio commentary of a boxing match – and at once a serene pastoral innocence was raucously ransacked by commentator Stewart MacPherson's breathless torrent of descriptive bloodletting from London's Harringay arena.

It was cold, metallic machine-gun stuff from MacPherson's mike as the Brit was hit to kingdom come. Dad said it was obvious the ration-booked country was not getting enough good red meat.

Freddie Mills was a popular and mettlesome, heart-of-oak little warrior, a former booth-fighter billed as 'the Bournemouth Milkman'. On 5 November 1946, he was pasteurized, semi-skimmed, jugged and mugged by Baksi, three stones heavier and without mercy in his soul. The referee found some at last and stopped the wretched one-sidedness after six rounds – trainer Tom Broadribb angrily demanding a seventh. Mills spent that night in King's College Hospital. At Christmas he was still complaining of 'dreadful and recurring headaches' and always being woken by his wife Chrissie 'as if out of a deep coma'. For weeks his speech was slurred. Faraway, us urchins cried out for vengeance.

The following April, Baksi was back at Harringay. He was waiting with a smile on his face for Bruce Woodcock. We knew Woodcock, two stones heavier than our Freddie, was a far more accomplished boxer in the classic English upright style, with a poker-stiff left jab and a strong right-cross. Not only us dressing-gowned kids faraway near a wireless were presuming that Bruce would shave that stubbled lantern-jaw; the contest pinned back the ears of the nation. Ringside seats were priced exorbitantly at twenty guineas, but more than 100,000 applications came in for 11,000 seats. The gross gate of £54,000 was a British record. Baksi's purse was £13,000, Woodcock's half that.

Although it was to last twenty minutes, the fight was to all intents over in seconds when Woodcock's jaw was broken by the American's first punch. Peter McInnes's vivid history of Harringay Stadium recalls the first bell sounding, whereupon 'Baksi came across the ring like a flyweight and with an ungainly left-hook caught the British champion in his corner. That one punch smashed Woodcock's jawbone and caused severe damage to his eye. Everyone except Bruce saw the blow coming . . .'

The referee was Moss Deyong, who later wrote an autobiography, *Everybody Boo!* He recalled that gruesome April night: 'I was more than a referee; I was a butcher's scales, weighing bleeding beef as if it was flayed . . . By the seventh, Woodcock's face was like a jam tart that had been trodden on. But I have never witnessed anything gamer than Bruce's recovery after that disastrous first round. With the subsequent knowledge that the first blow had broken the Doncastrian's jaw, it was a miracle of courage and fighting spirit.'

Woodcock was not fit to fight again for eighteen months. He won four fights and lost one before his defeat by Jack Gardner and retirement. In January 1965, James Mossop interviewed him in the *Sunday Express* when the former champion and hero was mine-host of the Tumbler Hotel at Edlington, near Doncaster.

Woodcock said he could remember nothing of the Baksi fight after the American's first blow, and it seemed news to him that he'd been down in that first round for counts of nine, seven and nine, and twice more for counts of nine in the second. 'I was only semi-conscious. From that first punch I was fighting like a robot,' he told Mossop, adding: 'Don't feel sorry. Someone has to have the luck. I had my chances.'

Whatever happened to Joe Baksi? Certainly Britain never heard of him again. But he destroyed childhood heroes, and innocence, did this

Bully of the Century
JOE BAKSI

> I went to a fight last night and an ice hockey game broke out. *Rodney Dangerfield, comedian*

> RENTAJOGGER – only $1.95. Rent me and I will jog for you at least one mile a day (weather permitting) for the next year. *Ad in* New York Times

Horse Racing

Jockey of the Century

Scattering the field

A great professional jockey has to pick his horses as well as ride them – and nine winning Derbies scatters the field and leaves no possible room even for discussion.

Jockey of the Century
LESTER PIGGOTT

> I did everything from leading the band to running races against horses. I had baseball teams, basketball teams and candy-bars named after me, sold soda pop and danced in dance marathons. None of these ventures turned out to be profitable. *Jesse Owens, US athlete, 1951, on his career after his Olympic triumph in 1936*

> Once a guy starts wearing silk pyjamas, it's hard to get up early. *Eddie Arcaro, US champion jockey*

> People think of me as an athlete, but I am not really. I am a businessman. *Jean Borotra, French tennis star, 1956*

Racehorse of the Century

Bird off the bit

If Ormonde is generally accepted as the horse of the nineteenth century, the horsebox for the following hundred years is so crammed with nominations as to seem, when the tailgate drops, to be signal for a charge of the light brigade. Even boldly dismissing a pair as 'best two of the century never to have won the Derby' – Alcide ('nobbled' in 1958) and Dancing Brave ('pilot error' in 1986) – does not clear the decks in any noticeable way.

The first half of the century was speckled with enduring four-footed grandeur. Neither did Bayardo, for instance, win his Derby, but he truly dominated the Turf for two or three seasons till 1910, just as the 1917 Derby winner Grey Crusader did all through his career. Bahram and Hyperion by all accounts had a breathtaking turn of foot in the 1930s, and a decade later as racing put itself back together after the War, at least the 1940s could boast about its wondrously gallant Alycidon, still considered the 'greatest stayer of the century'.

For the rest, an alphabetical Top Ten which cannot even squeeze in Blue Peter, Brown Jack, Pinza, Royal Palace, Grundy, Lamtarra . . .

BRIGADIER GERARD (born/foaled 1968) Won seventeen out of eighteen races, including 2,000 Guineas and Champion Stakes (twice). Only defeat to 1972 Derby winner Roberto in B&H Gold Cup. Named after a Conan Doyle character, owned by journalist John Hislop.

DANCING BRAVE (1982) Rated one of best never to have won the Derby. New jockey on board when won Eclipse, King George and Prix de l'Arc de Triomphe.

MILL REEF (1968) Brilliant colt with blistering acceleration. Won Derby, King George and Arc. Saved for stud after breaking a leg on the gallops. Has bred two Derby winners, Shirley Heights and Reference Point.

NASHWAN (1986) Nicknamed 'Nash The Dash'. Won the 2,000 Guineas, Derby, Eclipse and King George. Beaten only once.

NIJINKSY (1967) Late acceleration was his hallmark and won 2,000 Guineas, Derby and King George.

OH SO SHARP (1982) Lengthy filly that won from seven furlongs to a mile and three-quarters including the Fillies' Triple Crown of 1,000 Guineas, Oaks and St Leger. Of fillies, only Meld (1952) might have caught her.

PEBBLES (1981) Only British horse to win the Breeders' Cup in America and over £1 million. Temperament problems but abundant ability.

RIBOT (1952) Italian-trained colt named after nineteenth-century French painter. Won Prix de l'Arc de Triomphe and King George at Ascot in 1956. Unbeaten in sixteen races.

SEA BIRD II (1962) French colt, won Derby without coming off the bit and the Arc by six lengths. Fast finisher, slower at stud.

SHERGAR (1978) Easiest Derby winner of all time, scoring by ten lengths. Relentless galloper rather than quickener. Ended his days when kidnapped.

The latter may have won the Derby by the widest distance of the century, but the penultimate, French phenomenon Sea Bird II, won the great Epsom classic with such contemptuous ease that jockey Pat Glennon dropped his hands eighty yards from the pole and they almost trotted past the line, exuding disdain for those rolling and heaving four-footers behind with their nostrils flaring like cartoon trumpets. Three months later, the sumptuously haughty chestnut with the two white stockings behind did exactly the same back home in the Prix de l'Arc de Triomphe. On both occasions, you knew no horse in the world could have beaten him – indeed, no other horse in the century.

Racehorse of the Century
SEA BIRD II

> In fact, Sam the Gonoph says, I long ago came to the conclusion that all life is six to five against. *Damon Runyon*

> I will put it this way: Situations may arise in a good cricket or football team requiring a quick decision. Perhaps a shade quicker than a company commander with a line of skirmishers in the field. *Col O'Callaghan-Westropp, Member of the Royal Commission for Militia and Volunteers, 1904*

> Never forget that you have an appointment with a man with a chequered flag at the end. You can be late if you like, but if you don't keep that appointment you might just as well not have started. *Sammy Davis, racing driver, 1920*

National Hunter of the Century

Sure feet, soft humours

If the voluptuous Sea Bird II was so contemptuously fast on the track and so comparatively slow at stud, he did sire the remarkable and endearing all-rounder of the century, Sea Pigeon, who was winning the Ebor with a record ten stone at the age of nine, and then took merrily to life 'over the sticks' to win, each two times over, the Cheltenham, Scottish and Welsh Champion Hurdles between 1977 and 1980. Every time you saw him put in those held-back, sudden stirring finishes, all systems go, you thought, 'Well, how excitingly different from his dad.'

But the 'sticks' are for the See You Then speedsters, the hooraying hurdlers and the coming of spring, the Persian Warriors, you might say. The winter's murky, fogbound glories are for the great brave mudlarks of the high blackthorn hedges with their moated trenches fore and aft. The jury is *au fait* with every fact, each name happily trips off the tongue and is savoured – Troytown, Reynoldstown, and old favourite Freebooter; Golden Miller, Prince Regent, Cottage Rake; no end of familiar and true-great names, March after April, from Cheltenham and Aintree . . . dear bright-eyed Dawn Run, for sure, as well as the utterly glorious grey Desert Orchid . . . even Mill House till somebody beat him and he was never the same again. Nor was the century. Mill House, simply, had been beaten by the most courageous, gentle, intelligently sure-footed and soft-humoured fellow who was, indisputably, the all-time

National Hunter of the Century
ARKLE

Nationalist of the Century

Truly a darling fellow

In 1973, Red Rum won the Grand National in the fastest time ever. In 1974, he became the first dual winner of the race for 28 years. In 1977, he won the race for, uniquely in 140 years, the third time. In between, he was twice second.

Nationalist of the Century
RED RUM

> Then ye returned to your trinkets; then ye contented
>   your souls,
> With the flannelled fools at the wickets for the muddied
>   oafs at the goals.
> *Rudyard Kipling*

> You might as well praise me for not robbing a bank.
> *Bobby Jones, US golfer, 1923, after being congratulated on his good sportsmanship*

> Hail the conquering hero comes
> Surrounded by a bunch of bums.
> *Anon, 1920s*

Cock-up of the Century

The race that never was

There was only one man to talk to on the eve of the 1994 Grand National. The man who had started the 1993 Grand National – or rather, hadn't.

At 3.58pm on the last Saturday in April 1993, retired Captain Keith Brown, formerly of the Third Hussars, pulled the lever which should have hoisted the starting tape over the horses' heads and so set in motion the cavalry-charge gallop to the first fence of the Grand National, history's oldest steeplechase race. Seventy thousand people were there as he did so, and countless more millions watching live on television all around the world. There had been an 'animal rights' demonstration on the course during the previous race and the police had spent time clearing it before allowing Captain Brown to begin proceedings . . .

It was a filthy day, windy and very Irish Sea wet. He pulled, and the eighty yards of tape bucked slightly and then, for much of its length, billowed back to bandage and coil around some horses and jockeys. Half a dozen unaffected horses took off. The sixty-six-year-old Captain at once raised the red flag and waved it vigorously. Down the course, near the first fence, his NCO oppo, Ken Evans, saw it and in turn waved *his* flag. The six jockeys noticed this and pulled up, to return for another go at a mass start. At once, at 4.04pm, the good Captain tried again. Once more, some horses and/or riders were enmeshed in the rain-heavy starting tape. Captain Brown waved his flag again, but it did not unfurl. Eleven of the thirty-nine this time broke free and began to race – ignoring any pleas to stop from race-course stewards, for the horsemen presumed them to be animal rights demonstrators.

The eleven finished it, both circuits, before the race was declared null and void. There was no 1993 Grand National.

There was a Jockey (by now referred to by the nation as 'Jokey') Club inquiry, chaired by another military man, Brigadier Andrew Parker-Bowles, which produced, six months later, a thirty-four-page document exonerating the Captain – but blaming Evans, the £28-a-day part-time course flagman.

All £75 million worth of bets were off. The non-race had been non-won by Esha Ness non-ridden by John White. *The Times* called it 'a national scandal'. The *Daily Telegraph* said, 'Britain is a laughing stock.' The Treasury said it had forfeited £6 million in taxes. The racing industry lost over £1 million.

It was the last race Captain Brown 'started'. He had been due to retire that day anyway. He had a police escort from the course in his bowler hat and officer-issue belted gaberdine mac. Angry racegoers tried to jostle him and a trainer threatened all sorts of action in the courts.

Exactly a year minus a day later, now in his check cap, battered cords and a dog-haired old pullover, the Captain shivered momentarily at the memory as he amiably pottered around his potting-shed in suburban Surrey.

'Do I have nightmares about last year? To be truthful, yes, I do. I will wake up in a cold sweat. I bitterly regret what happened. Always will. But I have a clear conscience. I'd do the same again. There was nothing else I could have done. Well, what would you have done, eh? If I'd let the field go, someone might have been killed. It was utterly filthy weather. The jockeys were getting agitated, you know – "C'mon, guv, get us away, can't you?" – and the horses even more so.

'All around was absolute bedlam. It was like a bear pit. A few thousand amateur starters as well, all shouting "They're off!" and that sort of thing. Because of the rain, the tape was getting heavier and heavier. That's why it wouldn't go up properly when the time came. Then one horse looked to fly-jump the tape. Oh, it was all so horrid, absolutely horrid ... I dare say I did look officious in that hat. I only wore the bowler for the National or for Cheltenham. Simply because, with the masses milling about down there, the jockeys could recognize me as the starter by my hat.

'You do realize, don't you, that I had long been warning Aintree that the starting tackle was getting past it? So had all my predecessors. It was too old and too slow and the tapes, at sixty yards, were too long and sagging. It was only used this once a year and just loused up on the day. The National was the only race started from there. It was, in a way, a disaster waiting to happen.

'The only pity is that it happened on my retirement day. Yes, I'll always feel bitter that it did – and I'll never forget my long, lonely and thoroughly wretched drive through the filthy weather that night, home to Surrey and the dogs and my wife. Deirdre had watched it all on television and, bless her, it was past one o'clock when I got in and she'd left me a whacking great tumbler of scotch.'

Captain Brown, a jolly decent stick, profoundly hoped that, having been famous for his fifteen minutes, the world might leave him in peace. Another, more world-weary part of him, however, is resigned to going to his grave one day, cheerioed by just the one obituary headline in every public print the world over: 'CAPTAIN COCK-UP.'

Cock-up of the Century
AINTREE 1993

The so-called Golden Age of Sports, the twenties and early thirties, was really the Golden Age of Sportswriting. *Robert Lipsyte, US sportswriter*

When athletes are no longer heroes to you anymore, it's time to stop writing sports. *Grantland Rice, US sportswriter*

Athletics

Run of the Century

Sittin' in the armchair

Jim Thorpe, Eric Liddell and Harold Abrahams ... the remarkable Jesse Owens putting Hitler's racist nose out of joint in 1936 ... Fanny Blankers-Koen and Emil Zatopek ... swimmer Mark Spitz at Munich in 1972, discus-thrower Al Oerter and rower Steve Redgrave who won gold medals at four successive Olympics ... Seb Coe, all history's only winning defender of the blue riband 1500m title ... the immense all-rounder Carl Lewis, and any decathlete *victor ludorum* in any Games from the incomparable Daley Thompson downwards ...

But not Ben Johnson, disgraced at the Games of Seoul, or any of his shamed ilk who took performance-enhancing drugs. But how many cheats down the century did? Hundreds? Thousands? They smear the honours' board of sport. But some specific events, by all accounts, are 'drug-free' because no known stimulant can help: like the 'middle-distance' foot races and sprints. So another Johnson can be safely and honourably garlanded here with the laurel, bushes of it. In the last Olympic Games of the century, in Georgia, an upright, sober-sided Texan did what a man's gotta do ... or rather, what no man before had ever done. Not only the unique double winner, but world record holder and world champion at two distances. Not just great, it was phenomenal to smithereen your own world records in uniquely winning the 200 metres and 400 metres at the very same Olympics.

After we had watched Johnson's utterly breathtaking second run, in the 200 metres, a friend next to me in Atlanta's press box muttered in awe, 'I wish I could frame that 19.32 seconds and put it in a glass case at home; you'd have art galleries the world over queuing up to buy it for millions.'

Johnson afterwards actually bothered to smile. 'The world record is a bonus,' he said. 'The most important thing to me was making history. A lot of people hold a world record, and I did too before I arrived here. But nobody else can say they made history, the first man to win the 200 and 400. I stumbled – did you notice? – around my fourth step from the blocks, but then I got into gear pretty fast. By a dozen strides or so, I was just relaxed. I sat back in the armchair. I was feeling good and honestly felt I couldn't go any faster than I was already going. After about eighty or ninety metres, I felt totally in control and at that point I just went to my endurance tank and gave it all I had. I knew the time was faster than 19.66, but I didn't know how fast. To run 19.32 is unbelievable. If you want an analogy of the incredible thrill I felt, well, go out and get a go-kart, find a hill, a very steep one, and let it go, and you'll know how it feels. Pretty good, eh?'

Before the race, Jesse Owens's wife Ruth sent a fax to Johnson simply saying, 'Michael – run and deliver.' He did. With knobs on. Just like Jesse Owens had that day when Adolf Hitler petulantly walked out on him in Berlin nearly two-thirds of a century ago in 1936. Michael ran. Michael delivered.

Run of the Century
MICHAEL JOHNSON

There isn't anything on earth as depressing as an old sportswriter. *Ring Lardner, US sportswriter and humorist*

Mile of the Century

Double rainbow over Magdalen

The race was run in 3 minutes 59.4 seconds. Enough said, really. It was Event Nine on the programme: 'One Mile Footrace' to begin at 6pm on Thursday 6 May 1954, during Oxford University Athletic Club's annual match against the Amateur Athletic Association at the university's running track which rimmed its rugby field alongside Iffley Road. I was far away at school. It had been a cricket afternoon. In the refectory before saying grace, a priest, Father Norbert, announced reverently, 'You may like to know that Bannister has just broken the four-minute mile!' We let rip with soprano shrieks and piled into the common-room to listen, I suppose, to *Radio Newsreel* on the wireless.

By that time, in Oxford, Roger Bannister, our pale-faced hero with the showgirl's legs and severe National Service haircut, was in Vincent's Club celebrating with a wine glass of tap water laced with salt, followed by a half of shandy. His friends were urging him against his will that it was his duty to take up BBC TV's offer of a dash to their London studios in a specially hired blue sports car. In the end, the young man agreed.

Decisions, decisions: there had been a lot of them about for Bannister that famous May day in 1954. He had woken that morning in his parents' home in Harrow after yet another of his recently restless, sweaty nights. It was not long after dawn but already the wind he saw was gusting strong, surely excuse enough for him to put off the whole madcap enterprise.

The medical student arranged to catch a train around noon from Paddington and on the way popped into his hospital to get his heavy old leather running-shoes. He also sharpened the spikes of another pair on a graphite stone in the laboratory.

The early train would ensure he would not run into journalists. He knew the buzz was on about a record attempt. Fleet Street had been pests. He preferred the wind in his hair to his name in the headlines. These tiresome journalists were challenging him to steal a march on the Australian John Landy, Wes Santee, the US sophomore, or even Gordon Pirie, the 'serious' British athlete. No, he, Bannister, was a trainee medic first and would continue to run for fun where and when he chose.

In the train, Bannister met Franz Stampfl, an enthusiast, coach and visionary to whom he had been introduced by one of his prospective pacemakers that night, Chris Brasher. A month before, in a Lyons upstairs tea-shop in Sloane Square, Stampfl had insisted that four minutes was breakable and, on the back of the bill, had drawn up plans for the students. Now on the Great Western as Bucks became Berks and then Oxon, Bannister was still funking it and told Stampfl the wind was too high. He would go for the record in nine days' time at the White City. 'Your mind can overcome any adversity,' said Stampfl.

Charles Wenden, friend and athlete and later bursar at All Souls, met him at Oxford station. At Iffley Road, Bannister tried his spikes and liked especially the sharpened pair which had been given him by the Lancashire fell-walker Eustace Thomas. That made him feel better, though the wind still ripped at the flag of St George on the nearby church tower. Mrs Wenden had prepared him a late lunch of ham salad and stewed prunes. Metaphorically he kicked his heels, then went to agonize with his other pacemaker and friend, the carroty-haired Chris Chataway, who was languidly stretched out reading in a window-seat at his college, Magdalen. 'Let's call it off now,' said Bannister. 'Let's wait until five,' said Chataway.

At 5.30 they had changed and were warming up. 'We must go for it,' said Brasher, urged on by Stampfl. Chataway looked at Bannister who was shaking his head and mouthing a positive 'No.' There was a sharp shower, hardly conducive, followed by a bold double-rainbow arcing over Magdalen's mellow tower of ages. Then, suddenly, on the same tower, the flag of St George was still and limp on its pole.

Five minutes to the gun. 'Yes, yes,' insisted Brasher and Chataway. Bannister still shook his head. He broke away from his friends and loped into one last gentle 150-yard warm-up. He returned to his musketeers at the line. 'Yes,' he said. The starting-pistol cracked . . .

Less than four minutes later he fell almost unconscious into the arms of another friend, the Rev Nicholas Stacey. The athletes fell into one huddle holding Bannister upright for fear of his collapse. The timekeepers fretted over their watches.

After agonized gulping, the medical student opened his eyes: 'Did I do it?'

'I think so,' said Stampfl.

Then, with no more emotion than a porter announcing the next train to Crewe, the PA announcer, young Norris McWhirter, intoned: 'Ladies and Gentlemen, here is the result of Event Nine. Winner, in the time of three minutes fifty-nine point . . .'

Mile of the Century
ROGER BANNISTER

You can sweat out beer, you can sweat out whiskey, but you can't sweat out women. *Sam Langford, boxing champion, 1911*

Why should a woman wear shorts and look like a second-rate man when she can wear a dress and look like a first-rate woman? *Teddy Tinling, tennis costume designer, 1959*

There are two things no man will admit he can't do well, apparently: drive and make love. *Stirling Moss, British racing driver, 1963*

Motor Racing

Driver of the Century

Arms, elbows and thrills

I don't mind the trips to exotic places, but I have no particular affection for the fumes and vrooms of the motor racing itself. The excruciating noise, for one thing ... and once two or three laps have screeched diabolically past, the uninitiated have no remote idea of who's first and who's last. Who wants to stand for three hours on a motorway bridge making notes about braking-power and camshaft-ratios? And it's not real sport if the human is only as hooraying as his horsepower ...

But some of the nicest nuts love it – and with relishing obsessiveness – and if I don't know anything about motor racing, I know a man who does, and probably knows more than any man down the century. Fount of all this noisy wisdom is the great Murray Walker, who had a father who was a champion motor-cycle racer and Murray was scarcely out of nappies in 1928 when he had an oil-can put in his hand and Dad took him off round the tracks of the world. As the century wound to its end, we were at the Mexican Grand Prix and I sat Murray down and said, 'Okay, wisest guy of all, you've seen the lot, who's the greatest driver of them all?' Without a blink, no christian names needed, Murray answered:

'Nuvolari, no question about it, the all-time great of the century for me is "Il Mantovano Volante", the "Flying Mantuan". Second place on the grid has to be the near-incomparable Fangio.'

Then, for once and you've got to believe it, Murray pauses and seems genuinely lost for words ... You prompt him: 'What, Nuvolari and Fangio better than the two who bumper-to-bumpered it towards the end of the century, Schumacher and the late Senna?'

'Oh, sure, they will get into the Top Ten, but I was trying to put them in "order of finishing" and I'm already stymied nominating third place. Okay, I'll only sort of funk it and third on the podium just has to be a dead-heat between the two Germans, Rosemeyer (killed, Frankfurt 1938) and Caracciola (died 1959). Then comes Moss (alive and well and livening up London), Clark (killed, Hockenheim 1968) and Stewart (still geeing up the world).

'Nuvolari was the best who has ever lived. His manager was a family friend. I remember like yesterday him winning at Donnington in 1938 in an Auto-Union. A daredevil? Crikey, yes! And what a contrast to his supreme rival, another Italian, Varzi, who was ice-cold, aloof, expensively dressed and a brooding womanizer. Nuvolari was a right scruffy 'Erbert, an engaging, archetypal arm-waving, laughing, hysterical Latin. Where Varzi was neat, precise and cold, Nuvolari was all arms and elbows and thrills, four-wheeled drifts round corners and smiles as he realized he'd arrived fifty miles an hour quicker than he should have, all opposite-lock and brakes and dust. Nuvolari was the guy you queued up all night for, and he was unquestionably the greatest of them all.'

Varzi had settled in Argentina, where he helped encourage the young Fangio: 'Suddenly around 1948 this guy Fangio arrives in Europe. He's already in his late thirties but proceeds to blow everyone off the track. The furious Europeans just could not keep up with him.

'In such a list, you cannot ignore Prost, such a gritty little devil, a truly great thinking driver; so incredibly smooth, neat and unobtrusive, he never actually looked as if he was going fast – then "Crikey, he's gone past you and you never even saw him go" type of driver. His team-mate Rosberg rocketed round a corner rather like Nuvolari – full pelt, four-wheeled skid and all that – but afterwards you realized he was half a second slower through the corner than Prost.'

**Driver of the Century
TAZIO NUVOLARI**

Snooker

Potman of the Century

Lightening the darkness

They called him the Emperor of Pot and the Sultan of Sink. Joe Davis was undoubtedly the snooker player of the century for keeping alive the flickering flame of an old pastime when it seemed on the point of oblivion through the middle years. But the man who revived and enervated the game single-handedly was a mighty different kettle of cueman and cove.

Clinking whizz of the century was Ronnie O'Sullivan, who organized the fastest 147 cleanout break of all in an astonishing five minutes twenty seconds – thirty-six balls in 320 seconds – at the 1997 world championships in Sheffield. Match of the Century had been at those same championships a dozen years earlier, in 1985, when Dennis Taylor, a tubby little outsider with no hope but a perky mien and full-moon, nil-nil spectacles, kept the nation up half the night when, from 0–7 down, he sank the black, last ball of the last shot of the last gasp, and beat the next great Sultan called Davis, this one Steve and no relation. It was like Sgt Bilko beating Muhammad Ali over the full fifteen.

Such shared collective and grand 'national' dramas were made possible by one man. (Well, two if you count the inventor of colour television.) By 1972, nearly every household had a colour set. Snooker's green baize, white chalk and fancy wes'kits, the pinks and blues and yellows and greens and starbursts of red, were made for colour television. When a nervously pale, slight young fidget hustled in from Ulster in 1972, he so took a game and its threadbare old championship by technicolor storm that it just had to be covered live by television the following year. In so doing, this gloriously instinctive Parvenu of Pot resurrected, single-handedly, an ancient sport.

The game might have been 'invented' by British soldiers of the Devonshire Regiment in their mess at Jubbulpore more than 120 years ago, and the rules finessed by the officers of the Central India Horse at Ootacamund in the 1880s, but no doubt about it, the game was dramatically topsy-turvied when Alex Higgins, an unknown qualifier, lit up the world championship in the enforcedly dingy dancehall of the Selly Oak British Legion, just off the Bristol Road in Birmingham.

No television cameras covered that 1972 final. If a TV station had wanted to, transmissions would have been cancelled anyway because the Tory Government, confronting the mining unions, was sitting out a series of power cuts in the period known as 'Ted Heath's three-day weeks'. The head-to-head final between the champion, John Spencer, and the cavalier upstart, who called himself 'The Hurricane', lasted from Monday to Saturday. When power cuts came, which was frequently, the British Legion switched to its emergency generator. During the Tuesday evening session, even that failed, and the match continued under lights generated by car batteries. But Higgins's sparkling, manic play – tossing away a winning frame with the same abandon that would win him the next from an impossible position – illuminated not only that dingy dancehall. He won the marathon by 37–22, and snooker was never the same again. Nor was Higgins.

In his definitive history of the game (*The Story of Billiards and Snooker*, Cassell, 1979), Clive Everton recalled snooker's seminal week: 'Under the dull and inadequate lighting, the hall bulged with a jam-packed crowd, hanging precariously from any vantage point. Snooker was suddenly not used to the idea of paying customers – let alone thousands beating the doors down to get in and watch.'

Higgins took a winner's cheque of £480, but the new champion augmented that by lavishly backing himself through the week at, successively, 14–1, 12–1, 4–1, 2–1' and 6–4. Everton wrote with prescience: 'Could snooker ever be the same?' Higgins potted from every conceivable angle and missed only two pots all week that he might reasonably have been expected to get. Within six days, Higgins had put an ancient but ignored sport not only on the back pages but on the front ones too. And in no time, BBC television were making plans to give over hour upon hour to snooker – and its coloured balls and, suddenly, very colourful personalities.

Potman of the Century
ALEX HIGGINS

The only time to feel superstitious is when someone hits you hard on the chin. *Jack Dempsey, world heavyweight champion*

I'm black. They never let me forget it. Sure I'm black. And I'll never let *them* forget it. *Jack Johnson, first black heavyweight champion*

It's a funny thing about athletics; it transcends all prejudice. If only the government of South Africa, for instance, would recognize this and let their kids compete against each other, what a tremendous thing it would be for the unity of that country. *Jesse Owens*

Champions don't retire because they're through, they retire because they're just tired of it. They get tired of putting on their shoes. I did too, when I got to feeling bad. I don't feel that way now. I'd just love to get my shoes on once again. *Babe Didrickson, US athlete, 1956*

General

Commentator of the Century

First man in space

On 15 January 1927, the England rugby XV beat Wales 11–9 at Twickenham. Three items set a humdrum match apart: the England captain Len Corbett dropped a goal from a mark, the last time that was to happen in an international; at fly-half England fielded, at eighteen years four months, their still youngest player, HCC Laird, a student at the Nautical College, Pangbourne; and for the first time a live outside-broadcast commentary of a sports event was relayed by the BBC.

Since when a stream of voices (and then, with television, faces) have become household familiars down the decades in every country in the world – offhand in Britain such resonant names as Howard Marshall, John Snagge, Maurice Edelston, Freddie Grisewood, Stewart MacPherson, Raymond Glendenning, Peter O'Sullevan, Kenneth Wolstenholme, David Coleman, Brian Moore, Dan Maskell, Desmond Lynam and heaps more ... indeed, so familiar at cricket commentary that half the nation knew simply their nicknames such as Arlo, The Boil, Johnners, CMJ, Blowers and The Alderman. To be sure, that broadcast from Twickenham in the New Year of 1927 was the start of something so big it would alter the culture and economics of all sport. Star of that first show (neither seen nor heard) was an unnamed blind man.

Only on 1 January that year had the private British Broadcasting Company become a corporation when the Government took control. The head of programming was Lance Sieveking, whom John Arlott was to describe as 'probably the most outstanding and creative

229

pioneer of broadcasting'. Sieveking wasted no time.

On Friday 7 January he received from Commander Coopper, the RFU secretary, permission by letter to 'attempt the experiment'. On Monday 10 January, just five days before the match, Sieveking telephoned Captain HBT Wakelam out of the blue at his London engineering and contracts business. In his guest, Teddy Wakelam had been a decent sportsman at Marlborough and had narrowly missed a blue at Cambridge for both cricket and rugby, and then played five seasons for Harlequins after the First World War. Now he was a sometime steward and alikadoo around Twickenham. One must presume that Sieveking had been recommended to Wakelam by Coopper. In an essay in a sporting anthology, *The Game Goes On*, published in 1954, Wakelam remembered: 'I had no thought beyond the dull life of engineering and that Monday afternoon I was sitting at my business table working out some details of a tender when my telephone rang. An unknown voice at the other end asked me if I was the same Wakelam who had played rugger for the Harlequins, and upon my saying "Yes", went on to inform me that the owner of it was a BBC official and he would like to see me at once on a very urgent matter.'

By Wednesday, Sieveking had met Wakelam to conduct a 'field-trial' at the rugby ground at Guy's Hospital, but the engineer and microphone never appeared – they had been directed inadvertently to Greenwich Park and another midweek match. However, next afternoon – two days before the international – a dry run was managed at an inter-schools match at Richmond's Old Deer Park.

Thus to Twickenham on Saturday morning, and a climb to a 'rickety-looking hut mounted on a scaffold platform at the end of the then single-decker West Stand'. Sieveking nailed up a large piece of card on which he had written 'DO NOT SWEAR'. He also introduced Wakelam to his two new colleagues – 'my number two broadcaster, the cool and collected Charles Lapworth, whose job was to fill in my pauses with occasional "Doctor Watson-like" questions such as "Do they always play with an oval ball?", and also a blind rugger enthusiast from St Dunstan's Home who would be just outside the window of my box in order that I might imagine that I was explaining the action of the game directly to him and so perhaps lose some of my natural stage-fright.'

The teams kicked off. By all accounts, the pioneer Wakelam was terrific. A dozen years later he was to write an autobiography, *Half-Time*: 'Straight away I forgot all my nervousness and stage-fright, all the previously and arduously collected phrases of the past three days, and all the snappy and pithy expressions which I had so anxiously culled from the leading sportswriters of the day. I was so wrapped up in following the flight and fortunes of the ball down there and so desperately keen to keep my St Dunstan's man fully informed that I raced away like a maniac . . . It was, on the whole, a most curious experience, for at the end I had not the slightest recollection of what I had said or done, and I have never been able to remember one single incident of that game . . . but I shall carry the general memories of it to my dying day.'

At cricket, when the summer of 1927 arrived, Sieveking was far less certain about continuing his 'experiment'. For such a slow game, he knew he needed someone who was a master of waffle. He went to the Church of England. The Reverend Frank H Gillingham was a tall, lugubrious Anglican curate from Leyton who scored more than 9,000 runs in 307 innings for Essex between 1903 and 1928. In 1939, by then a canon, he was appointed chaplain to King George VI. However, on his death, aged 67, his claim to imperishable fame was that on 14 May 1927 he had delivered the first live broadcast in Britain of a cricket match for the fledgling BBC: Essex against the New Zealand tourists at Leyton.

His Essex confrère TN Pearce remembered Gillingham as 'a very nice chap, a terrific preacher who had his congregations absolutely with him'. The game's venerable, EW Swanton, himself a pioneer broadcaster in the thirties, recalled Gillingham as 'an avenging prophet of a preacher, a lantern-jawed fellow with, in repose, a face of unrelieved gloom'. Of course, no transcript of the famous first broadcast exists; the stentorian descriptions from the pavilion-balcony pulpit just rang across the new 'wire-less' airwaves of Britain and up into the murky East London ether, never to be heard again. Gillingham did not last much longer – his next broadcast was from The Oval where he incurred the Episcopalian Scottish wrath of the BBC's first general-manager, John Reith, when, during a particularly dull passage of play, the parson enlivened his observations by reading out the names of advertisers, plus catchy slogans, displaying their wares on billboards around the ground. Such heinous sacrilege had Gillingham fired forthwith.

Sieveking's serious doubts about cricket seemed to have been underlined. After Gillingham's first broadcast at Leyton the press notices were, as they say, mixed. The bold critic of the *Edinburgh Evening News* penned a rave, hailing the broadcasts as 'particularly successful in three short transmissions' with the commentator 'excellent', while in Bristol the *Western Daily Press* pronounced the experiment 'deadly dull'. It added, with an unapologetic swipe of local-hero nostalgia, that the broadcast was nevertheless 'useful' in showing that a clergyman-cricketer was 'not the man to rattle off a bright racy description, and unless there is a GL Jessop batting, running – crawling is the most applicable term – commentary on cricket will be a waste of ether. Alas, there is no player in first-class cricket able to emulate the deeds of Mr Jessop.'

But hip-hip-hooray for it, Canon Gillingham might have gone on to become chaplain to the king – but that was small fry to what he had launched the moment he said, 'Good morning, everybody,' on 14 May 1927. He was the precursor of *Test Match Special*.

Meanwhile, Teddy Wakelam was covering his ball games with increasing aplomb and relish. That summer of 1927, he broadcast from Wimbledon and the London Test matches. In less than ten years, Wakelam was also the pioneer commentator for the BBC's fledgling television unit (for the London area only) at the 1938 Calcutta Cup match at Twickenham and the Ashes Test at Lord's in the same year. By which time, Captain Teddy, the former engineering contractor, was also nationally famous as sports columnist for the *Morning Post*. In his second war, Wakelam was disabled and thereafter enjoyed his sport as a listener and not as a commentator. On the premise that pioneers are the greatest – that Gagarin and Armstrong will be remembered as finest of all astronauts, just because they were the first – there can only be one name submitted in this category.

Commentator of the Century
TEDDY WAKELAM

All-rounder of the Century

Kevin, the greatest name

When Johnny Arnold died, aged 77, in a Southampton hospital in April 1984, it left just two men living of a select band who had been 'double internationals', playing for England, that is, at both football and cricket – Willie Watson (born 1920) and Arthur Milton (born 1928). Before those three, the century's roll of honour read RE Foster, CB Fry, LH Gay, HTW Hardinge, Alfred Lyttleton, William Gunn, Jack Sharp, Harry Makepeace and Andy Ducat. Between 1940 and 1945, the two Middlesex and England batsmen Patsy Hendren and Denis Compton turned out at soccer for England XIs in wartime internationals.

With a romantic's timing, old Johnny Arnold died in the very week of the April changeover, the penultimate week of winter when in those expectant springs of long ago he would bung his football boots into his London landlady's cupboard and hot-foot to Waterloo to catch the Southern Belle and hurry to pad up for the nets at Hampshire's County Ground. He played 200 games on the left-wing for Fulham (and half as many again for Southampton) and scored 21,000 runs for Hampshire. He was chosen once for England at cricket (a duck and 34 against New Zealand at Lord's in 1931) and once at soccer, against Scotland at Hampden two years later. Arnold started his double career just as Andy Ducat was endinq his. Ducat, whose friends called him 'Mac', scored 23,000 runs for Surrey, though he failed in his one Test, making only 3 and 2 against Australia in 1921. His six soccer caps bridged the First World War. He died at the wicket, bat in hand, in a match at Lord's in 1942 between the Surrey and Sussex Home Guard XIs. *Wisden* records: 'He began his innings before lunch and was 17 at the interval. On resuming he scored steadily, then he hit a ball from Eaton to mid-on; the ball was returned to the bowler, who was about to send down the next delivery when Ducat fell forward and apparently died immediately.' The match was abandoned. In its tabulated scorecard, *Wisden*, usually the fount of all truth, wrote, 'Private A Ducat . . . not out 29' instead of the possibly correct 'retired dead 29'. As Benny Green noted in his whopping anthology of the great *Almanack*: 'Ducat is one of the very few sporting figures in English history of whom it could be said that the next ball was literally his dying thought.'

When Ducat died, Willie Watson, though away at the war, was already on the books of Yorkshire CCC and Sunderland AFC. He won six soccer caps for England in the 1950s as one of that long-gone breed 'the cultured wing-half'. His main job for those stars in stripes at Roker was as straight-man and feed for the relentless, crackling genius of Len Shackleton. Watson played in twenty-three cricket Tests as a left-handed number five, and his most glorious hour – or rather, six hours – was in 1953 when he batted all day with Trevor Bailey at Lord's to thwart Lindwall and Miller and a seemingly certain Australian victory. Incidentally, Bailey himself was not half a bad footballer. The game also provided him with his now universal nickname, 'The Boil'. Doug Insole, another England cricketer, started it when the two Cambridge double-blues were on a soccer tour of Switzerland with, I think, Dulwich Hamlet. A Swiss spectator kept shouting, in pidgin English, 'C'mon, *Boiley*, get rid of it!' or cuckoo-clock words to that effect.

Denis Compton might not have played in a full peacetime international, but like Ducat (with Aston Villa in 1926) and Sharp (Everton in 1906) he won an FA Cup winner's medal, with Arsenal in 1950. (CB Fry, by the way, missed out, getting a loser's medal with Southampton in 1902, where reports said, 'The one weakness of his game was the usual amateur's fault of heading with hunched shoulders.') Two years later, Compton's place as a wingman for the Gunners had been taken by Arthur Milton, who in twenty-six summers was also to score over 32,000 runs for Gloucestershire, hold 759 catches and score a century in the first of his six Test matches. In 1952, after just a dozen first-team games for Arsenal, Milton was picked for England against the Austrians at Wembley. Forty years later, Arthur remembers: 'I didn't play very well. At Arsenal I had little Jimmy Logie lining up glorious passes for me to run on to. For England my inside-right was Ivor Broadis and he didn't have a good game. Billy Wright was my half-back and he was one-footed on his right so kept slinging out passes to the left to Bailey and Medley. Within half an hour I had vanished from the match, and was too inexperienced to get back.' He was never chosen again.

Till the last decade of the century, when the game reinvented itself as one for full-time professionals, the carefreeness of rugby union allowed many more 'double internationals'. Sammy Woods was one early bold colonial who arrived from New South Wales and in no time was playing cricket and rugby for England. There was RO Schwartz who did it 'the other way'. An old Pauline and Cambridge blue, he was England's fly-half for a season at the exact turn of the century, only to turn up in sport's genuine gold-leaf record book seven years later as one of South Africa's mesmerizing purveyors of googlies on their 1907 tour to England, in which he took 143 wickets at a ludicrous 11 apiece. ('RO' went right through the Great War, and, frequently 'mentioned' for gallantry at the front, he won the Military Cross; he died seven days after the Armistice – of influenza.)

AE Stoddart, tragic hero, played both games for England. Maurice Turnbull won one rugby cap for Wales and nine for England at cricket. A Rhodes Scholarship seemed to oil the sporting wheels as well. Clive van Ryneveld played his rugby for England and his cricket for South Africa – and so did 'Tuppy' Owen-Smith. 'As a batsman,' wrote Pelham Warner, 'while no one would dream of calling Owen-Smith "sound", he had an eye like a hawk, hit a half-volley an awful long way, and could cut and hook.' He was fullback for England for four seasons, ending as captain and 'chaired' from the field at Twickenham after England's championship of 1937. A one-cap wonder to join the club was the sublime left-handed batsman Martin Donnelly (one game at rugby for England – he was up at Oxford – in 1947). England's last was Mike Smith, their cricket captain countless times in the 1960s. He played once for England at rugby in 1956. It was a none-too-happy occasion, but he had become a member of a rare freemasonry, an immortal.

Keeper of this particularly bright flame – and we all know Ian Botham played soccer for Scunthorpe, Viv Richards for Antigua, and Bob Willis for the Corinthian Casuals – irresistibly has to be Dr Kevin O'Flanagan. The All Black rugby winger-wizard Jeff Wilson pushed him hard, but one can safely forecast that in a century in which one-trick professionals increasingly prevailed, no man will ever remotely beat the record of Doctor Kev. On three successive December Saturdays of 1947, O'Flanagan played First Division soccer on the left-wing for Arsenal at Highbury; for All-Ireland against Australia on the right-wing at a totally different game, rugby union; and on the left-wing at soccer for the Republic of Ireland against Spain. The January before, he had played against France at rugby one week and against Scotland at soccer the next, both in Dublin.

The doctor was a natural, and self-taught. His Dublin school, Synge Street, played neither soccer nor rugby, just the Gaelic games. While studying medicine at University College, O'Flanagan was twice Ireland's 100m sprint champion (at which for years his national record stood at 10.1 seconds) and, also on two occasions, won the long-jump title (on the first leaping 22ft 10½in). In his forties he was playing golf off scratch for Ireland's amateur golfing team. For years he was his country's representative on the International Olympic Committee.

Working for two years in a Grosvenor Square clinic in London immediately after the War, he played on Saturdays for Arsenal, who were League champions in his second season. As an amateur, all he claimed as expenses from Arsenal each week was eightpence – the return fare by Tube from Victoria to Highbury on the Piccadilly Line. His work meant he could not train with the Arsenal players during the week – the Arsenal manager Tom Whittaker said that, had he done so, 'he could have been the greatest forward in history'. Whittaker said O'Flanagan was the hardest kicker of a dead-ball he had seen. By all accounts, the Highbury supporters called him 'Cannonball Kev' and the newspapers the 'Flying Doc', which was shorter. He once scored five goals in a Cup tie against Plymouth Argyle. When he scored against Bolton Wanderers, the *Daily Sketch* the following

Monday described: 'Before he was ready to carry out his elaborately advertised intention of trying an "impossible" direct free-kick from thirty-five yards, Dr O'Flanagan carefully wiped the mud off the wet ball, and did everything except chalk his cue. It scraped the underside of the bar as it whipped through into the net.' The only other man to be capped in the century in a full international at both soccer and rugby was another Irishman, later a well-known vintner, by the name of Michael O'Flanagan. A coincidence in the name? He was Dr 'Cannonball' Kev's younger brother.

All-rounder of the Century
DR KEVIN O'FLANAGAN

Nobody ever beats Wales at rugby, they just score more points. *Graham Mourie, New Zealand captain*

Tennis is a game where you give other people a chance to lose to you. We all hate the dinker, but he understands the definition best; at every level right up to Harold Solomon the dinker will win because he has a higher intellectual principle, a higher frustration-tolerance threshold, and a longer concentration span. *Jack Kramer*

In Spain, when little, the other caddies sat playing boy's games and laughed when my brother Sevvy came in – how you say? like a drowning rat maybe five hours afterwards. They no laugh today. They still carry golf bags. *Manuel Ballesteros*

Début Cock-up of the Century

Another fine mess, Stanley

In first-class cricket, no end of famous batsmen (as well as, agreed, even more not so famous) down the century began their careers with a first-ball 'golden' duck, although the most celebrated début 'pair' – that is being dismissed for 0 in *both* innings of a match – is probably the Pakistan batsman 'Mez' Ghazali's in 1954 at Old Trafford when, his side following-on against England, he made his two ducks in a minute less than two hours of each other, the century's record. (England's David Gower, incidentally, is the century's batsman who went most consecutive Test innings *without* a duck: 119 between 1982 and 1991.)

This jury finds it difficult to come to a decision on début cock-ups-best-forgotten – just as in cricket, there are limitless first first-round exits by 0–6, 0–6, 0–6 at Wimbledon, an inept majority of them by hitherto-expectant hometown British players. Début Cock-Up of the Century has therefore, alas (because they said he was a lovely fellow and very keen on his job), to be that of a footballer, Stan Milton of Halifax Town, who had played for years in the second XI awaiting his chance. It finally came against Stockport County on 6 January 1934. The score was 13–0 and Stan picked all thirteen of them out of his net. No other Football League goalkeeper has let in more, before or since.

Début Cock-up of the Century
STAN MILTON

Turn-up of the Century

Tile by tile by Tyson

Cheers! A nice thought would be to award this one to Guinness. The mighty West Indian tourists of 1969 had the better of a five-day draw against England at Lord's and immediately packed for a fleeting overseas missionary trip to spread the gospel – to non-cricketing Ireland. On 2 July they made the boat trip across the Irish Sea and, as ever, the Irish welcoming committee was deliciously hospitable. The one-day match was on the pretty Derry ground at Sion Mills. In the absence of captain Gary Sobers, Basil Butcher led the world champions and he agreed to dispense with the toss and bat first – the big crowd wanted to be sure to see some exciting batting from the likes of the captain himself and the lissom Clive Lloyd, both of whom had thrilled Lord's two days before. The stout had been dark with a froth of cream, the pitch was green. West Indies were all out for 25. Butcher made 2, Lloyd 1, there were four ducks, and top score was 9 by tail-ender Grayson Shillingford. For Ireland, Goodwin took 5 for 6, O'Riordan 4 for 18. Ireland knocked off the runs at a breeze, to win by nine wickets. And back to the clubhouse for more drinks all round. (Not only the name of Ireland is a chastising wink in the stupendous cricket record of the West Indies – they were also beaten by unlikely Kenya in the 1996 World Cup.)

Turn-up of the century? Possibly. Mind you, there have been a lot of those about since the century's very first year when a then-amateur north London football side quaintly calling themselves Tottenham Hotspur won the FA Cup in 1900. Then again, almost at the exact halfway point of the twentieth century, 29 June 1950, the part-timers of United States soccer beat England, founding fathers of the game, by 1–0 at Belo Horizonte in the 1950 World Cup.

The only 100–1 Derby winner of the century was Aboyeur in 1913. The hottest favourite for the Grand National's annual 'lottery' was Golden Miller, at a ludicrous 2–1, in 1935. He unseated his rider at the first. Tip-up of the century? The hottest favourite of the two-horse race Wimbledon men's final, at 6–1 on, was Jimmy Connors in 1975; Arthur Ashe beat him in that epic encounter. Turn-up? You bet.

In that same year that Ireland beat the West Indies at cricket, 1969, history's first 'expansion' (that is, newly founded) rookie baseball team, the New York Mets, won the World Series; you would have got 150–1 on them doing so at the beginning of the season. At basketball, the US Olympic team had sixty-three successive victories at the Games all down the century. They were 12–1 on for the final at Munich in 1972; the USSR beat them.

At lunchtime on the penultimate day of the third Ashes Test match at Headingley, the two Australian cricketers and natural gambling men Dennis Lillee and Rodney Marsh noticed on the scoreboard the odds posted at 500–1 against England winning, so perilously hopeless was the home side's position. Few Aussies resist 500–1, so England's two opponents 'had a bit of it'. They won their bet – England's victory next day through Ian Botham's revivalist batting and Bob Willis's blazing bowling proved as irresistible as the bet itself. The bet of the century? (On that November morning in 1953, you'd have happened on the very same odds for predicting Hungary's upcoming 6–3 score against England's soccer XI at Wembley.)

Bookmakers on any number of occasions have 'closed the book' and refused any more bets on a certain event so, well, certain was the outcome. The two most notable 'closed book' turn-ups were surely in the America's Cup yachting race in 1985 when the *Australia II* boat took the trophy from the New York Yacht Club for the first time in 132 years, and eleven years later when Australian Greg Norman teed off for his final round at the US Masters golf tournament all of six shots ahead. *Australia II* won in style, of course, and Greg Norman blew up to let Britain's Nick Faldo get measured for the famous green jacket.

In 1964, don't forget, the then Cassius Clay's defeat of the 'invincible' Sonny Liston was considered boxing's biggest upset of the century (Liston 14–1 on), and even outdid Jim Braddock's 12-1 chance of beating Max Baer in 1935. Before Braddock at once lost the title to all-time great Joe Louis, he had organized himself a tiny slice of Louis's future purses, so the Irishman continued a long life as a happy, rich man. Louis had begun his grand reign by shamelessly fighting a string of no-hopers, called his 'bum-of-the-month' club, and had any one of those unknowns beaten him we would have wrapped up this conversation here and now. The Welshman Tommy Farr and Irish-American Billy Conn came nearest genuinely to defeating Louis in his pomp, and they were fine boxers and by no means bums – but had they won, they would have been famous upsets, sure.

So must it all boil down to Buster? In 1990 the affable journeyman Buster Douglas was the rampagingly cruel champion Mike Tyson's presumed bum-of-the-year. Johnson, Dempsey, Marciano, Liston, Foreman ... of the century's scary and feared hitters-to-hurt, Tyson was terror of terrors. By Jove (the god of war), when Tyson punched, you stayed punched. Most of his opponents, you felt, *arrived* for the contest in an ambulance. They fought in Tokyo and Douglas didn't have a prayer had he even been the Pope. Back in Las Vegas, the odds opened at an unheard of 35–1 against Douglas winning, and on fight day, 11 February, dropped even further at 42–1. In his spare time, Douglas worked as a sports coach at the Department of Youth Services in his hometown of Columbus, Ohio. He said he knew how to deal with bullies. Only one boxing reporter in the whole world tipped Douglas to win – a Tim May of, you've guessed it, the *Columbus Dispatch*. May was the decisive verb. The almost portly Douglas had hands like telephone directories. In the first five rounds he hit Tyson with A–K, in the next five L–Z. In the tenth, the unfallable fell, and the seismic reverberations were heard all round the world.

That would unquestionably have been *it* – the turn-up of the century. But exactly two years to the month later, Tyson was convicted of the rape of a teenage beauty-queen contestant in Indianapolis. At his trial, for some defence reason or other, submission admitted a splurge of drink, pills, girls and more girls, and generally indisciplined living which took in no sports training whatsoever, during a particular period which precisely took in the Douglas fight. In other words, the world heavyweight champion's most dangerous opponent had become . . . himself. If you beat *yourself*, it can hardly be the sporting upset of the century, can it? Sorry, Buster.

Tyson, however, is still involved in this end-game. The great fighter served, to the day, three years in the Indiana State Penitentiary and emerged, he said, a reformed man and sportsman. He trained hard and impressively and in no time had dispatched four scared pacifists (including Britain's Frank Bruno) before a veteran thirty-four-year-old former champion, Evander Holyfield (diagnosed by some doctors to have had a 'dicky' heart, would you believe), came up to the scratch for a final benefit payday, and a presumed fifth walkover for Tyson, at Las Vegas on 9 November 1996. Tyson looked brutally awesome in training, flea-fit and dagger-sharp and nasty. Holyfield went about praising God's goodness, and no wonder. You genuinely feared for him, his health and, truth known, his very life.

Again, only one single boxing writer, Ron Borges, came up with the remotest of chances for Holyfield, this time from the *Boston Globe*. So this was around 5,000–1. Fight day, I booked an earlier flight back to Gatwick, knowing the one- or at most two-rounder would give me ample time to tidy up all the post-fight hospital reports and file my copy. No problems, for hadn't even America's finest boxing writer, Pat Putnam, that very morning assured me and the world, 'You can put your house on it: it will be a very short night. Just two, or perhaps three, Tyson uppercuts should do it.'

I had to scramble on a far later plane. And when I went for it, there was an eerie buzz of astonished disbelief still swirling around the Nevada valleys and all through the stunned crowds on the Strip's vast gaming floors. Here was a jackpot with knobs on, an epic for the annals, the all-time turn-up. Holyfield not only beat the ogre Tyson, he beat him up, mercilessly, for round after round after round. Till the referee had mercy after a gruesome half-hour.

This was no flukey one-punch aberration. Tyson was dismantled piece by piece, brick by brick and tile by tile. The three judges, two Americans and a Venezuelan, all had Holyfield miles in front (96–92, 96–92, 100–93) when the end came in the eleventh round. One judge, indeed, gave him every round. No future opponent would ever be intimidated by Tyson. End of an aura. Holyfield dedicated his victory to God, and in sporting terms it was a victory blessed by all the gods. From the first bell Holyfield gave far more than he got. The bully was out-bullied, and then he was hit some more.

Tyson was still on his feet at the end, but it was obvious his feet did not know where they were. Even to the throng in the distant bleachers it was plain to see that a semi-conscious fighter was receiving the sort of comeuppance he had inflicted on others so often in the past.

Same ring, seven months later, and the measure of that greivous beating-up was plain to see when, in the return fight and being measured up for another clinical bashing by Holyfield, the bully-boy grotesquely resorted to biting ears and was disqualified in the third.

Turn-up of the Century
EVANDER HOLYFIELD v MIKE TYSON, November 1996

> Life was a damned muddle … a football game with everyone offside and the referee gotten rid of – everyone claiming the referee would have been on his side. *F Scott Fitzgerald, 1920*

> The fascination of shooting as a sport depends almost wholly on whether you are at the right or wrong end of the gun. *PG Wodehouse, 1925*

> To think of football as merely 22 hirelings kicking a ball is merely to say that a violin is wood and cat gut. *Hamlet* is so much ink and paper. It is Conflict and Art. *JB Priestley*

Outsider of the Century

Running with wings on

She ran it as an afterthought. An Olympic final almost for the fun of it – as you could in those days. Tokyo, 20 October 1964, the 800 metres Olympic final for women. Ann Packer had run only five two-lap races in her life, which included the Tokyo heats. Her fiancé, Robbie Brightwell, was the England team captain. They had both been favourites for their individual 400m races – in Fleet Street's terms, anyway. But they had been disappointed, Robbie coming fourth and Anne being beaten into second place by the gritty, hard-nut Australian flier Betty Cuthbert. Packer had only been given the chance for an 800m run because no-one else in Britain had managed the qualifying time.

'Yes, I suppose the disappointment that Robbie and I had in our first races made me determined to ensure we had something a bit more glittery than silver for our mantelpiece,' she remembers. 'I was sharing a room with the hurdler Pat Pryce and the two Marys, Rand and Peters. The first thing I did when we arrived was to bang up a nail on the wall for our gold medals. And lo and behold, of course, Mary R went out and won the long jump with a world record on the first day. Well, you can imagine what an inspiration that was. Here we were, four ordinary girls who had found ourselves tossed into this incredible conglomeration of talent from around the world, and at the first time of asking one of us had come back with a gold medal and world record.

'Only getting a silver in the 400 ludicrously did seem a blow at the time, even though I'd run faster than I'd ever run before, which should have been a real consolation. The room-mates, and Robbie, and Dennis (Watts), my darling coach, all bucked me up that I had a real chance in the 800. Qualifying for the two finals meant six races in six days. But somehow I knew I was strong enough.

'When I was leaving the village for the 800 final, I was in the lift with that wonderful Indian runner Milka Singh, you know, with his little top-knot pakta on his head. He insisted in his rich Indian accent, "Ann, you vill vin." Also in the lift was that eccentric old Aussie coach Percy Cerruty, and he agreed: "There's no one else in it, girl." If they were being serious, I was none the wiser, really – for never having remotely followed the event before, I didn't really have a clue who I was up against. All I knew was that as a 400–er, I'd have some basic speed left unless they dragged it all out of me in the first lap.

'And that first lap was just right, just fast enough for me. They called out the time at the bell, or did it come up on the stadium board, I can't remember. I read somewhere once that they saw me glance up at the board and obviously decide to get a move on. But by then it had all seemed to go to pot as everyone else coiled up for the final push for home. I was way adrift, terribly placed, last I suppose. I was just about in touch, and remember thinking, "Do a bit more for the last bend and then give it all you've got down the straight."

'I had to take the long way round on the outside, didn't I? Then, all of a sudden – oh, I just can't really describe or even remember the feeling when, off the bend, I suddenly realized that everyone else seemed to be running backwards. It was such an incredible feeling of utter power. I'd never felt the same before or since – not a trace of churning lactic acid or any tiredness at all or any semblance of the headaches that would have hit me in similar stages of an all-out 400. In fact, no pain at all, like running on air, running with wings on.

'There is a photograph showing the utter serenity of my smile as I crossed the line. Well, I had plenty to smile about, hadn't I? I was just enjoying and savouring the sublime moment, that's all.'

Outsider of the Century
ANN PACKER

Picture of the Century

Evidence in camera

The evening shadows were lengthening on the Gabba cricket ground at Brisbane just before Christmas of 1960. An exciting cricket match was coming to an end: Australia versus West Indies. Exciting? One of the most thrilling of all history. High up on a gantry behind the bowler's arm, hunched over their ancient bazooka-like 'Long Tom' plate-cameras were two deadly professional rivals – Ron Lovitt, of the Melbourne *Age*, and Harry Matlin, of the *Sydney Morning Herald*. The excitement of the closing overs of the Test match meant that they had used up all but one of their glass plates. Thus, with one ball left to be bowled by the Caribbean demon Wes Hall, Australia needed one to win, with one wicket standing – and, more to the point, the two opposing snappers up on the faraway rim of the stand had this precious one plate each left for the final delivery.

Big Wes fingered the gold crucifix which always dangled from his neck, and turned nervously at the end of his run-up. His captain Frank Worrell had already spent minutes saying, whatever, don't bowl a no-ball which would at once forfeit the victory. The last Aussie batsman, Kline, settled uneasily into his stance at the distant crease. Up at their station, the two photographers looked at each other with helpless shrugs. At last, in the long history of Oz newspapers' dog-eat-dog hatreds, the *Age* agreed with the *Herald* and decided a compromise. One plate each, and four results possible.

These two had been weaned on the bitter rivalry from the first day of their respective apprenticeships in the darkroom. Now they came to their agreement and tossed up: 'Tails!' Martin would photograph the actual stroke, no matter what happened. He would thus take the winning run, or Kline being bowled or leg-before or caught at the wicket or in the slips. Lovitt would take the action following the stroke – catch, run out or victory salute.

Hall bowled. Kline pushed to square-leg and ran like a rabbit. Martin clicked his shutter – 1/50th at *f*11. Lovitt, heart-attack tense, still waited. Joe Solomon swooped in and threw the wicket down, as the umpire's finger goes up, and – SNAP! – Lovitt of the *Age* takes the most famous cricket picture of all time. It went round the world and for the first time a sports photographer became a household name.

Picture of the Century
RON LOVITT

> Right or wrong is all the same
> When baby needs new shoes.
> It isn't how you play the game,
> It's whether you win or lose.
> *John Lardner, US writer*

> He can run, but he can't hide. *Joe Louis, world heavy-weight champion, 1941, on his fight with Billy Conn*

> The climate of victory in tennis is created long before a match starts, and clothes play a big part. Players dressed by me have an advantage over opponents. *Teddy Tinling, tennis costume designer, 1962*

Southpaw of the Century

Each a hero of the left

At one and the same time, a decade and a half or so before the century ended, the world's two best tennis players were Martina Navratilova and John McEnroe. They were both left-handers. So was the third best, Jimmy Connors. Simultaneously, the captains and best batsmen of the world's three leading international cricket teams were southpaws – West Indian Clive Lloyd, Australia's Allan Border and England's David Gower.

Some say Rodney Laver was the most complete tennis player of the century. He was left-handed. And who was the best ever cricketing all-rounder? Was he the leftie who came from Cleckheaton? Or the leftie who came from Barbados? Wilfred Rhodes and Sir Garfield Sobers are mighty near the top of this poll already. Is the sumptuous young batsman who, not long before century's end, made the highest first-class cricket score and the highest Test match score, respectively 501 and 375, already an all-time great or merely yet 'a prospective genius?' What is for sure is that the wondrous Brian Lara is left-handed.

I don't know about Michelangelo's cover drive, but he painted left-handed. So did Leonardo and Holbein. How good at squash was Jack the Ripper? Or Paul McCartney? No idea – but I do know Jonah Barrington's left arm won him six world squash championships. Mark Spitz, of swimming's six gold medals, was a leftie, although I can't think it helped his crawl. The Hall of Fame's most shiny baseball diamonds, Babe Ruth and Reggie Jackson, both swung the truncheon from left to right, although the Babe *wrote* with his right. Only one cack-handed golfer has ever won the Open, the taciturn Kiwi Bob Charles.

All forms of footballer, of course, should be, as they say, 'two-footed'. But at rugby, Welshman John Taylor made his mark on the century with his immortal last-second left-footer at Murrayfield in 1971 – 'the greatest conversion since St Paul' – because he only chose to take it from the right touchline *because* he was a leftie. The all-time soccer star who broke all the tenets and seemed to use *only* his left foot in whatever circumstance was the maestro Ferenc Puskas, and only his can be named as Left Foot of the Century. It helps, too, in boxing to be 'two-fisted', though if I ran a poll among the snorting fraternity, I daresay they would make the left-hook the killingest kayo of all. You don't see it coming. 'Enery's 'ammer was the upward sinistral. As Hemingway once said: 'I suppose Life itself is the most savage left-hooker of all – but after that comes Charley White of Chicago.'

Ice hockey coaches are said to prefer left-handed players. As the Boston Bruin Wayne Cashman, a leftie and accomplished silver-blade brawler, once put it: 'The key to a hockey match is the first punch. Most players carry their stick in their right. When you're left-handed and they're looking for the right, it helps a lot.' Fishing champions are usually southpaws. Right-handers along a bank always cast the same way. A leftie can cast into places other baits cannot reach. The Irish hammer-thrower who could not get his ball and chain out of the cage at the 1984 Los Angeles Olympics was, I seem to remember, the only left-hand whirler in the competition, which must give him some sort of excuse.

But helps not with our shortlist. It has to whittle down to the cricketers Rhodes and Sobers, shining vice-presidents of the immortals both, and Lara; and the tennis aces Laver, McEnroe, and multi-Wimbledon winner Navratilova.

Take your own pick . . . while having no complaints about

Southpaw of the Century
SIR GARFIELD SOBERS

Southpawess of the Century
MARTINA NAVRATILOVA

The Race of the Century

Eyes down for *Le Tour*

Only twice, and briefly, have I dipped into *Le Tour*. 'Dipped' is the word: both times I hurried back to Dover as sponsored as a newt.

Britons think we've got problems with corporate hospitality? Silly us. Mind you, in France through July you need the relieving strong liquids to quieten the gorgeous din as commerce, sport and nationhood collide in a screeching, head-on, three-week, full-pelt major road accident.

En velo! On yer bikes! Ringa dat bell! – except not a solitary soul can hear it above the adrenalin-charged honking, tonking, tyre-tearing tunes of 7,000 accredited advertising vans and trucks and scooters and faded-green 2CVs, full to the gunwales of *flics*, film men, freeloaders, physicians and physios and phonies. Not to mention pharmacists, agents and a jangle of journos from *L'Equipe*, all waving their arms in an effort to attract attention like Jacques Tati's postman when he was attacked by that swarm of bees. Not forgetting the bod with the puncture kit.

C'est le Tour. This year and every year. *Jamais* they close.

In the midst of this jangling jamboree, the pack, the gladiators, the chasers and the chased – vests and pants and gloves and hats, a kalei-doscope of tiny advertising billboards: eyes down and sunk in sallow, straining, waxwork faces; shins and ankles a rotating egg-whisk blur; reds and greens and purples and mauves and blacks and whites . . .

But only one yellow jersey. Did you know, by the way, why the overall leader each day is robed in *le maillot jaune*? Nothing to do with Jason and the Golden Fleece or any classical Olympian baloney like that. The tradition arose simply as a publicity stunt by the French sports paper *L'Auto* in 1903 – for as London's *FT* is pink and old Green 'Uns of a Saturday teatime were green, so the literal colour of *L'Auto*'s pages in those days was yellow. It has ever been fast bikes and fast bucks.

The editor then of *L'Auto* (now evolved into the present sports paper *L'Equipe*) was Henri Desgrange, the WG of the sport, and without a doubt cycling's first nutter (and there are a lot of them about on this side of the Channel too). In the 1890s, Desgrange, a failed Parisian law student, published a series of homilies as testament to his passion. At the turn of the century it was brought out as a single volume, *Tête Et Jambes*, urging the French as a nation first to discover and then retain the soul and romance of the sport for all time. It became the biker's bible, the besotted Desgrange covering everything from saddle-sores to sex:

'To excel, the rider must eat, live and breathe his bicycle; his emotional commitment must overwhelm him; once that moment is acknowledged, the rider is saved and he will have no more need of a woman than of his first pair of socks. The rider's self-denial is all . . . but, oh, in the winter, with the tracks closed and the sun departed, then go to the ball with one, two, three, four women, as many as you want, to make up for lost time in any way you can.'

In 1911, Desgrange (who lived till 1940, aptly and for obvious reasons the first time *Le Tour* was not run since its beginning) published his *Acte d'Adoration* to his 'divine' bicycle and his nation's debt 'for the precious and ineffable love it has given us, and the host of memories sown over our whole life. I love it for its having given me a soul capable of appreciating it; I love it for having taken my heart within its spokes, for having encircled part of my life within its harmonious frame.'

It remains any sports freak's credo.

Le Tour will be ninety-seven when the bells ring out the old century. *Vraiment* it is

The Race of the Century
LE TOUR DE FRANCE

Film Clip of the Century

'Slight, balding Bobby.'

In Jacques Tati's glistening gem, *Monsieur Hulot's Holiday*, the tennis sequence is one of the all-time classics for sport on the silver screen. Aiming to impress his girl, Hulot goes into a tiny shop with no room to swing a cat let alone a catgut racket, and the crone behind the counter illustrates in the restricted space an arthriticly jabbing service action – which Hulot takes onto court and proceeds to serve ace after ace. Superb. Tati also displays his genius with a minute or two on cycle racing and ping-pong.

In the 1980s, Hollywood had a crack at a tennis film, called *Players*. It was a ritzy, multi-million job, but was pretty dire. They shot most of it at Wimbledon. One day the casting director came up to the press bar where Fleet Street's heavy mob hang out. Looking for authenticity, he chose a mate of mine, John Jackson, then at the *Daily Mirror*, to ask a question in full wide-screen Technicolor close-up. He did it brilliantly, forgot to ask for any fee, but next day when the beautiful Ali McGraw passed him she whispered huskily, 'Hiya, star!' and one-take Jacko blushed for the only time in his life.

Tennis is an international sport, but I often wonder what the Americans think of cricketing references in British films, when we used to make them. I daresay they re-ran *The Lady Vanishes* for the umpteenth time over Christmas, and Charters still didn't manage to tell Caldicott precisely what field Grimmett had set for Hammond at Old Trafford before dotty old Miss Froy borrowed back the sugar-lumps again. Or what about this in *The Four Feathers* during a dusty blood-curdling skirmish in the Sudan?

> General Burrows: Remember Wilmington? Father killed at Inkerman, grandfather blown up with Nelson, uncle scalped by Indians. Splendid record, what?
> *General Faversham*: What happened to the fellow?
> *General Burrows*: Blighter ordered to gallop through front line to deliver message. Fellow paralysed with funk, dammit. Sent his adjutant. Killed before he'd got thirty yards. Sent his ADC. Head blown off at once. Finally went himself. Lost an arm. Alas, quite ruined his cricket . . .

Harold Pinter's devotion to the great game had him including cricketing sequences in his screenplays for *Accident* and *The Go-Between*. the only trouble was that the actors, Michael York in the first, and Alan Bates in the second, didn't seem very good at batting or catching. Still, it is even worse when real sportsmen try to be actors. The only film devoted entirely to cricket, I suppose, was Anthony Asquith's disastrous, *The Final Test* in which a veteran England batsman, played by Jack Warner, goes out for his last innings at The Oval. A real-life Len Hutton was hired to pat Warner on the back and say, a 'You've done it before – let's do it again.' Hutton, a shy man, was nervous and couldn't get it right.

There was a nice story told by the late John Arlott, which has Asquith 'wrapping' the studio after Hutton had botched take after take on the Friday and telling him to spend the weekend rehearsing the line over and over again. Hutton did so, to the extent of repeating it in his sleep – and on the Saturday morning he was awakened by a nudge in the ribs and his wife exclaiming, 'That's all very well, Len, but you have to co-operate!'

Which makes the decision not to name a whole film itself in this category – leave that to the Academy and give the shared palm to the Oscar-winning *Chariots of Fire* and *Raging Bull*. So, like the one-liner Len Hutton had trouble with, go for the one sporting scene, the glistening little cameo en passant.

The film on Aussie Rules rugby, *The Club*, had a lighter touch than Lindsay Anderson's gritty classic on the same game, *This Sporting Life*. But neither had one particular scene you could tweezer out and present as the all-time memory. You could with the end of the cross-country race in Tony Richardson's *Loneliness of the Long Distance Runner* when Tom Courtney gloriously V-signs the headmaster by not winning for the school when he could have. Same actor in John Schlesinger's *Billy Liar* and I whooped with recognition at the 20-second silhouette longshot of teenager Billy charging down the curve of a slag-heap and, just for the hell of it, essaying at full lick FS Trueman's bowling action.

Surprisingly, horsey films have flopped, from *National Velvet* remakes through drearily middling *Dead Cert*, to the yawnworthy *Champions*. I suppose *The Charge of the Light Brigade* and *Tom Jones* tally-hoing were best for four-footers' flared-nostril sequences. Best horse-sport sequence of all remains the Marx Brothers' beaut when Groucho goes nuts in a horsedrawn chariot all over a US football pitch.

Off the top of my head, I'd say the best two 'games' films were *The Hustler* with Paul Newman, about the thrusting young pool player, and *The Cincinatti Kid*, with Steve McQueen as the likewise card sharp, though, on second thoughts, they were about gambling, not games playing. Those two also indulged in their hobby of car racing with, respectively, *Grand Prix* and *Le Mans*, but they were drearily more about machines than even macho men. Newman did make the literally smashing *Slap Shot*, about ice hockey, which I could readily see again, but not enjoyably hear: the 'script' consisted of 80 per cent 'fucks'.

Soccer? Forget it. Every one of the few has been a dud. Only a few because there is no sale, nor understanding of, for soccer films to a US audience. I suppose the same goes for Hollywood films on the three most popular American sports – a shame in fact because, for instance the baseball pix, *Bull Durham*, *Field of Dreams* and, certainly, Tommy Lee Jones's bio of Ty Cobb were each in their way terrific.

Prizefighting and the flickering silvery screen sheet have been soulmates since 1914 when boxer-actor Jimmy Clabby starred in Hollywood's *The Kidnapped Pugilist*. Jack Palance was a great champion. So was Kirk Douglas. Your man Newman looked a bit of a choirboy for the real Rocky Graziano, but young Marlon really looked and spoke like he 'coulda bin a real con-ten-dah' in *On the Waterfront*. I resisted all the umpteen Sons of Rocky, but I rather enjoyed the first. *The Great White Hope*, biopic of Jack Johnson, was garlanded by fine central performances by James Earl Jones and Jane Alexander but, for me, Martin Scorcese squeezed far too much tomato ketchup out of that bottle for his *Raging Bull*; it was dripping off the ropes at one time. Britain's best shot has been Liam Neeson in 1990 playing *The Big Man* in David Leland's adaptation of William McIlvanney's granitey novel. Best boxing film for a long time remained the uncompromising *The Set-Up*, played and directed respectively by the Roberts Ryan and Wise (1948) – till a quarter of a century later, that is, when John Huston dragged gloriously touching performances out of the washed-up Stacy Keach and the beginner Jeff Bridges in *Fat City*.

There was a wonderful passage in *Fat City* when the two boxers were being driven to the fights in a van which evocatively painted the mix of adrenalined anticipation and vomit-inducing fear a prizefighter must go through each time, however big or small his 'show'.

That nearly made this shortlist of three. Tough, literally. I also thought, an Olympic sport after all, of including the Irish bowmen in Olivier's *Henry V* – but it was, on second thoughts, really Walton's score that made that sequence. I insist on Jacques Tati's tennis cameo, but buying his racket from the crone and then arriving on court with it to serve all those Sampras-like aces meant the two passages have to be laced together – so that, alas, disqualifies it as one entity.

Hugh Hudson's *Chariots of Fire* was a good film for all the right, as well as wrong, reasons. The gleaming little sequence which lifted it into great was when Harold Abrahams (played by Ben Cross) won the Olympic gold medal in the 1924 Olympic sprint at Colombes. His coach Sam Massabini (Ian Holm) was a professional so not allowed in the stadium. He rented a bedsitter nearby. He heard the cheers for the race. But who had won? He fretted and fannied. Of a sudden, the strains of 'God Save the King' . . . and old Sam, all alone and overjoyed, cannot think what to do – but bash to bits against the bedpost his battered old Panama hat in serene and silent celebration.

Great stuff. Sir Ian Holm deserved his knighthood just for that. Great, but not the greatest. The wonderful Ken Loach's *Kes* was a modest little film with a grand big heart pumping life all through it. Of all unlikely juxtaposes, it involves falconry, futility, friendlessness – and, quite resplendently, football in a voluptuous sequence in which forlorn schoolboy no-hoper Billy Caspar plays a miming gymnast monkey at one set of playing-field goalposts while, at the other, the egg-bald ego-tripping sportsmaster 'Sir' (played with chillingly humorous, you might say, humour by Brian Glover) imagines himself to be 'slight balding Bobby Charlton in the Number Nine shirt' as he acts out his Old Trafford fantasies on a windswept field among the desultory 13-year-olds. Quite superb. I have never seen it in a cinema without a round of applause involuntarily breaking out – or watched it on video without wiping my eyes, and then pressing REW to watch it once more.

Film Clip of the Century
BRIAN GLOVER IN *KES*

I withdrew the word 'cheating' although aren't the alternative words, 'professionalism' and 'gamesmanship', only euphemisms? *Christopher Martin-Jenkins*

Footballers are not wordy people, they are movement people. When distinguished professor Freddie Ayer spoke about football he sounded as moronic as anyone, talking about 'tight at the back'. *Dr Desmond Morris*

Danny Blanchflower said football was all about glory, doing things in style and with a flourish. Danny never played for Aldershot. *Michael Herd*

---

100 Best Sports Books of the Century

76 *Masters of Golf*, Pat Ward-Thomas
75 *Sports*, Keith Dunstan
74 *The Great Bike Race*, Geoffrey Nicholson
73 *The Champions of Formula 1*, Keith Botsford
72 *A Lot of Hard Yakka*, Simon Hughes
71 *The Sweet Science*, AJ Liebling
70 *Blue Blood on the Mat*, Sir Athol Oakley
69 *England on Tour*, Peter Wynne-Thomas
68 *Rugger, a Man's Game*, EHD Sewell
67 *Hirst & Rhodes*, AA Thompson
66 *A Wayward Genius*, Greg Growden
65 *Goodbye to Glory*, Terry McLean
64 *Rugby Recollections*, WG Townsend Collins
63 *Horsesweat & Tears*, Simon Barnes
62 *Association Football & How To Play It*, John Cameron
61 *Dragon In Exile*, Paul Beken
60 *The Inner Game*, Timothy Gallwey
59 *The Sportspages Almanacs 1990–92*, Ian Morrison & Matthew Engel
58 *Hedley Verity*, Alan Hill
57 *Barnsley: a Study in Football*, Ian Alister & Andrew Ward
56 *Playing on their Nerves*, Angela Patmore
55 *The Ashes Crown the Year*, Jack Fingleton
54 *Running from A–Z*, Cliff Temple
53 *Association Football & the Men Who Made It*, A Gibson & W Pickford
52 *Percy Fender*, Richard Streeton
51 *The Tennis Set*, Rex Bellamy
50 *The Croucher*, Gerald Broadribb
49 *Ball By Ball*, Christopher Martin-Jenkins
48 *Hobbs*, Ronald Mason
47 *Ten for 66 and all that*, Arthur Mailey
46 *Gone to the Cricket*, John Arlott
45 *Illustrated History of Boxing*, Harry Mullan
44 *The Art of Coarse Rugby*, Michael Green
43 *A Rough Ride*, Paul Kimmage
42 *Jack Dempsey*, Randy Roberts

41 *Gentlemen & Players*, Michael Marshall
40 *The Best Loved Game*, Geoffrey Moorhouse
39 *At the George*, Geoffrey Moorhouse
38 *The Art of Captaincy*, Michael Brearley
37 *Coming Back*, Sebastian Coe & David Miller
36 *Only a Game*, Eamon Dunphy & Peter Ball
35 *Fred*, John Arlott
34 *The Death of Ayrton Senna*, Richard Williams
33 *My Life & Hard Times*, Henry Longhurst
32 *The Players*, Ric Sissons
31 *Why Life Begins on Opening Day*, Thomas Boswell
30 *Gettin' to the Dancefloor*, Al Berkow
29 *Percy*, Pat Pocock & Patrick Collins
28 *'My Dear Victorious Stod'*, David Frith
27 *It Never Rains . . .*, Peter Roebuck
26 *All Played Out*, Pete Davies
25 *A Season in the Sun*, Roger Kahn
24 *Fever Pitch*, Nick Hornby
23 *Portrait in Motion*, Arthur Ashe
22 *Harold Gimblett – Tortured Genius*, David Foot
21 *Muhammad Ali*, Thomas Hauser
20 *A–Z of World Boxing*, Bert Blewett
19 *Testament of a Runner*, WR Loader
18 *The Great Fight of the French XV*, Denis Lalanne
17 *A la Recherche du Cricket Perdu*, Simon Barnes
16 *Days in the Sun*, Neville Cardus
15 *You've Got to be Crazy*, Bob Wilson
14 *The Oxford & Cambridge Boat Race*, Christopher Dodd
13 *The Soccer Syndrome*, John Moynihan
12 *The Football Man*, Arthur Hopcraft
11 *Match Play & the Spin of the Ball*, Bill Tilden
10 *Association Football & English Society 1863–1915*, Tony Mason
9 *Sods I Have Cut on the Turf*, Jack Leach
8 *The Summer Game*, Roger Angell
7 *Beyond a Boundary*, CLR James
6 *Haunts of the Black Masseur*, Charles Sprawson
5 *Crusoe on Cricket*, ed. Alan Ross

4   *In This Corner*, Peter Heller and *The Glory Game*, Hunter Davies
3   *A Handful of Summers*, Gordon Forbes
2   *Fields of Praise*, David Smith & Gareth Williams
1   *The Football Grounds of Britain*, Simon Inglis

Sports Book of the Century

THE FOOTBALL GROUNDS OF BRITAIN, Simon Inglis

Novels

3   *Polo*, Jilly Cooper
2   *The Blinder*, Barry Hines
1   *Mike*, P G Woodhouse